# Sail Away!

## A Guide to
## Outfitting and Provisioning
## for Cruising

by

Paul and Sheryl Shard

*Illustrations by Paul Shard*

### Pelagic Press
Mississauga, Ontario, Canada

**Canadian Cataloguing in Publication Data**

Shard, Paul, 1960-    .
    Sail away! A guide to outfitting and provisioning for cruising

2nd ed.
Includes bibliographical references and index.
ISBN 1-896575-06-4

1. Sailboats - Equipment and supplies. I. Shard, Sheryl, 1959-   . II. Title.

GV811.4.S53 1998        623.8'223        C98-931340-9

Published by:
*Pelagic Press*
3376 Enniskillen Circle,
Mississauga, Ontario, Canada  L5C 2N1
Phone:        (905) 279-7640
Fax:           (905) 279-1223
Email:        shard@interlog.com
Web Site:    http://www.interlog.com/~shard
Printed in Canada by Webcom, Toronto, Ontario.

---

**Warning**

Every effort has been made to insure that the information contained in this guide is accurate however the publisher makes no warranty, expressed or implied, for any errors or omissions in this publication. It is the responsibility of every sailor to act in the most seamanlike fashion and disregard any information that appears contrary to the safety of his or her vessel.

---

*This book is dedicated to our parents,*
*John and Cynthia Shard,*
*May Woolfe and the late Dr. Clifford Woolfe,*
*who have always encouraged us to live our dreams.*

# TABLE OF CONTENTS

# Introduction to the Second Edition

Three years have passed since *Sail Away! A Guide to Outfitting and Provisioning for Cruising* was first published and the response has been heart-warming. The book became a bestseller in the marine market and the letters, e-mails and calls we have received from readers show that passion for the cruising life is alive and well.

As we continue to cruise aboard *Two-Step*, we are always learning and making changes to our boat, to our equipment, to our routines and to our style of cruising. We have incorporated these changes into the Second Edition of *Sail Away!* as well as new developments in marine technology that we have benefitted from while sailing and living aboard our boat. We have updated old material and have added lots of new information as well as numerous photographs and illustrations to add to the book's value as an onboard quick-reference guide. The basic format remains the same with lots of detailed checklists and tables that you can adapt to suit your own personal cruising style. As before, the book has a special waterproof cover and lay-flat binding so it is practical to use on a vessel underway.

Since the publishing of the First Edition in 1995, we have taken *Two-Step* on two more voyages to the Bahamas, survived a direct hit from a hurricane in North Carolina and completed our third transatlantic passage to the magical islands of the Azores. It's hard to believe that *Two-Step* has 30,000 miles under her keel and that we have been sailing internationally for almost a decade.

The cruising life continues to fill our lives with challenge, adventure and wonder. We hope that in some small way this book will help add to the enjoyment of your next cruise.


Paul and Sheryl Shard
Terceira, Azores
June 1998

# Acknowledgements

This book started out as a collection of lists that we developed during our years of voyaging to countries around the Atlantic Ocean. We relied on them as checklists to ensure that our boat was properly outfitted and provisioned at all times. The contents were based on our needs and experiences, as well as on the advice given to us by cruising friends around the world. When we began giving presentations and seminars, we were often asked for copies of our lists and we began using them as handouts. Still more information was requested as well as stories that would help people visualize the experience of being at sea. The book grew from there and our thanks go to all the enthusiastic sailors who encouraged us, especially Richard Bodt on *Partout* (now a transatlantic sailor himself) who called or wrote every few months to ask, "Is it finished yet?!"

Our gratitude goes to all of our cruising friends who, over the years, have generously shared their knowledge and experience with us. They have contributed in no small way to this book. In particular, we would like to thank circumnavigators Keith Braint on *Happy Girl*, Phil Corridan on *Alleda,* and Alan and Gill Brookes on *Passage West*, and transatlantic sailors Matthew and Lisa Buckle on *Caribee*, Brian and Dorothy Goring on *Radnor*, Siw and Christer Johansson aboard *Svenska Bjorn*, Michael Guy and Lise St Germain on *Blue Dragon*, and Herb and Bridgette Hilgenberg on *Southbound II*. Special thanks to Herb who encouraged us while we were still building *Two-Step* and who helped us re-install our HAM radio properly when we arrived in Bermuda in 1990. Herb stayed in touch with us over the radio across the Atlantic providing weather information and passing on messages to our worried families. He continues to be a great source of information and support for us and all other sailors.

We would also like to thank Penny Caldwell, former editor of *Canadian Yachting* magazine who first encouraged us to write about our voyages in 1992 and for the continued support of subsequent CY editors Iain MacMillan and Graham Jones, and Heather Ormerod. Some of the material in this book has appeared in our monthly CY column, "Cruising Notebook".

Special thanks go to Ross Wilson and Dorothy LeBaron, owners of The Nautical Mind, Marine Booksellers and Chart Agents, in Toronto for their encouragement to pursue various projects from books to videos. Ross and Dorothy are strong believers that, for the marine industry to grow and thrive, everyone must support each other. They give generously of their time and use their networks to promote all marine activities. Thanks also to Lori Mason of "The Store", Mason's Chandlery, who recommended resource people and loaned us reference material.

Thanks also to Muriel Smith of Women for Sail for her feedback, to marine filmmaker Peter Rowe for help with this, and also our filmmaking projects, to Janis and Ila Priedkalns whose advice has helped us in many situations, Gaye and Lionel for their technical advice and to Ron Hopkins who couldn't bear to scribble on our manuscript with the red pen we gave him, but who always had great suggestions which he carefully wrote on a separate piece of paper with page references. And thanks to Heather Sipprell and authors Dave Hunter and Liza Copeland who helped us navigate through the treacherous seas of book publishing.

And finally, we would like to thank our friends and family who spent hours proof reading our manuscript, bringing us tea and lunch, and running around for us while we stayed glued to our computers finishing the book, especially Sheryl's mother, May Woolfe; Paul's parents, John and Cynthia Shard and Paul's grandmother, Winifred Simpson. Thanks to you all. We couldn't have done it without you!

# Introduction

The turquoise water sparkled merrily in the tropical sunshine as we navigated our way past the coral heads into the Tobago Cays anchorage. Palm-clad islands fringed with white sand beaches circled the anchorage and ahead of us the surf crashed over Horseshoe Reef breaking the ocean swell. The water in the anchorage was calm and boats of all sizes and nationalities swung gently on their anchors, bows to the trade winds.

It was a welcome sight. In the last two months, Paul and I had spent more time at sea than within sight of land. For weeks we had been doing four-hour watches around the clock as we travelled south on a 20 day passage from the Canary Islands to Brazil aboard *Two-Step*, the Classic 37 sailboat we had built together back home in Canada. Then, after a short stop to film the spectacular marine life of Fernando do Noronha, we had continued on to the Caribbean - 14 days straight through. Now we were working our way north, day sailing and island hopping. Protected waters and a full night's sleep still felt like luxuries after 34 days at sea and I was filled with contentment at the sight of boats swinging peacefully at anchor in this magnificent setting.

Standing at the bow, I scanned the collection of yachts looking for familiar silhouettes. A couple of days ago, we had made radio contact with our British friend, Keith Braint, who at age 71 had just completed his third transatlantic passage aboard *Happy Girl*, the Nicolson 32 he had owned for 25 years. We had first met Keith in Bermuda two years before and together had set sail for the Azores with another Nicolson 32, *Caribee*, owned by our 25-year-old Australian friends, Matthew and Lisa Buckle. *Two-Step*, *Happy Girl* and *Caribee* got separated in a terrible gale early in the passage (see the Appendix for a chapter from our upcoming book *Call of the Ocean*) but met up again in the Azores two weeks later. From there, Keith returned home to England and Matthew and Lisa left their boat in Portugal to return to Australia to work for a while. We had all kept in touch and now, two years later, everyone was back aboard and cruising the Caribbean.

"There they are! There they are!" I shouted to Paul. "Just ahead of that charter boat to port."

My heart was pounding. When you're so far from home, it means a lot to meet up with friends you have shared adventures with.

Paul wove *Two-Step* through the anchored boats and before I could get on the radio, I saw Keith, his nephew Richard, and crew member Lisette standing on deck waving a welcome. In no time at all, we were anchored and on board *Happy Girl*, animated with our reunion. *Caribee* arrived shortly afterwards and we sat up late into the night laughing and joking as we caught up on news and shared the experiences of our passages.

"I thought you had swallowed the anchor, Keith," said Paul. "You were going to quit long-distance sailing when you left the Azores for England I seem to recall."

He laughed. "Retirement life ashore is such a bore! My trip around the Atlantic just whet my appetite for a trip around the world."

"You've added some new toys since we saw you last, mate," Matthew said admiringly.

"Matthew!" Lisa wagged her finger at him. "You're not going to get into hours of Nic' talk tonight I hope," she said, referring to his passionate interest in Nicolson 32's.

But she knew it was impossible to get sailors together and not talk about boats and equipment.

Keith laughed again. "Well, I thought the old girl could use some treats if she's going to take me around the world," he replied to Matthew's comment, "and besides, I *won* this solar panel in the ARC rally last month!"

"Ah... the <u>racing</u> *Happy Girl*!" said Matthew and, as we admired Keith's new wind generator and SSB radio, we got to talking about what kind of boat and gear was good for long-distance cruising.

We had all come from different places, cruising in different ways on small boats. Matthew and Lisa were cruising in stages, leaving *Caribee* to work for a while, then returning to continue their voyage. The plan worked well and enabled them to travel at a young age. Keith loved passage-making and, restless after his voyage around the Atlantic, was taking on the challenge of a circumnavigation with crew to assist him. We were cruising long-term on savings and with money we earned from writing and photography. Compared to the fancy yachts and charter boats surrounding us, our boats were not large, yet we had all travelled great distances in comfort and safety. Learning to outfit and provision our boats to meet our own needs gave us the freedom to cross oceans.

When Paul and I first started cruising, we were hungry for information. We talked to every experienced sailor we knew in search of answers. Now, when we meet new cruisers they ask us the same questions: "How much does it cost?", "What spare parts do you take?", "What do you eat and how do you know what quantities to stow?", "How do you get money from home?", "What safety equipment do you carry?"

We answer what we can and pass along copies of our stores lists as other sailors did for us. On our visits home, we are invited to give

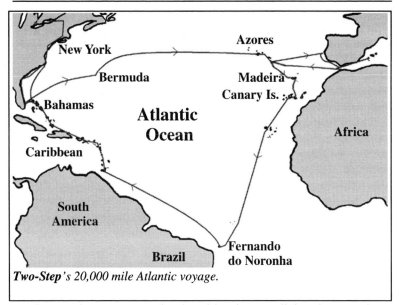

*Two-Step's 20,000 mile Atlantic voyage.*

seminars and upon request developed handouts outlining the procedures for planning an extended cruise. Still people asked for more information and this guide book was born.

*Sail Away! A Guide to Outfitting and Provisioning for Cruising* focuses on the *process* of outfitting and provisioning your boat. Using our experiences and the knowledge that other long-distance cruisers have shared with us over the years, we take you through the steps we find helpful when planning a cruise. We discuss the reasons for choosing the equipment and supplies we have on *Two-Step* and give tips on how to define your needs so you can equip your boat in the best way possible for you and your crew. Every crew has different requirements based on boat design and size, destination, budget and personal goals.

We have included our checklists and maintenance schedules as examples, but provide forms for you to build your own custom inventory manual. Since many sailors now have computers on board, these forms and checklists are also available on computer disk for fast processing and customization. See the Appendix for more information.

The exchange of information between sailors is one of the things we enjoy about cruising. This occurs in many forms - over dinners on board, at dockside cafés, in eagerly awaited correspondence or over hundreds of miles in radio waves. You never stop learning.

That night on *Happy Girl* as the moon cast a silvery path on the water, I looked at the smiling faces around me in the lamp light. Despite our differences in nationality, age and experience we all shared a common bond and had learned much from each other. Keith, a modern-minded engineer, had impressed us with the fact that we should never reject traditional ideas or tools for new methods until we are satisfied for ourselves that the new ways are more efficient. Matthew, who has crewed on the prestigious Sydney-Hobart race in Australia taught us valuable sail-handling techniques that have increased our performance and safety at sea. Lisa, a medical technician, taught us important first aid skills. We, in turn, have shared our skills in boat building and computer communications and applications.

We hope you will share your expertise and ideas with us too. We have included a comment card at the end of the book and encourage you to write to us with suggestions for future editions. Like all cruisers, we love to get mail!

In the meantime, we hope you enjoy this book and we look forward to meeting you out on the water.

Until then, fair winds and happy cruising!


Paul and Sheryl Shard

# Part 1 : Planning Your Cruise

# Secrets of Successful Cruisers

It was amazing how much cooler it was on the south coast of Spain. Although it was 34°C, the wind felt cool on our faces compared to the lifeless air we'd had coming down the Rio Guadalquivir from Seville.

Paul and I had just spent a hot, but heady, couple of weeks in that magnificent city where, 500 years ago, Christopher Columbus had sailed up the same river and convinced the Spanish royalty to fund his voyage to America. We were used to ocean breezes and being 55 miles inland in Seville made a big difference in September. The thermometer had read 37°C when we sought out the shade in Parc Maria Louisa at siesta. Thank goodness we hadn't decided to explore this historic city in July when it's even hotter!

Our trip back down the river had been a cooling one and now as we headed into the bay of Cadiz our minds were on the ports ahead. We were headed for Puerto Sherry to explore the Jerez region where for centuries the finest sherries and brandies had been produced. My 31$^{st}$ birthday was coming up and we had planned a tour of the wineries. Then we would leave the Atlantic behind and enter the Mediterranean Sea through the Strait of Gibraltar.

We had a fast beam reach for the rest of the day and as we rounded the point we picked up the light at the Puerto Sherry breakwater.

We were surprised when we entered the harbour to find the brand new marina almost empty. Then I caught sight of a boat I recognized.

"Hey! There's *Mic-L-Mac*."

A woman in her late forties with short sandy red hair was hosing the deck of a white steel-hulled sailboat. Her teenaged daughter slooshed the water with a mop, scrubbing it clean. They both looked up when I called and a moment later John popped up from the companionway and came running down the dock to help us with our lines.

Later that evening, we joined fellow Canadians, John Wilson, his wife Marian, and daughter Jejo (short for Jessica) for a delicious dinner on board *Mic-L-Mac*.

We had met the Wilson family in Bermuda the previous spring and, although we had left for the Azores a few days before them, we had been in radio contact throughout our transatlantic passage. Then, they were our neighbours in several ports in the Azores, again in Lisbon, Portugal, and now we were happy to discover they would once again be our neighbours in this Spanish port.

People cruise for different reasons and the Wilsons seem to be motivated by the same things we are - the thrill of harnessing a breeze and flying across the waves, the adventure of travelling oceans and waterways to reach exotic ports around the world, the good health we enjoy from living in the outdoors, the opportunity to see marine life in its natural environment, the relaxing pace of life and the wonderful people we meet along the way.

That night as we exchanged news over a hearty beef dinner, we got talking about the ingredients of a successful cruise. We all enjoyed the ups and downs of life aboard but, sadly had witnessed other cruises ending in disappointment or disaster. We tried to identify what had gone wrong.

"I think some people give up on cruising because they miss their families," said Marian as she passed around a bowl of fresh green peas.

"Family and friends are very important to us", she continued, "so we fly home regularly to see the family and attend to business matters that are hard to deal with long distance. Then Jejo can write her exams -- she's doing grade nine by correspondence -- and can see her school friends at home."

"I love the challenge of passage-making" said John enthusiastically, "but Marian gets seasick so she plans visits home when there is a big passage coming up. Friends and family members, usually our other daughter and son who are in university, come to help me."

Marian nodded.

"I love travelling and living on the boat but long passages make me miserable so this is a compromise that keeps everyone happy and gives us all lots of time with people who mean a lot to us."

We were impressed. This family had been cruising full-time for five years and even though they faced many factors that caused other cruises to fail, they had worked out compromises that became positive experiences for other members of the crew.

If we made a dollar every time a cruising sailor introduced themselves and immediately confessed that cruising wasn't *their* idea, we'd have quite a few dollars by now. For happy cruising, the whole crew has to be ready and willing.

Resentment builds easily in the confines of a small boat. We have witnessed several cruising divorces because some well-meaning individual sacrificed their job, home or family life to go cruising with their mate and then got traumatized or fed up living a lifestyle they were unhappy with.

Children over the age of 10 value their peers and can be sulky and miserable if stuck in paradise with their parents when they know their friends at home are meeting at the mall. (Hard to believe, I know, but we've spoken to a couple of kids sitting in tropical splendour and wishing they were at the mall back home.)

There are two solutions to this predicament - make a deal or make alternative arrangements. The deals are usually "you come cruising with me and then next year/next vacation we'll do what you want" or some other form of give and take. If deals and compromises don't do the trick then alternative plans must be made if you value the relationship. Miserable kids have been restored to happy individuals who still love their parents by staying at home with grandparents or going to boarding school if the dream cruise is to be long-term. Nervous sailing wives who know how important the cruising dream is to their men often watch them sail off single-handed or with crew and fly to meet them at various destinations. Sometimes the plan for a long-term cruise becomes a series of short-term cruises instead.

The bottom line seems to be, *if it's not fun for everyone, it's not going to be fun for anyone.*

As we said goodnight to our friends, and walked back to *Two-Step* under the starry Spanish sky, I realized how fortunate we were to also have found compromises for our differences in experience, strength and needs for comfort. We both have a good sense of humour too, which helps us cope with the frustrations of culture shock.

"I certainly don't mind compromising... so long as I get my way in the end!" Paul quipped, and gave me a hug.

Well, I think it was a quip. I gave him a shove, just in case.

# Crew Harmony and Expectations

Worksheet 1 - Crew Harmony and Expectations

> The following questionnaire has been designed by a team of nautical experts to test crew compatibility. Each member of the crew should answer separately... you have 10 minutes!

**When I think of a cruise south to the Bahamas via the Intracoastal Waterway, I think of ...**

A)  a languid voyage of discovery, seaside towns, getting to know coastal America.

B)  being in the Bahamas before November 1. If we go offshore from Charleston we can get some night passages in and test the new autopilot.

C)  missing the family at home! Maybe they'll come to visit at Christmas, or maybe we can lay the boat up in Fort Lauderdale for a month over the holidays.

**Cooking on board our boat will be...**

A)  a fun way to try food along the route. If we can install a bigger spice rack I can bring my whole collection.

B)  difficult offshore! But I've put in a gimballed 1-burner kerosene stove near the companionway to heat a can of stew for night watches. Who needs vegetables.

C)  not like home. I miss my food-processor already!

**I think Captain Bligh was...**

A)  a miserable and unfortunate man. Luckily in this enlightened age of equality we can both take turns running the ship.

B)  unlucky to have such reprobates for a crew! A little discipline never hurt. Imagine a committee in charge of the *Nimitz*! They'd never get out of port.

C)  I never did see that movie. If we bring a VCR can we still rent movies even if we don't have a membership at all those foreign places.

**The idea of being offshore, out of sight of land in my own sailboat...**

A) is something to think about. If we watch the weather carefully we can probably make the 60 miles to Bimini. I think I remember from Power Squadron how to calculate the current.

B) is what I live for!! The smell of the ocean. Challenging the wild sea! Maybe I should get an earring.

C) I don't have a sailboat. It's really my husband's boat. He can take it offshore if he wants.

**Managing the finances for our big cruise will be...**

A) very organized. We'll take along traveller's cheques for 3 months at a time. If we don't spend any money in a day we get a gold star!

B) no problem! We should live very economically. Once we get offshore we can catch fish. I heard you can make a nutritious salad by catching plankton in a net.

C) actually I think we're over budget already! We spent a lot on some new thing for the sail. We'd better have enough for the cell-phone though or I'm not going!

---

### Tabulating your answers

If the majority of your answers were "A" you are organized, adventurous and a born explorer. Buy lots of guide books. If there are any "B" types on board consider the implications of mutiny.

Mostly "B" ? The sea life certainly agrees with you. If there are any "A" types on board with you, consider downscaling your plans for a non-stop circumnavigation and watch the more sensitive, Mel Gibson version of *Mutiny on the Bounty*. If there are any "C" types along, discuss your plans to get an earring and consider a vacation to Seaworld instead.

If you put "C" for most questions, do you have enough frequent flyer points to meet the ship in foreign ports? Europe uses a different TV standard than North America so you'll have to bring your own movies. Don't rent *Dead Calm* or *Titanic*.

# Where Are You Going?

Most cruises are based on a destination: "When school finishes, we are going to take the kids on a summer cruise through the Thousand Islands." "When I retire, I want to cruise the Caribbean for a couple of years." "We want to take the boat over to Europe and cruise the Med for a few seasons." "We're going to sail around the world."

Even if you change your plans along the way, having a specific destination in mind will give you a starting point for designing your cruise.

When we made the decision to build our boat and "go cruising", our plan was to take a one year sabbatical and sail to the Caribbean. We had several friends who had done it, had seen several inspiring slide shows about doing it, and finally made the decision to do it ourselves when we took a bareboat vacation in the Caribbean one winter. We were hooked!

Having a plan gave us direction and incentive. Knowing we were headed for the tropics helped us make decisions about boat design, cabin layout, our rig, safety equipment - everything down to the smallest detail. It even helped us make valuable career decisions that increased our incomes so we could achieve our goal more easily.

We chose to build a Classic 37 because of the stability the full keel provides in big seas (safety), the large amount of storage space it has for living aboard (comfort) and its simple design which made it possible for the two of us to build her ourselves (manageability). We knew we wouldn't save any money building our own boat but it meant we could put money into it gradually. We had just finished university and didn't have a lot of capital. We would get to know our boat intimately and develop skills that would make us self-sufficient at sea or when cruising in remote areas. Also, we knew that if we put in the huge amount of time it would require to finish building it, we would stay committed to our dream. When we launched that boat, gosh darn it, we were going to enjoy it!

We started to build our cruising boat in the summer of 1986. We kept our first boat, a snappy little BIC Trilantic 410, so we could get out on the water when we needed a fix of sailing. We developed our keelboat skills by crewing for friends at the Port Credit Yacht Club and, in the cool of autumn, worked on navigation courses given by the Port Credit Power and Sail Squadron. Thoughts of hot sunshine and tropic blue water rushing past the hull of our new boat kept us down at the boat yard on cold winter nights working on completing her.

We launched *Two-Step* in the summer of 1988, a year ahead of schedule, and sailed her on Lake Ontario for two seasons. On September 21, 1989, we set sail from Lake Ontario and headed south.

Our plans did change along the way. We spent the first winter in the Bahamas and, as we gained experience and confidence, our wanderlust grew. Before we knew it, we were crossing the Atlantic Ocean headed for Europe. Our one year sabbatical stretched into a three year, 20,000 mile voyage that took us to 23 countries in Europe, South America and the Caribbean. At each stage of the way, we designed a new plan that would get us happily to our next destination.

We found it was best to plan things a step at a time. Then you don't commit yourself to more than you can handle. We have met many sailors who announce when they leave home that they are sailing around the world. Then, after cruising for a while, they change their plans for one reason or another and end up feeling like failures. Instead, they should be very proud of their accomplishments. It takes a lot of gumption and skill to get your boat to the Caribbean or all the way to Australia. Better to plan a challenging but achievable cruise and expand your plans gradually.

## Do You Really Want to Go There?

One of our favourite cruising destinations is the Bahamas. We have sailed there three times now - and still want to go back! The crystal clear water, vibrant reefs, endless white sand beaches, abundant wildlife and numerous picturesque anchorages make the Bahamas the ideal cruising grounds for us.

But we have friends who found cruising these islands very disappointing. We were surprised that they felt this way. We had all made the long journey from Toronto because we had heard so much about the Bahamas and were anxious to explore them ourselves. We had found paradise and were ready to tell everyone to go there! They were telling everyone to consider other cruising destinations. How could we all be reacting so differently?!

What it got down to was expectations. Our friends are adventurous sailors with a lot of cruising experience but, in the Out Islands of the Bahamas, there isn't a whole lot more to do than swim, fish and snorkel. Besides sailing, most other water sports don't interest them. We are certified scuba divers and love sailing because we can get to great dive sites! They felt confined by the shallow water, reefs and sandbars. We liked the navigational challenges and didn't worry if we had to push through the sand occasionally to reach a safe harbour (*Two-Step* draws 6 feet). We love remote anchorages; they do to a point but are more comfortable if they can stop in marinas occasionally for a break. In the

Out Islands, marinas are few and far between and, in most cases, offer pretty basic facilities.

It was a valuable lesson for us. We are now very careful when people ask us for recommendations on cruising destinations. We do our best to determine their interests, attitudes, comfort levels and cruising style so we don't wax poetic about a place they would find boring or uncomfortable. We keep the same things in mind when asking other sailors for information about destinations we haven't been to, but are considering.

Despite these difficulties, we still think the best way to research a destination is to talk to someone who has been there. Keeping your own criteria in mind, you can ask lots of specific questions and get a good feel for a place.

Other good sources are cruising guides, sailing magazines, boat shows, tourist boards, cruising videos and books by long-distance cruisers. We enjoyed autobiographies by Miles and Beryl Smeeton, Paul Howard and Fiona McCall, Tristan Jones, and Lin and Larry Pardey when preparing for our first cruise. (See Appendix for more recommended reading.)

Long-distance cruising requires a lot of energy, preparation and planning so it pays to be sure the destination you have chosen is a place *you* will enjoy sailing to and exploring. The more thorough you are with your research, the more you will get out of your cruise. There will be fewer surprises (there are always some) and, when you do set sail, you will be confident *that you really want to go there!*

# Part 2 : The Cost of Cruising

# Estimating Costs

"How much does it cost to go cruising?" is a question we are asked continually when we give presentations on our sailing adventures.

The answer is, like all things about cruising, dependant on several factors - the style in which you like to cruise (marinas versus anchoring, cooking on board versus eating in restaurants, coastal cruising versus passage-making), the size of your boat and whether or not you can handle repairs yourself, the cost of additional activities (scuba diving, sightseeing, etc.), the cost of living in the cruising grounds you are sailing in, how good you are about keeping a budget, and so it goes.

But we're not just going to leave it at that. It *is* possible to estimate the cost of your cruise with a little research and number-crunching.

The first thing we would like to say is that, once you have your boat, the cost of cruising is surprisingly low compared to living on land. At sea and at anchor, there is no rent to pay. You require few services on a regular basis such as telephone and cable TV hook-up. You won't have the regular cost of running a car, and since it will be more of an effort to get to the stores, you probably won't go shopping as often. Your wardrobe won't need to be so extensive and will be more casual. Your basic expenses will be groceries, water, fuel, boat maintenance, marina fees and entertainment. The more self-sufficient you are, the more affordable cruising is.

In our three year Atlantic cruise (1989 to 1992), we lived on a budget of $1,000 US ($1,300 CAN) per month and travelled very comfortably. We anchored most of the time and enjoyed some pretty magical surroundings. We both love to cook so only ate out once or twice a month, preferring to shop in local markets and entertain on board. Our favourite activities were hiking and snorkelling which cost nothing, kept us fit and led us to some amazing places. We rented cars in the countries where it was affordable which was helpful when doing big provisioning runs or where sights we wanted to see were further inland. Otherwise we walked or relied on public transit - both great for meeting the locals! Life became more simple, yet richer and more stimulating at the same time.

Our recent cruise from Toronto to the Bahamas (1994-95) cost us even less - about $800 U.S. per month. It was our third trip there and it cost us less this time because we anchored more, went offshore down the U.S. coast whenever we could rather than exploring the towns along the Intracoastal Waterway, and spent all our time in the Bahamas fishing and diving rather than sightseeing.

Some cruisers we know, live on very little - $400 to $500 U.S. per month - but this is bare bones cruising and only possible in certain third world countries or out-of-the-way places where they can anchor and live on simple diets such as fish and rice. They never go to marinas or eat in restaurants. They don't rent cars or scuba equipment or go to museums. Yet they live happy contented lives and enjoy freedom that others only dream of. It is not for everyone though.

At the other extreme, there are cruisers with enormous boats who stay in marinas every night, eat in restaurants, have paid crew on board to cook and manage the boat -- and live a different life than we do!

Since there are so many cost variables when cruising (and the longer your cruise is, the more variables there are), a good strategy is to find people who have a similar size boat to yours and who have done long-distance cruises in the same style you would like to. This was how we estimated the cost of our first cruise and it worked well for us.

We found these experienced sailors at our yacht club; at the boat building club we belonged to; at the Power and Sail Squadron navigation classes we attended and at boat shows or chandleries where they came to speak, show their slides or conduct seminars. Cruisers are proud of their accomplishments and are usually eager to share their adventures and knowledge with others. In fact, the information exchanges that take place over dinners on board or drinks at dockside cafés are one of the many things we enjoy about cruising. Networking, it seems, improves your cruising life as well as your business life!

The criteria we set for our first cruise in 1989 were threefold. The major purpose was to travel and learn about people in other lands, so we wanted to be able to rent cars or travel inland by bus or train and go sightseeing. We also wanted to be able to stay at marinas occasionally to make provisioning easier or if anchorages were too crowded. Finally, we wanted to eat out once in a while to sample the foods in new countries, and as a treat after a passage or a rough day at the helm.

Almost every experienced cruiser we spoke to who had the same agenda as us, said they spent about $10,000 to $12,000 US per year for two people cruising full-time, or about $1,000 US per month. On our three year cruise from 1989 to 1992, our expenses were the same.

We did not keep a strict budget allotting so much money for food, or so much money for marina fees and boat expenses. We just tried not to spend more than $1,000 U.S. per month. If we wanted to go out for dinner, we did. If we wanted to stay at a marina, we did. We would just go easy on other expenses to balance our spending for the month. We would only rent a car in places where it was affordable and at times when we needed a car to find supplies, too. If we did a large provisioning, we amortized the cost over the time we had provisioned for. If we really blew the budget, we'd stay at anchor or head out to sea for a while! (It's amazing how little you spend when you don't see land for three weeks!)

As we gained more confidence and experience, our spending declined without effort. We learned how to anchor comfortably in all conditions and found we preferred swinging on the hook to staying in marinas. We discovered we met more people and experienced the culture of a foreign land more directly by taking public transportation instead of renting a car. Shopping in local markets and trying new foods in our galley was often more fun than eating out, especially if new friends came aboard to teach us how to prepare the traditional dishes of their country.

We built our boat so we have the skills to do all our own repairs and are diligent about preventative maintenance. This saves a lot of money. We find that most long-term cruisers are handy at repairs even if they didn't start out that way. When you are cruising, you have the time and incentive to learn these skills but it is still best to develop as many as you can before you leave home. Self-sufficiency gives you the comfort, safety and freedom to sail wherever the winds blow.

It is important to know the comforts you need for happiness and to maintain the standard of living you enjoy when cruising. If, after your research, you find the estimated cost of your cruise is higher than expected, it is better to plan a shorter cruise than cut costs drastically. Cruising is for pleasure! If you are feeling constrained by finances and living in a fashion that feels substandard, it won't be fun.

## Cruising Cost Profile (in U.S. dollars - 1995)

Table 1 - Cruising Cost Profile.

| Monthly Budget | Lifestyle |
|---|---|
| <$500 | Depending on how much less than $500, the budget for food is either merely restrained, or only beans and rice! Treats like beef, wine, etc. are very carefully budgeted. The budget cruiser maintains his own boat - sail repair, engine and electric, etc. To stay in budget, a major purchase such as an anchor will have to be planned well in advance. If the boat needs a new sail it must be second-hand. It will be difficult to sustain this budget for long especially if the yacht needs much maintenance. Almost any repairs will push expenses over $500. |
| $500 to $700 | The food budget is less restrained. There could be a couple of nights a month in marinas *if necessary*. Cruisers on this budget shop around carefully for inexpensive haulout facilities and still do all their own repairs. A major repair will be difficult to afford. |
| $700 to $1000 | The boat can take most of the extra money here. A new anchor, some replacement rope or a rebuild kit for the water pump are not such a strain on the budget. A couple of rolls of film a month, a dinner out, a few visits to the pub and a night in a marina every two weeks to do laundry will spend the rest. *Two-Step* cruises at around the $1000 mark. |
| $1000 to $1500 | The $100 needed to rent a car and go off sightseeing for 2 days won't be too hard to find. Where phone calls are expensive, you can still afford to call home (but still not on the cell phone if you want to say more than "Hi!"). If the dinghy wears out, you can afford a new one if you live cheaply for the next while. |
| >$1500 | Luxury cruising begins here! You still cannot afford marinas every night ($30 x 30 nights is almost $1000 a month!) but then anchoring is so nice anyway. If you spend only $1200 a month, you can have treats like a flight home or a new sail once in a while with your savings. Heck, buy a video camera! Call home for someone's birthday ON THE CELL PHONE! |

**Notes:**  The preceding table was drawn up from a large number of cruising sailors over a wide range of budgets. (although we dropped by the *Trump Princess*, Donald wasn't on board, so his 200' yacht isn't included).

Most people cruise on boats from 28-40 feet long. Some money can be saved on a smaller boat since all boat related expenses are less. The problem is that they are generally not able to stock up on food to save that way since the boat is too small.

Larger than 40' will definitely add to the monthly cost. Almost everything on a 45 footer is double the cost of a 30 footer. Fuel will be twice the cost, a new sail will be much more expensive and marinas will be more too. Figure on an extra $200 U.S. a month for a boat over 40 feet. If you don't spend it, you can save up for when there is a major boat expense one day.

Expenses such as insurance (health, boat, life) will all be extra. Many cruisers keep a nest egg to cover themselves in the event of needing medical attention or something expensive such as a new engine. This can substantially reduce insurance premiums if you are willing to bear some risk yourself in this way.

# Tracking Expenses Underway

Keeping track of expenses while you are underway is not always an easy task. Dealing with different currencies can be confusing, communications with the person paying your bills at home can be difficult in remote places and the cost of goods can vary wildly from one country to another.

We got a real shock when Paul's mother sent us a copy of our cell phone bill to the Bahamas. She had dutifully paid the bill when it arrived a month after we made some business calls from the islands to Toronto. It took another month for the mail from home to get to us, so when we finally got a copy of the bill and saw how much those calls cost, two months had elapsed.

A twelve minute call to Canada from the Bahamas during prime business hours in 1995 cost $89 with air time and long-distance charges! A fifteen minute call was over $100! If we had known sooner, we would have shut off the phone and sailed for the nearest public telephone centre but we were almost at the end of our cruise by then and had been merrily making calls in the meantime. There was no way for Paul's mother to warn us either. By the time she got the bill, we were filming in an isolated area of the Family Islands and couldn't be reached by phone or fax. We knew cell phone costs would be more expensive than the costs we incurred using the phone in the U.S. but we had no idea it would be *that* much more. Now we rarely use the cell phone out of the U.S. or Canada and check "roamer" charges and long-distance rates *carefully* when we do.

It is very important to track expenses while you are cruising because there are so few fixed costs compared to living ashore. You need to keep tabs on how much you've spent and how much you've got left so that you don't find yourself stranded and short of funds in a foreign country. The records you keep will help you make decisions about the future as well. You may find that cruising costs more than you thought after several months of record keeping, and decide to change your cruising style a little or choose a destination where the cost of living is less. After our first year living aboard, we discovered cruising *did not* cost as much as we thought it would and were able to extend our cruise another year with careful money management.

The secret to tracking your expenses while cruising is to design a system that is easy to carry out. Our cruising budget is $1,000 U.S. a month. We have some fixed costs we need to pay at home such as insurance, so have arranged for those payments to be automatically withdrawn from our bank account. We don't like to carry more than about $400 U.S. cash at one time, so use our credit cards a lot. We keep tabs on all the credit card and cash receipts and convert the totals into dollars so we know what we've spent. Simple.

# Getting Cash While Travelling

We keep our money in investments that pay a good interest rate at home. Both our mothers have power of attorney and every month one of them transfers money from our account to pay our bills -- credit cards, cell phone, yacht club dues, etc. and makes sure there is a $1,000 U.S. *credit* balance in our VISA credit card account. Whenever we need cash, we go to the nearest bank machine and withdraw what cash we need by making an *interest-free* cash advance on our VISA card. It is interest-free because we have a credit balance. There are high interest charges if you don't put the money in first.

We used to just go to a bank in person, but if we arrived in a foreign country late on Friday, it meant we couldn't get our money until the bank opened on Monday. With the bank machines we can get money on any day, at any hour, in the local currency and in small amounts -- $200 U.S. to $400 U.S. -- so we're not carrying around a lot of cash on the boat. There is a $2 service charge (1995) for using the bank machines but for the convenience and security we feel it is not an unreasonable charge.

If we do need a large amount for provisioning or a major repair, we go into the bank and make a larger cash advance (there are daily limits on the bank machines). We check with the Moms first to be sure there is a sufficient credit balance in our Visa account and, if not, one of them transfers the necessary funds into the account. This takes less time and trouble than having money transferred from your bank at home to the foreign bank where you are.

Some of our cruising friends have opted to put all their cruising funds for the year -- $10,000 to $15,000 -- into travellers cheques before they leave home. But their money isn't growing while they're travelling. It costs them to put their money into travellers cheques and many stores won't even accept them. Banks charge from 3% up to a high of $10 to cash just one! (In Gibraltar we tried to cash some $20 and $50 travellers cheques and the rate was $10 per cheque -- even for the $20 ones!!) Although travellers cheques are secure, we only bought them once, and have been very happy with the Visa method instead. Since the Gibraltar experience we have opted to carry a hidden stash of $300 US dollars as an emergency fund in place of travellers cheques.

We try to use our credit cards whenever possible so we don't have to carry a lot of cash. Visa was accepted everywhere we travelled in the U.S., Europe and the Caribbean. In Brazil, we wished we had a Mastercard. The credit card bills are also backup records of our spending habits and the exchange rates at the time. We have separate credit card accounts in case one of our wallets is stolen and we have to freeze that account. Then we're not stranded. (See Important Documents on page 252 for more info.)

We enter all our expenses in a monthly expense record (sample follows) so we know if we've overspent, and what we're spending our money on. As I mentioned earlier, we don't stick to a rigid budget. We just try not to spend more than $1,000 U.S. per month and cut back for a while if we do.

Our expense records have been invaluable for planning future cruises. Careful money management has allowed us to travel farther and longer than we first imagined we could. If you keep your record keeping simple, tracking your expenses will be easy. Financial worries can ruin a cruise. When you know where you stand, it gives you freedom and peace of mind.

# Monthly Expense Record

Worksheet 2 - Monthly Expense Record

| Boat | Amounts |
|---|---|
| Customs and Immigration<br>        e.g. cruising permits, visas, canal fees | |
| Boat Maintenance and Services | |
| Supplies and Spares | |
| Fuel (boat, dinghy, stove, lamp) | |
| Marina Fees | |
| Insurance (boat, contents, towing) | |
| Personal | |
| Clothing | |
| Communications (phone, fax, postage, radio license fees) | |
| Health (medicine, check-ups, insurance) | |
| Laundry | |
| Provisions | |
| Water | |
| Transportation | |
| Financial (exchange, surcharges, management fees) | |
| Entertainment (attractions, hobbies, meals out) | |
| Gifts and Souvenirs | |
| Expenses at home (home insurance, mortgage, etc) | |
| Other: | |
| | |
| | |
| **TOTAL EXPENSES:** | |

| Balance at the end of the month in: | |
|---|---|
| Savings Account | |
| Chequing Account | |
| Credit Card Account | |
| Investments | |
| Other: | |
| | |
| **TOTAL ASSETS:** | |

Photocopy for your own use. Also available on disk. See Appendix.

# Part 3 : Outfitting

# Outfitting

I should admit at the outset that I (Paul) am a gadgeteer! Outfitting for me means an opportunity to wander the aisles at boat shows and to peruse the fantastic marine catalogues looking at new gear. But it also is about equipping our relatively small boat (wandering at a boat show makes *Two-Step* feel positively *minuscule*) on a relatively small budget. I am always trying to strike a balance between improving the safety and performance of our yacht and having enough money left over to cruise. To that end I feel it makes sense to stay up to date on new technologies that affect sailing, but to be quite cautious about purchasing additional equipment.

There are probably few aspects of sailing that have not been examined by a budding entrepreneur to determine if a market exists to sell more gadgets. From fender line adjusters and gimballed drink holders to electric winches and computer monitored wind indicators, there is no shortage of potential "essential gear" to outfit your boat.

Not even a 100' mega yacht has room for all of them! Upscale inventors have bigger inventions for mega yachts -- our favourite was an automatic retractable gangplank that we saw on a mega-yacht that sailed in when we were docked at Marina Bay in Gibraltar. The gangplank slid out from a covered garage extending 15 feet astern, then handrails folded up on either side with discreet lights shining on the walkway. Finally a computer system monitored the height of the end of the gangplank above the dock. This controlled a motor that kept the tip exactly 2 inches above the dock surface when surge and tide moved the boat. I'm not recommending one of these: I just had to describe this gadget!

For us spending the winter on board in Gibraltar, walking the dock was good exercise and provided an insight into the rarified heights of extravagant yachting as well.

But we also saw the other end of the spectrum. We met countless cruisers happily living and sailing on boats from 22 to 30 feet long -- boats without many of the modern conveniences we have on board. The owners are sailing about, some of them travelling great distances, enjoying their boats. Meanwhile, many of the largest yachts are being tended by crew -- their owners are only able to spend a short time each year sailing.

The typical cruising boat is between 25 and 40 feet in length - and whether it has sailed the Bahamas or around the world, most skippers are still looking at adding an extra gadget or two. Few people have it all. Most of us have to carefully choose how to outfit our boats, do it reasonably, and get to the important business of going off cruising!

# What Boat is Right for Voyaging

If you don't have a boat already, or are considering a different one for voyaging, the question of outfitting is secondary to the selection of the boat itself.

Choosing a cruising boat is naturally a very personal matter. If it weren't, I suppose we would all be sailing in the same cookie-cutter cruisers. Instead, a typical anchorage is populated by a wide variety of boats ranging from sleek multihulls to fiberglass sloops to small pirate-style schooners (some flying the "skull and crossbones"!).

Where and how you plan to cruise will definitely play a large part in your decision. The multihull with a shallow draft can reach many more places in the shallow islands of the Bahamas than can any traditional deep keeled boat like ours. A tough steel hull won't mind bumping into the odd ice floe in Alaska, and a light fiberglass racer/cruiser will probably make the fastest passages offshore (unless the multihull has really kept the weight down). No one boat can be all things to all people.

A look through any of today's sailing magazines will reveal a number of "purpose-built" ocean voyaging yachts, ranging from a scant 20 feet to an opulent 70 feet or more. One great thing about the proliferation of ocean voyaging yachts is that they have encouraged a fresh look at yacht design. Instead of designing boats to cheat a racing rule, the "voyaging yacht" designer can try to get the best mix of interior space, seaworthiness, and other factors he thinks are good for the voyaging sailor. These boats often look like the best choice, but even if you have the luxury of choosing a boat without worrying about price, it makes sense to really evaluate where you will be cruising. A trip through the Caribbean with a couple of short offshore passages may not justify a boat built for Cape Horn, with the restrictions of that sort of boat, in terms of draft, weight and expense.

In the final evaluation, cruising plans, liveaboard lifestyle, the number of crew and of course financial constraints, will help to decide which is the best voyaging yacht.

## Hull Material

In considering a sailboat for cruising, the choice of hull goes along with the choice of hull material. Before jumping into the sailboat market, it makes sense to understand the basic properties of the various construction materials that are available, especially since there is such a wide range of options. I know of no other item except a boat that is available in all the materials listed below. And that is not including the one *stainless steel* yacht we saw in Gibraltar. Even bronze has been used to build a hull!

## Aluminum

Many cruisers consider aluminum to be the best choice of boat-building materials. It is strong and relatively light, allowing a very tough boat to be built. Marine grade aluminum will not rust in seawater since aluminum protects itself against seawater corrosion by forming a thin layer of oxide on the surface. A welded unit exterior means a dry leak-free boat and the resulting boat requires relatively little maintenance.

Why doesn't everyone cruise in aluminum yachts? Cost is certainly a major reason! Aluminum is one of the most expensive materials, and there is also the fact that it doesn't lend itself to mass production. Galvanic action with other common marine metals means the boat must be very well protected against electrolysis. Aluminum boat owners are extra nervous of stray currents in marinas (we should all be somewhat nervous) since electrolysis will attack the whole hull.

Aluminum boats remain relatively rare but it is a good choice for custom construction, where the added cost of a "one-off" project conceals the expense of the material.

## Ferrocement

Concrete boats became popular more than 20 years ago, mainly with home builders, and chiefly for the low cost of the raw materials. Although a well constructed ferrocement boat is very strong, many were built by amateurs who did not know the material well enough. It was easy to produce an overweight hull.

Today very few boats are built of ferrocement and it cannot be recommended as a construction material.

## Fiberglass

The correct name is really Fiberglass Reinforced Plastic since it is a plastic resin reinforced with glass (or now Kevlar™) strands in various woven and matt forms. More popular than all the other construction techniques combined, fiberglass is the obvious choice for a mass-production yacht since it can be easily moulded into a hull. The end product is strong and light.

Although it was initially promoted as requiring no maintenance, fiberglass has its own special problems. Polyester resin absorbs water through osmosis, with boats kept year-round in tropical water being especially vulnerable. The absorbed water can form blisters where small pockets of the plastic deteriorate into a sticky mess. This is rarely a structural problem but can be expensive to repair.

Having competent workmen lay up the hull under the correct conditions, and with the proper materials are all important factors to achieving a sound fiberglass boat. With these prerequisites met, fiberglass sailboats are the most cost-effective way to go voyaging. In fact, their longevity has forced a worldwide depression in the sailboat market.

### Steel

Steel is definitely the strongest material for boatbuilding. Steel boats have been known to bounce up and down on a reef and be pulled off un-punctured hours later -- bang out the dents and apply a coat of paint and they're back in business. It's the stuff of legends, but realistically there are problems with steel.

Susceptibility to rust means that most steel boats less than 50 feet are made thicker than they would need to be for strength alone. The extra thickness increases weight and reduces performance - but that's where the stories of super-strong hulls come from. Like

*Michael and Lise on Blue Dragon chose steel for strength and are sailing here in the iceberg strewn waters of Newfoundland.*

aluminum, producing a steel boat is much more labour intensive than fiberglass and the cost is proportionally higher. Rust is a problem and the surface preparation and coatings must be applied well.

Despite all that, steel can make a good choice for a voyaging yacht. Many long-term voyagers admire the steel boat's bullet-proof reputation. One dark night on our passage to Bermuda, we listened to the drama of a 53' yacht that had struck a submerged object 50 miles north of us and was taking on water. We were too far away to hear the skipper's call for help, but we heard Bermuda Radio's powerful signal asking vessels in the area for assistance. As *Two-Step* sailed on through the black waters, the yacht in distress sank and we heard the report that a freighter picked up four people in a liferaft.

It really shook us. Since that experience, we have done numerous projects on *Two-Step* to increase her ability to withstand such a collision including adding a forward waterproof bulkhead, and strengthening the front edge of the keel.

Steel provides a peace-of-mind for voyagers who are willing to live with the increased weight and the rust problem.

## *Wood*

Plywood and epoxy used in "cold-moulded" construction are a viable option for one-off boatbuilding, and are especially favoured for multihulls since it yields a very light and strong vessel.

Care must be taken when working with such large quantities of epoxy resin however, since it is not unusual to develop a violent allergic reaction to the material in its uncured state. Purchasing one of these modern wood boats can be a cost effective way to get out sailing. Annie Hill wrote *Voyaging on a Small Income* to describe her cruising lifestyle on *Badger*, a 33 foot plywood cruiser she built with husband Pete. The book is a great source of inspiration for those who don't have a lot of resources but just want to get away sailing.

September of 1997 Sheryl and I woke up one sunny morning on Two-Step on the hard in the port of Angra do Heroismo in the Azores. Most cruising yachts had left already and we hadn't seen another cruiser in two weeks. We had just hauled out and were preparing to fly home for the winter. I poked my head out the companionway and noticed a trim black junk-rigged ketch at anchor in the harbour, under the watchful eye of the 17th century fort on the hill. It was *Badger*. Later when Annie and Pete Hill rowed ashore we shared a few beers up on Two-Step in the late summer sun. We talked about their lifestyle and the decision to build *Badger* in plywood.

"Well we just got in last night and haven't sussed out the town yet" said Annie, looking fit and trim, red hair framing a pretty face.

"Did you come from Horta?" I ask.

"Baffin Island actually" Pete says, eyes twinkling at my surprise.

"So you were at sea 5 days ago" I ponder "what weather did you get when Hurricane Erika came by. We battened down here and had quite a blow!"

Annie looked over at Pete. "Ahhhh, that explains it, we had some dirty weather a few days ago. We don't have a radio or any way to get weather you know."

I asked them how they decided to build *Badger* in plywood.

"Well, it was economics really" Annie smiled. "We could build the boat cheaply and quickly, put the rest of our money away in investments and use the investment income to cruise on. We've cruised for years, made numerous circuits of the Atlantic in *Badger* and kept to a budget of just $2,500 per year."

"What about your book, has that changed anything for you?" Sheryl asked.

"Yes, we earned a bit on that, in fact we were able to give ourselves a raise. Now we cruise on $3,500 a year!"

Later Sheryl and I agreed that the plywood *Badger* was one of the most successful cruising boats we had seen that summer. They had been living happily on her for eight years. She looked trim and seaworthy after a stormy passage from Baffin Island (near Greenland!) and it hadn't broken the bank to get her out on the water.

I believe traditional wood planked construction is no longer a viable method of building a cruising boat. It is beautiful and easy to repair but the skills and time necessary to produce a good product, combined with the high maintenance required, make planked wooden boats a labour of love only. If you choose to purchase a traditional wooden vessel, be aware that maintenance requirements rise substantially in the tropics where rot, teredo worm and sun are all more active.

# What Size Boat?

We have met sailors cruising happily aboard boats from 21 feet right up to a family cruising on a 101 foot sloop. Under 28 feet the boats are generally single-handed. Longer than 50 feet is quite rare for a liveaboard cruiser.

Yachts 30 to 40 feet long make up the great majority in anchorages around the world. Ten years ago the average was in the lower 30-35 foot range and now it has crept up to the 35-40 foot range. The key here is that these boats are all actually out cruising - if you look at boats just tied up in marinas you get a different answer!

Choosing a boat for cruising, and living aboard must obviously involve compromises. The smaller boat will be more affordable but may feel cramped and make slower passages because of a shorter waterline length. The larger boat will be more comfortable at sea but will cost more to purchase, maintain and dock in a marina.

There are other factors less obvious. A large gleaming yacht will look like more of a target in a harbour in one of the poorer nations. If you plan to cruise "the road less travelled" it may be a good idea not to look like a multimillionaire as you cruise in on a boat where any one of a dozen deck fittings costs more than double the annual salary of the locals.

The dimensions of a boat can restrict her cruising grounds as well. For example, a sailboat with a mast more than 65 feet off the water will not be able to transit the Intracoastal Waterway on the American east coast. Fixed bridges restrict passage to 65 feet height, and in fact, boats over about 62 feet must watch the tides or be ready to collect things like masthead lights, wind instruments etc as they rain down on the deck!

Choosing the right boat for a cruise is important, but there are so many unknowns if you haven't done it before. How much gear will be needed? How much personal space should there be to live aboard and cruise full time? These are difficult questions, and when we tried to answer them in preparation for our first cruise we looked through boat design books and went to boat shows. After deciding to build a spacious 50 footer (!!) reality intervened and we started looking in the 32-38 foot range. The choice has been perfect for us. At 37' Two-Step is cosy and comfortable belowdecks, and has lots of storage space. Sailing mostly in warm weather, we find we are outside a lot and don't miss the extra living space in the cabin.

The size of boat will be a very personal choice, and very affected by financial considerations. A 40 foot boat will cost substantially more than a 35 footer since it is much bigger not only in length, but beam and depth. On average a 40 footer is 50% larger than a 35 foot sailboat of similar design, since the volume increases by the cube of the length. The extra space inside will definitely cost more!

No matter what kind of boat you choose, the key factors are that the hull is sound, the gear and rigging are able to withstand the strains of voyaging and that the crew are comfortable and confident handling her.

# On Deck

When Sheryl and I were building and outfitting *Two-Step* we tried to imagine sailing her in a storm. As a result, we designed the deck layout so we could handle most tasks from the cockpit, and bought heavy weather sails.

It is interesting to look back on our trip and see just how much heavy weather we encountered. In three years --1050 days of living aboard during an Atlantic circle trip -- we were under way for a total of 4500 hours or nearly 200 days full time. Of that time, 120 days were spent out of sight of land on passages ranging from 2 to 20 days in length and only 9 days were spent in heavy weather! Less than 1 percent of the cruise (8% of the time offshore) was spent in the storm conditions we had thought so much about.

In retrospect, it might seem strange to have put so much effort and expense into arrangements to benefit us for such a rare occurrence. But the time was certainly not misspent! The heavy sails and rigging helped *Two-Step* to avoid problems -- a form of insurance that paid out, without an accident happening.

And by planning the deck layout for easy single-handing, we simplified the sailing at all times.

One of the most common "on deck" problems we have seen on cruising boats is too much clutter. We fell into this trap when we left Florida on our first blue water passage to Bermuda. We bought extra jerry jugs for fuel, water and gasoline, and even an extra propane can (besides the two in the vented propane locker). We set sail with nine 5-gallon jugs, the extra propane can and some teak boards (never know when you might need them), lashed on deck. This was more than 300 pounds of weight well above our centre of gravity! *Two-Step* wallowed off into the Gulf Stream, taking noticeably longer to recover when the seas slapped her.

In a moderate blow 2 days later, a boarding wave tore the lashings and swept the gasoline jug and the propane can over the side. I prefer to think that I was being told to keep the deck clear. Since then we have eliminated all but two of the Jerry cans -- they each contain 5 gallons of water to be grabbed in case we ever have to abandon ship.

Setting up a boat "on-deck" for long-term and ocean cruising is really an exercise in common sense. If you plan to sail short-handed, as we and most cruisers do, organizing the deck for single-handing will allow the off-watch crew to get an undisturbed rest on passages. If you plan offshore passages it is important to consider heavy weather. Preparation is the best insurance you can get.

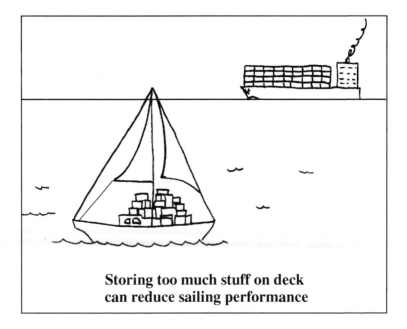

**Storing too much stuff on deck
can reduce sailing performance**

## Deck Layout

The deck of any boat must be a safe place for the crew to efficiently manage the operation of the craft. On a sailboat, that generally means sail handling and no matter how cleverly the boat is set up, sailors still need to be on deck to deal with the sails.

Given that venturing up to the foredeck is much more dangerous than staying in the cockpit or below, then the best way for a crew to safely and efficiently operate the boat is to:

1) Perform most operations from the cockpit.
2) Maximize the safety factor when crew must go forward.

On *Two-Step* we have led most lines back to the cockpit. We can set, reef and furl the headsail, and even reef the mainsail all without leaving the cockpit. The ability to reef both the main and the jib has been a great feature. It means that whoever is on watch can tuck in a reef without having to disturb the off-watch crew. We have agreed that neither of us will go forward in bad weather unless the other is on deck, and never without a safety harness. Setting and gibing the downwind pole, dealing with a spinnaker, and changing headsails, are jobs that must be done on deck, but by reducing the number of trips forward, we feel we have a safer boat.

A roller-furling headsail will be simple to handle from the cockpit but what about the mainsail? *Two-Step* has a conventional slab reefed main, and normally these require that an eye at the tack be put over a hook near the boom gooseneck fitting. Instead, we have a line tied into that eye so that both the clew and the tack can be pulled down remotely (see below). Both these lines could be led aft but there is a tricky arrangement in our Isomat™ boom that means only one line need be led aft -- pull it and both corners of the sail are pulled down tight.

When the trip forward cannot be put off, you will be grateful you have done everything possible to make it a safe trip. In fact, it is not just during a storm or at night that a safe efficient deck layout is important. Coming alongside a dock, setting an anchor and just living on a boat all require a seaworthy, safe platform.

An unobstructed walkway is important. Too much gear tied on deck is bound to trip someone up at exactly the wrong moment. The route must have plenty of handholds -- an extra handrail might be added to the cabin top if there are places where you feel you have to scurry from one safe place to the next.

The stanchions and lifelines are often overlooked and sometimes not as structurally sound as they should be. What might feel sturdy when you just wiggle it, may give way if a crew member fell against it. Check

Figure 1 - Single line reefing option.

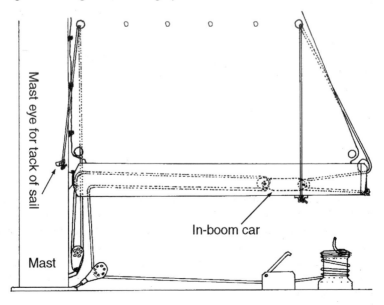

that the stanchion bases are through-bolted with backing plates, or at least large "fender washers". Check that the stanchions are secured in the bases and not corroded, and that the lifelines themselves are not about to part.

On *Two-Step* we rigged jacklines from the bow to the stern. These are lines that we can attach our safety harnesses to, so we can walk right to the bow without ever unclipping the harness (We have used regular 5/8" rope but many people are now using a flat webbing to eliminate the problem of the line rolling underfoot.) The jackline is run along the deck where we walk, so I can nip right up forward with my safety line dragging along behind. And when I'm lying below, off watch, it is a reassuring sound to hear Sheryl dragging the clip along the deck -- I know she's safely tied on!

In rough weather we put in the washboards (companionway door panels). These should be able to be secured so that they cannot be knocked out or lost somehow. There were yachts lost in the British Fastnet race solely due to losing washboards, then taking on water through the open companionway.

## Comfort on Deck

Protection from sun, spray, wind and rain must also be provided for the crew of a cruising sailboat. Where Dennis Conner and the boys can just paint zinc on their noses, the cruising live-aboard will want more protection. There are very few cruising sailboats without a good dodger -- we consider it a necessity especially since Sheryl, a fair-skinned redhead, burns easily. The ultimate luxury would be an inside steering station but the real need is a place where the crew can hide from the sun and spray.

We extended our dodger about a foot past the companionway so you can sit against the back of the cabin trunk, looking aft and be in the shade much of the time. A forward opening window is a necessity to provide ventilation in port.

In fact, we recently replaced the old canvas dodger with a hard fiberglass one of our own creation. The solid Plexiglas™ windows are much clearer than the old flexible ones so we can actually see out through it!

A bimini to protect the helmsman is a great idea as well, especially for tropical sailing and motoring through canals such as the Intracoastal Waterway. We cannot rig a bimini on *Two-Step* since it would interfere with the mainsheet. We miss it most in waterways since someone must be at the helm constantly, handling her in close quarters. Offshore the auto-pilot steers all the time and we sit under the dodger and peer out every few minutes.

Weather cloths are another option to improve crew comfort at sea. These are canvas panels that hang from the lifelines around the cockpit area to protect the crew from spray. Sheryl made these out of Sunbrella™ synthetic canvas and used grommets for attachment points. They are attached onto the lifelines and toe-rail using light cord.

Weather cloths make sailing much more pleasant on *Two-Step*, which tends to be a wet boat, with her narrow beam and low freeboard. They also give a little more privacy in marinas and at anchor. (Incidentally the British call these *dodgers*, and would call our dodger a *sprayhood*)

A sun awning is another great idea for use in port to keep sun off the crew and heat out of the boat. We have rigged ours so it can be easily taken down if the wind gets too boisterous -- more than 20 knots is our limit. It has also been useful as a rain catcher.

*A moulded fiberglass dodger replaces our old canvas one. A Plexiglas™ front window hinges up for ventilation.*

Table 2 - Features and Gear for Safety on Deck

| Safety Features | Comments |
|---|---|
| dodger | Indispensable for sheltering from sun as well as spray and wind. |
| bimini | Protects the helmsman from the sun and makes the cockpit more comfortable. |
| awning | Almost essential for sailing in the tropics. |
| mooring cleats | Oversize cleats with large backing plates. We attach our jacklines from the bow cleat to the stern one. |
| jacklines | Heavy line or flat webbing from bow to stern on both sides of the boat to which crew members hook their safety harness before leaving the cockpit. They remain connected to the ship as they venture forward. |
| lines led aft | Reducing the number of trips forward improves safety, so leading halyards, reefing lines, etc. back to the cockpit is a good idea. |
| headsail furling | Simplifies sail handling and allows the jib to be handled from the cockpit. We bought our Profurl$^{TM}$ to make short-handed sailing safer and it is terrific. |
| secure stanchions and lifelines | Check that stanchions are through-bolted and in good condition and that lifelines are not weak. |
| clear decks | For safer decks and improved performance by keeping weight low. |
| secure washboards | Companionway washboards should not just lie in place. Find a method to secure them. |

# Storing Items on Deck

As mentioned earlier, we have substantially reduced the clutter on *Two-Step's* deck. She is a safer boat now and handles better, but we do still keep **some** things on deck. Following is the list of gear we store on deck.

Table 3 - On Deck Storage

| Items | Comments |
|-------|----------|
| life raft | Lashed on deck. See *"**Safety Equipment**"* on page *134"*. |
| dinghy | Almost essential. Ours (and 80% of long-term cruisers) is inflatable but you'll never convince the other group to switch. We store it inflated and lashed down in front of the mast for immediate use in an emergency. |
| outboard | We like the freedom of exploring in the dinghy so we got an 8 HP engine to allow the dinghy to plane. |
| barbecue | A nice option. It keeps the heat outside when cooking on a hot day. |
| boat hooks | An 8' one and a 6' one. |
| 5 gal. water jugs | We carry two 5-gallon plastic jugs of water on deck only on offshore passages. It's extra water and could be grabbed in an emergency. |

# Dinghies

Some kind of tender is a necessity for long-term cruising. I suppose that in some areas a yacht could move from marina to marina and avoid needing one, but that would mean foregoing the joy and independence of time spent at anchor!

We have an inflatable dinghy with floorboards and a transom. The transom allows use of larger motors (such as our 8HP), not just the little 2-3HP engines that the "inner tube" style inflatable dinghies can handle. I should mention that we are so happy with our Avon R3.10 and Yamaha 8HP motor that it might be hard to make objective comparisons to other choices.

But if you should choose the *unstable*, *slow* and *difficult-to-store* option of a hard dinghy, what can you expect? Well, for one thing, there are many less thefts of hard dinghies than of inflatables. And realistically, a hard dinghy with a good set of oars is the cheapest and most durable option. There, I tried to be objective!

Most long-term cruisers have chosen an inflatable dinghy. Over 80% of North American cruisers have an inflatable with an outboard motor. Of these, nearly half are the rigid-inflatable type (or RIB), with a solid fiberglass floor and transom. The RIB offers the best performance of any small tender and addresses one of the "hard dinghy" peoples' concerns as well -- they fare better in the being-dragged-up-a-rocky-beach test. Their shortcomings are weight and storage. We think it is essential that the tender can be carried on board, not only towed, and if there isn't room for a RIB to be stored on deck, consider another option.

Our rules for towing the dink are as follows:

- never tow the dinghy at night.
- never tow the dinghy if there is a chance of rough seas.
- never tow the dinghy if the passage is more than 15 miles.
- always tow with a bridle through the dinghy's bow towing eye and back to the transom. We put a "U"-bolt in the transom for this purpose after tearing off one of the towing rings that was bonded to the bow. I don't believe any of these bonded rings are really up to the task of towing a dinghy. The transom can easily handle the strain.

This may be difficult to believe, but we met a yacht in the Azores who complained that they had been towing their dinghy and had lost it -- *on their way across the Atlantic!!*

The main reason we are so happy with our dinghy and motor combination, is that it provides such a great way to explore. With the two of us aboard, the dinghy will easily reach a plane (maybe 15 knots), so we can, and often have travelled more than 3-4 miles from *Two-Step*. We've explored up rivers and creeks, over shallow areas where we couldn't take the "mother ship". And for our major passion, skin diving, an inflatable is the best choice. We carry a small anchor and some line, and can easily climb in and out of the inflatable when we anchor near a reef.

Our Avon R3.10 is the type with three large pieces of plywood that assemble into a floor, then the dinghy is inflated around it. This is a 20 minute operation, but most of the time we store the dinghy inflated, secured upside-down on the foredeck. It can be

*Most cruisers choose inflatable dinghies for convenience and speed.*

launched in minutes and stands ready as a life-platform in case of emergencies.

No dinghy is maintenance-free. We have never had a puncture, but when the dinghy was four years old some of the seams were showing wear, so we had some new seam-tape bonded over the trouble spots. Repairs *can* be made on board but numerous conditions must be met to achieve a good bond. For Hypalon dinghies (Avon, Achilles etc.), the material must be sanded to roughen it first. It should be cleaned, and then wiped with toluene to soften the rubber. Temperature and humidity should also be within the normal indoor range (Apparently PVC dinghies are even trickier to glue.) We found it was easier to take it to a repair shop where all this could be more easily controlled.

The outboard motor must also be maintained and this is an area where it is easy to do the normal tasks oneself. Every few months I remove the cover and apply grease to all the grease-points as specified in the manual. Then I spray Boeing T-9™ on other likely looking places and close it up again. Once a year I change the oil in the lower unit.

Probably the biggest problem with outboard motors is corrosion and a good rinse with fresh water is the best therapy. If the motor is going to be out of use for a couple of weeks or more, I flush the cooling passages out with fresh water using a motor flusher (This is a simple device that allows a hose to feed water directly into the intake vents in the motor's lower unit)

We store the outboard on deck as well as the dinghy itself. The motor lives on a bracket on the stern rail, locked with a non-corrosive lock.

Table 4 - Dinghy Maintenance

| Dinghy Maintenance | Comments |
|---|---|
| basic repair kit | (comes with most inflatables) Includes one-part glue and some patches. |
| outboard manual | |
| motor flusher | |
| lower unit oil | |
| spark plugs | |
| shear pins | our Yamaha doesn't use a shear pin but if yours does, bring some spares. |
| basic tools | A spark plug wrench is all that is likely to be needed above regular tools for the diesel engine. |

Table 5 - Dinghy Gear

| Dinghy Gear | Comments |
|---|---|
| oars | |
| lifejackets | |
| bailing bucket | |
| anchor and 60' rode | We keep ours in a canvas bucket to protect the floorboards. |
| dinghy depth sounder | This is a marked cord with a lead sinker on the end (see page 99) |
| fuel tank | We use a 3-gallon plastic tank. We keep it lashed on deck near the transom when not in use. Do not store gasoline below decks unless in vented locker. |
| lock and cable | Honestly we don't use ours that much, but dinghy theft definitely does occur. |
| small fenders | We keep two 3½" diameter fenders for use coming alongside rough docks and walls. |
| air pump | We don't carry it with us in the dinghy -- maybe we're tempting fate. |

*Exploring a deserted cay in the Bahamas. Our 10 foot dinghy with 8HP motor planes easily even loaded with supplies.*

## Below Deck

Organizing the cabin space will be covered in "Organizing the Space Below" on page 207. Following are some hints for safety and comfort for living in the cabin -- offshore and at anchor.

## Living Aboard

### Ventilation

Ventilation is often overlooked in boats built for northern waters. But some provision must be made to get air down below, especially for sailing in the tropics.

Most boats are more comfortable at anchor since there are fewer obstructions to block the wind. The boat will usually face the breeze and tend to catch it with open hatches. Many cruisers use a WindScoop™ in a main hatch to get even more air in but the winds in the Caribbean and Bahamas are often too strong for them. We have found we don't need one because we have a reversing hatch lid which acts like a scoop, and six opening ports which provide

*A proper Dorade vent can bring a surprising amount of air below. We have never had a drop of water enter even in heavy weather.*

plenty of cross breeze. There are often areas in the cabin that are out of the main breeze that flows in the hatch and out the companionway. A fan can help here -- we use one for the forward cabin to make the hot sticky nights a bit more breathable.

### Rain and Insect Protection

Some form of rain protection for the hatches will help out on a stormy day as well. Until we built a rainproof hatch cover, on *Two-Step* we were forced to close all hatches except the companionway in a storm and it gets hot quite quickly on a tropical evening.

One extremely hot June night in the Bahamas the wind died almost completely. We had spent 3 days alone anchored in a narrow cut of swimming pool blue water that wound like a river between the sugar sand beaches of the low green islands on either side. Our only visitor had been a wild pink flamingo, hooked beak chasing dinner in the shallow waters of the cut. But as darkness fell the mosquitoes began to come out. With the wind gone there was nothing to keep them near home and they literally swarmed *Two-Step*. As I pulled our bug screen hatch out of the cockpit locker they covered me. I could swat 3 at a time -- with one swat!

Down below the evening took on a surrealistic Alfred Hitchcock quality. We were under siege! When we had finished swatting the mosquitoes that came back below with me, I started noticing they were coming in around the hatch! I watched in fascination as one after another sidled through a ¼ " tear in the screen. The only noise in the still night air was the buzzing of the 50-60 that were flying vainly against the rest of the screen -- only 1½ square feet.

We taped up the hatch to try to seal it. We taped the port screens and still they found their way in. Then, I saw one sneak out from under the ceiling panel! He had flown in the dorade vent and towards the screen attached to the inside of the ceiling. Meeting this obstacle he must have

escaped through a crack between the vent and the screen and into the space between the cabin and the ceiling. We went and hid in the forward cabin and swatted mosquitoes who found us under the sheets.

I recommend this experience if you want to learn the shortcomings of your bug defences. Or if you want to write a horror novel!

Now the new tent I've designed for the forward hatch allows us to leave the hatch open even in fairly heavy rain. The forward edge is lower than the hatch when it is folded down in the "rainy" position. The hatch itself supports the cover which just snaps on to the frame. I sewed a wooden

*Our new "hatch tent" in its fairweather configuration. Folded down it allows the hatch to remain open even in moderate rain and wind.*

dowel into the leading edge of the cover and grommets so it could be tied to the toerail or inner forestay. In the photo it is tied up to the inner forestay where it acts like a windscoop.

### Condensation

A more subtle threat to comfort below decks is condensation. We were shocked to find that the underside of our mattress was mildewed after 6 months of living aboard. We now air the mattress every few days by taking the bedding off and propping it up to get air to both sides and this has helped. Friends Michael and Lise on *Blue Dragon*, place a plastic open weave mat between their mattress and the berth, and this has prolonged the life of the mattress. Another thing for our "to-do" list!

Warm air can hold more water than cool air. If air is humid, water vapour held in the air will condense onto a cooler surface since the cooled air can no longer hold so much moisture. This situation happens if a hull with no insulation has cool (or worse, cold) water on one side and moist air on the other. On *Two-Step*, the hull is insulated with Airex™ foam from the settee level up to 3 inches from the deck. The area below the Airex™ is often quite damp when we're sailing in cold northern waters. Even the narrow strip above the Airex™ can be damp on some days although it is not in the water. The insulated area is never damp. In warm tropical water, we rarely experience problems.

Fiberglass and metal boats are all prone to condensation. Most metal boats are insulated as a method of preventing the condensation from becoming a corrosion problem. Fiberglass boats do not need this and many have been built with a solid glass hull with no core material to act as insulation. In this case it is easiest to line the areas that suffer worst with a foam-backed "Nauga-hyde" type of material for insulation, or plastic open weave mat to keep stored items off the wet surface. (I know the conservationists will hate me for this since I understand the Nauga is nearly extinct!)

# Offshore

Being in the cabin of a yacht in a storm has been likened to being inside a washing machine -- but not everything comes out clean! Even on a fairly pleasant sailing day the larger ocean swells can occasionally group together and give the hull a slap that will send an unwary crew member flying if they're not holding on.

### Handholds

When on passage we often find that there are days on end when we go from place to place in the boat always holding on to something. We added handholds below decks as well as above so we could more easily brace ourselves. I installed one long handrail beneath the coach house windows that runs the length of the saloon. Since *Two-Step* is fairly narrow this has been all we needed. Wider boats might need some handholds on the ceiling as well.

We have also tried to round off all corners that might catch someone below decks. The edge of the icebox and the galley and companionway were areas where I sanded some corners down a little. Nevertheless Sheryl still seems to get bruises from being jostled around by the motion of the boat at sea.

### Lee Cloths or Bunk-boards

*Leeclothes or leeboards are essential for safe and secure sleeping at sea.*

Some form of protection must be provided for crew in their bunks. On *Two-Step* the saloon settees are the most comfortable place when the boat is pitching since there is the least motion near the centre of the boat. We use these as pilot berths. To prevent rolling off when the boat heels, we made lee clothes to keep the sleeping crew member in place. These are made from a piece of canvas 18" high that is fastened

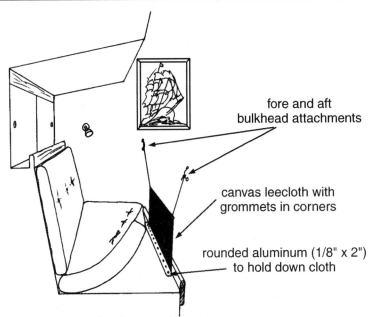

fore and aft
bulkhead attachments

canvas leecloth with
grommets in corners

rounded aluminum (1/8" x 2")
to hold down cloth

down on the outside edge of the bunk. We run them most of the length of the bunk, leaving 1 foot open at each end so you have a place to breathe and look out from whichever way you sleep in them. The canvas is fastened down to the bunk under a piece of aluminum (sanded smooth to prevent chafe) and attached up to the bulkhead at each end by lines tied in the upper corners. When not in use these fold neatly under the settee cushions.

### Securing Hatches and Lockers

Gear must also be stowed well. In some cases, designs that work well for everyday sailing conditions will not be sufficient for a rough offshore passage. We put sturdy twist latches on all the settee lockers so they couldn't be opened by gear banging against them from the inside.

The worst nightmare is for the boat to be knocked down, or even pitchpoled. In this case, the mess of gear that would empty out of lockers and from under floorboards doesn't bear thinking about. For an accurate and chilling first-hand description of this, I recommend Miles and Beryl Smeeton's tale of being pitchpoled near Cape Horn (*Once is Enough*). It should be enough to get anyone to purchase a few strong latches and to think about securing floorboards. Nothing will be proof against all disasters of course, but anything that helps is worth doing. I find that projects like this tend to help me keep *Two-Step* tidier below as well.

## Summary

- Good ventilation will be especially important in hot climates.
- Consider rain protection so hatches can remain open on a damp day.
- Install bug screens on dorade vents as well as for hatches.
- Condensation can ruin gear and upholstery. Insulation added to lockers will reduce this problem.
- Plan enough handholds below decks.
- Consider lee cloths to make pilot bunks secure if offshore sailing is planned.

# Generating and Storing Electrical Power

There's something in the smell of the spring air that will always remind me of sailing to the Azores. Smell creates powerful associations and our 1990 voyage from Bermuda to Faial was as much a rite of passage as a passage itself for me and Sheryl and Two-Step. The journey took 18 days and forged a bond between the three of us as we learned the feeling of the hull in the sea and the power of the wind pushing us along - the movements, sounds, sensations of a boat under sail on an ocean swell.

Subtle clues in the boat's motion, the particular sound of the water rushing past the hull tell me, even lying in my bunk, how well we're sailing. I know when something is amiss. It must be that communion of a boat and crew sailing well but I am always trying to postpone starting the engine as if it breaks the spell.

The engine you say?? Why start the engine?! Well, like the majority of sailboats today, *Two-Step* uses a fair bit of electrical power in a day of cruising and the alternator is the primary method of charging up the batteries when away from the dock (which for us is most of the time). We have to run the engine even if it's just enough to charge the batteries, but how much is enough?

We used to do two 1 hour sessions a day at sea but on this year's cruise of the Bahamas we decided to get a handle on what was really needed and see if there was something we could do to reduce that.

Before spending lots of money on improvements to our electrical system, I decided to see if we could economize on power use. I reasoned that if I could learn where all our battery power was going I might find an area where we were using more than was really needed.

Electrical power is measured in watts and many devices are rated for the number of watts of power they use. But I didn't want to just read the data sheets. I wanted to measure the power *Two-Step* was using at any given time. The answer was an ammeter. (Since the wattage used is equal to the voltage times the amperage, you can use an ammeter in a 12 volt system where the voltage will always be 12, e.g. a 12 watt bulb will draw 1 amp, an 18 watt bulb will draw 1.5 amps). I decided to install an ammeter (sometimes called an "amp meter") in the line from the battery to the circuit breaker panel - I'd see all the power that left the battery to go to the breakers.

$$Watts = Voltage \times Amps$$
$$18 \; Watts = 12 \; V \times 1.5A$$

Then the fun began. *Two-Step* was swinging at anchor and the sun was just setting as I finished installing the meter. We turned off everything in the boat and in the gathering dusk I played a flashlight on the ammeter. Sure enough we were drawing zero amps. For the next half hour Sheryl systematically turned on and off everything in the boat while I noted down the amps used in the logbook.

Figure 2 - Connecting an Ammeter to monitor current used out of ship's main house battery.

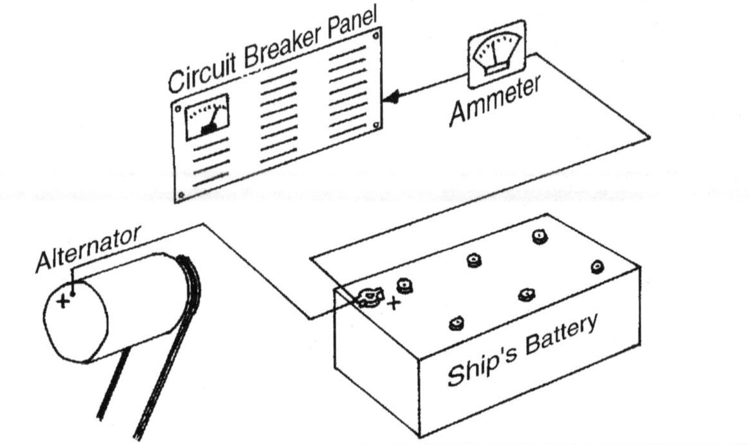

What an education! Some appliances such as the refrigeration system, used exactly what we thought they did - 5 amps for the fridge as specified in the user's manual. The solenoid for the stove on the other hand was a shock! I had somehow decided that it used 2-3 amps (since it has a 5 amp circuit breaker and no owner's manual). The ammeter shows it draws less than 1/2 amp! The cabin lights were another major surprise. With just 3 of our quaint yacht-style brass reading lamps burning we were going through 5 amps continuously !! Ouch!

Over the following few months of cruising the Bahamas we used our new ammeter to get in touch with a part of the boat that is a bit more elusive than the trim of the sails. By peering at it whenever I was near the nav-station I got a picture of electrical use on board *Two-Step*. I cut down our light use by installing 2 Aqua Signal™ halogen "Mini-Spotlights" beside the quaint brass reading lamps. The focused beam is better for reading by and uses only half as much power. A 10 watt bulb has replaced the 25 watt masthead light we use for night sailing, saving more power than the Autohelm™ uses in the same period. Our standard of living has improved greatly without adding expensive new batteries or a solar panel.

*Solar panels in a suitable place where they won't be stepped on. They provide most of our power at anchor, and insurance against losing battery power due to an an engine failure at sea.*

The wind that had hardly ruffled the shallow water as we left Great Harbour had built and given us a nice gentle sail back towards the Gulf Stream. Now it was dusk and the south wind was blowing 15 to 20 as we entered the stream itself with just 60 miles to go to West Palm Beach. Great Stirrup light blinked astern and was already seeming to drift to the south as we felt the powerful Gulf Stream current lift us northward. I checked the sails and felt the new rhythm of the waves as *Two-Step* danced towards Florida. We were moving well and I glanced around again at compass and telltales, and scanned the horizon before going below for 5 minutes to check the chart and brew a cup of tea. In the nav centre, I glanced at the ammeter and saw we were using just 3 ½ amps. We would not need to disrupt the night by starting the engine until docking at West Palm in the morning.

## Solar and Wind Power

Most long-term voyagers add some form of alternative power generation to cut down their dependance on the engine. The most popular methods are solar and wind generators and, although there are champions for either method, we believe that the determining factor is the climate of your cruising grounds.

Walking the docks in Gibraltar we saw a lot of boats with solar panels, and a number of the smaller wind generators such as the British "Rutland" wind turbine. We installed a Rutland while we were there, and found it a good way to top up the battery. Because these small generators are made for high winds, they do not have to be turned off when you leave the boat. Some of the larger propeller units would self-destruct if not stopped in a gale so you can't leave them unattended.

Our little wind generator was a reasonable way to <u>augment</u> our power needs although it could not be relied upon in all conditions. If the wind didn't blow, it didn't produce power. The Mediterranean, with unpredictable winds and lots of summer sun, would seem to be ideal for solar panels. Similarly, as we sailed across the Atlantic to the Caribbean via Brazil, we found the wind generator produced very little. Although we had plenty of wind, it was all downwind sailing and in the rolling seas, the generator couldn't seem to find the wind and stay with it. We got less than 1 amp per hour on that crossing.

*Solar and wind power working together. Alapa's stern posts keep both the dangerous windmill and the fragile solar panels out of the way.*

When we dropped anchor in the protected harbour of Prickly Bay, Grenada, we entered a different world. For day after day the trade winds blew steadily from the east from 10 to 20 knots. Truly the perfect place for a wind generator. It seemed so predictable that anything out of the tradewind range was worthy of mention. For days on end we collected 2 amps every hour from the wind generator, enough that *Two-Step* (without refrigeration at that time) did not have to have her engine run at all to charge the batteries. Here is the key point -- our intake was greater than our outflow -- and, just as in finances, that is essential. Other boats in the anchorage were in the same situation. The larger generators such as the Wind-Bugger™ were able to provide full power, even for boats with refrigeration.

Where you plan to sail will help to make the decision between solar and wind generators. Anywhere far north will be better for wind generators since the sun is not powerful enough to provide much power. Places like the Med and other non-tradewind locations will be better for solar power. Here a wind generator could sit idle for days at a time.

Of course the easiest way out of this dilemma is to have both! Many cruisers install a couple of solar panels and a small wind generator and have the best of both worlds. Keith on *Happy Girl* has a 50 watt solar panel and a Aerogen™ wind generator and says he seldom needed to charge batteries with the engine during his circumnavigation.

# A Solar Array

In 1996 we added 2 large solar panels to the roof of our hard dodger. With our refrigeration we decided we needed more power than the little Rutland WindCharger was giving. The panels are Siemens M65 from West Marine and each produce 3.5 amps in full sun. I installed an ammeter in the line from the panels to the battery to see what we were getting. The surprise for us was just how often that output was reached!

Swinging at anchor in Flores, Azores in July 1997 we saw over 2.5 amps *per panel* by 9 in the morning until after 4 in the afternoon. Of course the shadow of the boom on the dodger sometimes cut one panel off entirely. Nevertheless I'm glad I mounted the panels on the dodger and just left them. The idea of adjusting the angle of the panels to the sun as the day goes by isn't for me. Besides, you're just as likely to find the boat has swung on her anchor and can't be set optimally anyway. Just buy another panel and mount them securely. A dodger or bimini or cabintop arrangement can be quite tidy and is also less inviting for thieves.

I calculate we get 15 amp/hours per day from each panel on sunny summer days. Bright cloudy days provide roughly 10 ah/day per panel. If it looks like rain you won't get almost anything but the panels are surprisingly good in light overcast conditions.

The new harbour of Lajes on the island of Flores in the Azores is a snug anchorage against tall cliffs. Red roofed houses wind up along the steep lanes from the harbour to the town above. Floating on the warm sea air are enticing fragrances of the flowers for which this island is named. We have just finished a passage from Bermuda in a record (for *Two-Step*) 14 days and are longing to stretch our legs. The climb from the harbour up the cobbled streets is rough on our sea legs and we take a break at a bench with a breathtaking view high over the port. Looking like a model yacht far below, *Two-Step* hangs at her anchor soaking up the sun. I've left the refrigeration running to chill down some of the excellent Portuguese beer we've just bought and the solar panels are actually producing enough power to top up the batteries as well as run the refrigeration. Paradise indeed!

# Calculating Battery System Capacity

A good sized battery bank is essential.  It must provide ship's power for at least 24 hours and not reach less than 50% charge. Regularly discharging lead acid batteries below 50% will reduce their life substantially.

So how do you determine the amount of battery power used over 24 hours? Of course if you look at the ammeter we just installed it will give you the answer, but you can get a reasonably good idea by putting together an electrical budget. Write down all the electrical equipment and make columns for "amps used" and also for "hours run per day". Now the part that proves science is largely an art -- estimate how many hours each piece of equipment will be used per day. This can be quite difficult if you are trying to estimate for new equipment. I use a method that involves trying to imagine how much you will use something, working out the final number and then fudging it to work with the resources you have. For example, you imagine you might have cabin lights on for 3 hours every night. These three lights use 5 amps altogether. This means 15 amp-hours per day for cabin lights. Then, if that is too much, plan to turn out the brightest light and go to bed 1 hour earlier. Bingo, you cut power use to only 6 amp-hours. (Alternatively you could get fluorescent or halogen lights to replace the power hungry incandescents).

The following table shows *Two-Step's* electrical budget as a sample:

| Device | Current Draw (amps) | Hours Used | Consumption per day (amp-hours) |
|---|---|---|---|
| At Anchor | | | |
| Cabin lights | 4 | 3 | 12 |
| Anchor light | 0.8 | 10 | 8 |
| Refrigeration | 5 | 8 | 40 |
| Stove solenoid | 0.25 | 2 | 0.5 |
| Stereo | 1 | 3 | 3 |
| Cabin fan | 0.5 | 12 | 6 |
| Total amp-hours | | | 69.5 |

| Device | Current Draw (amps) | Hours Used | Consumption per day (amp-hours) |
|---|---|---|---|
| At Sea | | | |
| Cabin lights: saloon | 0.8 | 10 | 8 |
| galley | 1 | 3 | 3 |
| Masthead tricolour | 0.8 | 10 | 8 |
| Refrigeration | 5 | 8 | 40 ** |
| Stove solenoid | 0.25 | 2 | 0.5 |
| Autopilot | 1 | 24 | 24 |
| VHF radio | 0.5 | 24 | 12 |
| Instruments | 0.5 | 24 | 12 |
| Total amp-hours | | | 48.5 |

** To save power, we often do not run the refrigeration at sea.

Having determined the power required per day, you can consider how much battery capacity you will need to supply it. It is not so simple as having a 60 amp-hour battery to supply 60 amp-hours of power in one day. Normal lead acid batteries shouldn't be discharged more than 50% very often since it will reduce their useful life. Similarly, it is difficult to charge a battery right up to 100%. As the battery gets closer to full charge, it accepts current more slowly so that the last 10% is difficult to achieve unless the battery is charged over many hours. This means that a battery has roughly 40% of its stated capacity available for use on a regular basis.

For the example above, a battery with a stated capacity of 175 amp-hours or more, would be able to supply the 70 amp-hours of power needed for 1 day at anchor (175 X 40% = 70). A battery bank totalling 267 amp-hour capacity would supply sufficient power at sea (267 X 40% = 107).

Of course, these are basic minimums and any additional capacity would not be wasted. Cruising sailors rarely seem to complain they have too much battery capacity.

When installing additional batteries, they must be put in a vented box and secured in the event of a 360° roll. Batteries should not be connected in parallel since they will discharge each other. The best way around this is to connect them to the engine with either a battery combiner (that connects them all together if it senses more than 13 volts) or using diodes in the lines so that the batteries cannot drain though each other when the engine is not charging. A battery selector switch on the output side allows you to choose which battery will supply power for the ship.

On modern gadget-laden sailboats, adding a battery and additional charging capacity are not simple projects but provide a great payback in cruising comfort and peace of mind.

# Electrical System Problems

### Corrosion

The most common electrical problem, especially in saltwater, is corrosion causing a bad connection. This problem is not confined to wet bilges and areas where saltwater leaks onto and actually touches the connections. Even the salt air holds sufficient moisture and salt to start corrosion on terminals.

Different metals react to this corrosive environment in different ways. Plain copper wire, for instance, is very susceptible to corrosion -- it turns the characteristic green of copper roofs. The best wire for use on a boat headed for saltwater is "tinned, stranded copper wire" . Stranded copper wire refers to the fact that a large number of fine strands of wire are run together inside the insulating core. This means the wire is much more flexible and less likely to fatigue and break if bent repeatedly. (Single strand wire commonly used in houses should not be used!) Tinned copper wire has a fine coating of tin on the outside of each strand and this is far more resistant to corrosion than plain copper. Any projects where gear is added to a boat should be done using tinned copper wire.

A surprising amount of marine electrical gear comes with regular copper wire. I usually solder these bare connections before doing anything else. Even if I am not installing a new pump right away I lightly twist up the exposed strands and melt a drop of solder onto the wire. It protects it while waiting in the locker to be installed.

### Connections

Many boats are wired up with crimp connections and I believe this is the best solution to the question of how to connect two wires. Experience on *Two-Step* has shown that these connections last well BUT only when the wire being crimped is tinned first. If you don't have tinned copper wire then it is essential to protect the ends of the wires first by soldering them before crimping, when adding equipment. Then crimp a connection onto the wire and get a much better connection between the wire and the crimp fitting. Use closed end crimp connectors since they are more reliable in the event of a connection becoming loose.

Caution: Do not use acid core flux solder on any electrical connections. It will cause failure when least expected! Use rosin core solder only.

If the boat's original wiring involves regular untinned wire with crimp connections, it is worth considering running solder into the crimp connections to protect them before going into saltwater. If the insulation is damaged by this, slip an insulating piece of heat shrink tubing over the terminal.

Incidentally, a copper wire that has gone green will not accept solder until it has been cleaned first -- I sometimes pull the strands between a piece of fine sandpaper a couple of times to clean them.

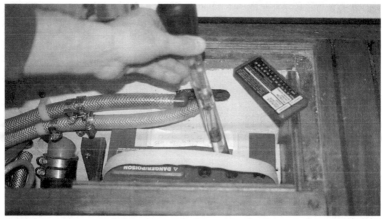

*A hydrometer tests the amount of charge in the battery by weighing a sample of battery acid drawn up into it. This doesn't work on sealed batteries or gel-cells.*

### Battery Health

For day to day fitness of the electrical system, it is important to know just what is going on in your batteries. At the risk of over-simplifying things, a voltmeter tells how much energy is still in a battery, and an ammeter monitors how much energy is going in and out of the battery. (See previous pages for ammeter information)

A voltmeter is not like a gas gauge that goes from zero to full. A difference of less than 1 volt (from roughly 12.6 down to 11.8 volts) represents the full range of charge. A battery that shows less than 11.8 volts is dead! *It is therefore important to have a voltmeter that allows you to see a difference of 0.1 volt.* A digital meter or an "expanded scale" analog meter can be used. The DVM or digital voltmeter is best . It has less than 1% error as opposed to an expanded scale meter at roughly 3%.

Table 6 - Checking Battery Voltage

| Battery Voltage -- How to check it | |
| --- | --- |
| To judge the battery condition with a voltmeter or hydrometer there must be no load - anything that is switched on will lower the voltage and give a false reading. Switch everything off and wait at least half an hour. The following table shows the percentage of charge remaining in the battery. | |
| 12.6 | fully charged |
| 12.4 | 75% |
| 12.2 | 50% |
| 12.0 | 25% |
| below 11.8 | dead |

Voltage does not always represent the charge in a battery. Many factors affect the voltage of the common lead acid battery. A cold battery will show a slightly lower voltage than a warm battery even though both have the same charge. A load (drawing a current out of the battery by having things turned on) will reduce the voltage of a battery in two ways. First of all, the load will take energy out of the battery so that the level of charge will be reduced after the device is turned off. Secondly, the fact that the battery is being discharged will dramatically reduce the voltage shown at the moment. The voltage of the battery will jump back up as soon as the load is removed and then will gradually climb even higher for up to an hour until it reaches equilibrium. **The state of the battery cannot be accurately judged while there is anything switched on.** Like any tool, you must practice with it to get good results. See example below and "Battery Voltage -- How to check it" above.

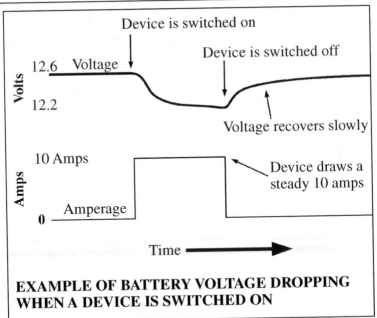

**EXAMPLE OF BATTERY VOLTAGE DROPPING WHEN A DEVICE IS SWITCHED ON**

Tip 1 - Tidy up with Tie-Wraps

| HINT - Tie Wraps: |
|---|
| If I'm feeling really saintly I sometimes grab 4 or 5 tie wraps and just wander the boat installing them to tidy up. I check the engine compartment and might add one to secure a loose wire. A spare alternator belt can be tie-wrapped close to the alternator in the engine compartment in case of emergencies. I also look on deck at the pulpit and stern rail where wires go to running lights and GPS/LORAN antennas. I use tie-wraps here to hold these wires snugly against the rail and out of harms way. A tidy boat is a happy boat! Michael on *Blue Dragon* suggests black ones last better in the sun than white ones. |

*A soldering iron is an essential tool. I have a small inverter so we can run the iron at anchor or at sea.*

Table 7 - Electrical System Spares

| Electrical Spares | Comments |
|---|---|
| ~50' stranded tinned wire | In two colours -- one for positive and one for negative. |
| crimp fittings | Assorted sizes and end types for repairs. |
| butt connectors | To be used to join two wires. |
| terminal blocks | |
| circuit breakers | Carry spares for each size in electrical panel. |
| electrical tape | |
| coaxial terminal fittings | 2 spares - they seem prone to corrosion. |
| white electrical tape and marker | For labelling wires - e.g. "bilge pump +" on positive wire to bilge pump where it connects to the electrical panel. |
| amalgamating tape | For waterproofing connections. |
| petroleum jelly, wire brush and #600 sandpaper | For cleaning and waterproofing battery terminals. |
| tie wraps | For tidying up wiring. Can also be used to attach wires to pulpits etc. outside. Also for marking depths on an anchor rode. 100 would not be too many. |
| bulbs | At least one of each type on board - especially nav lights. |

Table 8 - Electrical Spares for Self-Sufficiency

| Tools/Spares | Comments |
|---|---|
| reference book | |
| soldering iron, gun type | |
| soldering iron, traditional | The old type that is basically a block of metal on the end of a screwdriver handle. This can be heated up on the stove and then used for about a minute. I have found ours to be a good backup for the electrical type and is also capable of soldering a big wire - e.g. 6 gauge. |
| solder | Cored solder is nice for small jobs and electrical work. It must be rosin cored, not acid cored. |
| rosin flux | |
| voltmeter | |
| wire stripper | |
| crimper | |
| wire cutter | |
| hydrometer | Specific gravity is a more accurate method of testing battery condition than by voltage since you can check the condition of each individual cell. As with a voltmeter, you have to remove all loads and wait for the electrolyte to stabilize when testing with a hydrometer. They don't work for any sealed batteries such as gel cells. |

# Diesel Engines

I lay upside down in the cockpit locker with my head stuck in the cramped access space above the diesel tank. The boat rolled through 30 degrees as an old ocean swell lifted her up and dropped her again, the sails slatting in only a breath of wind. Our Kingston Anchor™ made an impression on my shoulder as I braced myself against the bulkhead and *Two-Step* lurched in the seaway. I wondered how I had got into this situation.

Sheryl and I had been underway for two months already - taking *Two-Step* south to the Bahamas. We had gone through the Intracoastal Waterway from Norfolk to Beaufort, North Carolina but now we wanted to pick up the pace. We had anchored in the protected bight of Cape Lookout near Beaufort to wait for the winds to drop to 20 knots. At one in the morning we had set off sailing wing and wing downwind towards Charleston, 200 miles southwest. There was no moon and the stars did little to light the scene. Wave crests hissed out of the dark, lifting the stern as we raced through the night. After using the engine to help raise the anchor I had left it running to charge the batteries. Then, two hours later, the boat rolling as we sailed downwind, the engine had slowed down and grumbled to a halt. By the gradual way it stopped I suspected the fuel filter was clogged. What had gone wrong?

Diesel engines are extremely reliable and well suited to operation on a boat and, more often than not, "dirty fuel" is the cause of engine problems. Sure enough, as I lay in the cockpit locker peering in at the glass bowl of the fuel filter I could see it was half full of water. I would have to drain out the water, replace the filter element and then bleed the air out of the system.

There are only a limited number of ways that water can get into the fuel tank:

- Pumped in with a load of fuel. Since most marina operators filter their product and stake their reputation on clean fuel, I believe this is the least likely culprit.

- Condensation in the tank from humid air that enters the breather. This is almost eliminated by keeping the tank full, thereby reducing the air space.

- If the tank vent is susceptible to splashes in rough weather, water could enter the tank directly.

- Leakage through the filler cap due to a worn O-ring, loose cap or even a hole in the cap itself.

*Changing a fuel filter on Two-Step requires a certain athletic ability*

It's what happens when the water gets into the fuel that is most interesting. Stuff can grow in it! There are algae that can live in the interface between water and diesel. They clog fuel filters with black algae-corpses. I believe this is commonly mistaken for "dirty fuel". The water can get into the filter as well. Since water is heavier than fuel, it will settle below the fuel but will lie waiting to be drawn up when the motion of the boat stirs it around. So it's more than Murphy's law that problems are more likely to occur when it's rough rather than on a calm day!

Tip 2 - Keeping Water Out of the Fuel Tank

| **Keeping Water out of the Fuel Tank** |
| --- |
| • Keep the tank full. Air expands and contracts with normal weather changes. A full tank provides a smaller space for air to be drawn into and subsequently reduces the potential condensation. |
| • Fill the tank completely before long term storage. |
| • Check filler cap for any potential leaks. |
| • Make sure the breather hose is looped high above the vent so any water that gets in will tend to drain back out, rather than into the tank. |
| • Install a fuel/water separator if you don't already have one. |
| • Carry lots of spare filters and keep them dry. |

I haven't heard diesel maintenance recommended as a cure for seasickness and by the time I had changed the filter, drained the water from the separator and bled the fuel system, I was ready for some clean air. When we were safely at anchor the next day I removed the inspection port from the tank. With the water sitting in a tidy puddle at the bottom of the fuel tank, I was able to pump it out from underneath 25 gallons of clean fuel with my oil scavenging pump. If you don't have an inspection port you probably have a drain in the bottom of the tank for this purpose. And here in the calm of a sunny day at anchor, I saw my problem. The O-ring was cracked and had been letting a little water in whenever some puddled on top of the filler cap.

Fuel problems are the most common ailment afflicting marine diesel engines - they're also largely avoidable. A little preventative maintenance will keep the water hissing past the bow rather than sloshing in your tank waiting to clog up fuel filters.

# Make Friends With Your Engine

If your engine was a person would it be a reliable friend waiting to help you out? A cranky old codger you can't depend on? How about a hooded stranger you can neither understand nor really come to trust? I have finally come to view our Volvo™ 2003 as a well meaning friend with whom I have difficulty communicating (after all he speaks English with a very heavy Swedish accent). He is strong and hardworking but depends on me for all regular check-ups and emergency care. We've become a pretty good team.

Diesel engines are a good choice for a boat since they are very fuel efficient, they run well at high output and their fuel is much safer than gasoline especially in the confines of a boat since it is less volatile. If anything, their fuel system is their weak point. The fuel injection system on a diesel engine is a finely machined work of engineering and won't tolerate dirt or water in the works. The best way to stay on your engine's good side is to follow the maintenance procedures in the owner's manual and make sure it has good air and clean fuel to run on.

There is a modern philosophy that goes something like this --

*You don't need to know radio-wave propagation theory and transistor electronics to watch a television -- just how to turn it on.*

Some sailors apply this school of thought to diesel engines. I know people who have motored their boats out of the harbour without knowing where the engine *was* on their boat, let alone how to fix it!

## The Owner's Manual

Somewhere between struggling to check and top-up the oil, to happily stripping an engine down and rebuilding it, is a place where you can be comfortable with your level of knowledge. I recommend familiarity with all the basic jobs in the owner's manual. This normally includes changing the oil and fuel filters, bleeding the fuel system, tightening belts, adjusting the valve clearance, changing the thermostat and checking zincs. With some basic tools and possibly some help the first time, this list is not beyond the scope of most boat owners. With these tasks mastered, half of the engine problems will never happen in the first place and many of the rest will be solvable without calling for help.

*Working on Two-Step's Volvo 2003 engine. This can be quite rewarding with a great sense of accomplishment if you can figure out what needs doing - and do it without skinning too many knuckles. A good reference book will be a great help.*

The engine owner's manual and a reference text are crucial tools. I use <u>Marine Diesel Engines</u> by Nigel Calder as a reference source for basic diesel theory and it also has a fine section on troubleshooting. (See Appendix)

The original manufacturer's parts manual is a great tool for ordering parts (especially if you can't visit the dealer in person) but also to show exactly what parts go where. *Two-Step* didn't always have a parts manual on board. Now that she does, it has virtually eliminated the problem of where those spare springs or washers go, that are sitting around after everything is put back together.

## Maintenance

Doing regular maintenance is a good way to learn about an engine and to catch potential problems at the early stage. When I check the engine before starting it up for the day, I am never hoping to see a problem. That is a psychologically difficult time!

*"Say, was that twisted piece of "Volvo green" metal lying under the motor always there?"*

*"Sure! It probably fell out of my toolbox the last time I did an oil change!!"*

Sometimes it takes an act of willpower to face a problem but it will always be better to deal with it at the first opportunity. Listen for "funny sounds" and fix them before they become "expensive sounds". Better still, look for any early signs of trouble such as a loose nut, a worn belt, a spongy or swollen hose, or signs of a leak of oil or coolant.

Having learned more about your engine, choosing a set of spares to carry along will be easier. I have included a full list of practically every possible spare for outfitting but I should note that it will be expensive and that we do not have this full list. Listed under "spares" are the minimal requirements. Most can be installed without help. The "extra spares" section are more expensive and some will require help installing but could save weeks of waiting for a part in a remote location.

We find that the best place to buy parts is at home before we leave for a cruise! We know where all the suppliers are. We have time to wait for things to come in and we have a car to pick up spares. Once under way, it is always harder to track down and get parts. I bought 7 oil filters before our last cruise and for more than a year did not have to worry about finding a Volvo™ dealer just to do an oil change.

Pack spares carefully. Some filters are just packed in a cardboard box -- fine for the store but not good enough for a damp atmosphere. After finding 3 filters, each worth $15, rusting inside their boxes, I now repackage them in Ziploc™ plastic bags.

*You don't need to be a diesel mechanic to operate a marine diesel engine... but it couldn't hurt.*

*Removing an injector for testing. Injectors are highly precise and very expensive - Reinstall with "Never-Seize" or similar lubricant.*

## Summary

- Keep the fuel clean.

- Do all regular maintenance as per your manual.

- Learn your engine. Consider a course if you don't feel comfortable with engines.

- Look for signs of trouble and try to fix them. Shine a light in around the engine on a regular basis, in port and at sea.

    - Check for oil or coolant leaks.

    - Check belts for tightness.

    - Look for parts loose or under the motor.

- Be vigilant. Listen for "funny sounds" before they become "expensive".

- Spares can be hard to find away from home. Take lots.

Table 9 - Tools for Engine Repair

| Tools | Comments |
|---|---|
| service manual | Get one you are comfortable with. Possibly an after-market manual will be better than the original manufacturer's. |
| Marine Diesel Engines by Nigel Calder | A reference text like this will help fill in some of the blanks about diesel operation and also with troubleshooting. |
| manufacturer's parts manual | The parts manual has excellent diagrams showing how everything fits together. Knowing the part number helps when ordering parts from a distance. |
| dealer list | Find a dealer list for your cruising area. |
| filter wrench | Webbing ones are good for any size filter. |
| combination wrenches | 6 to 22 mm should cover most needs. |
| sockets and drives | Optional |
| screwdrivers | Get good ones! |
| feeler gauges | For setting valve clearance and aligning prop shaft. |
| oil scavenging pump | |
| fuel bleeding accessories | E.g. I have a favourite plastic container for catching fuel when bleeding air from the fuel system. |
| any special tools | E.g. a piece of hardwood to lever the alternator belt tight. |

Table 10 - Engine Spares

| Spares | Comments |
|---|---|
| oil filters | Our Volvo™ uses 1 per hundred hours - we ran 400 hours from Toronto to Exuma in the Bahamas in 1994. |
| primary fuel filters | E.g. Racor™ - see hints above. |
| secondary fuel filters | Probably will not need to replace these more than once a year since the primary filter will catch everything - take two or three just to be safe. |
| fuel pump diaphragm | |

| Spares | Comments |
|---|---|
| alternator belts | Take several if you have an oversize alternator. |
| additional belts | E.g. if you have belts driving refrigeration or water pump etc. |
| water pump impellers | Note down the part numbers for all spares -- especially if you don't have a parts manual. Try getting one by description alone! |
| water pump rebuild kit | |
| thermostat & gasket | |
| zinc anodes for engine | I check this every 3 months and replace it when it is half gone. The Intracoastal Waterway seems to be especially hard on zincs. Take at least 2-3 per year in tropical saltwater. |
| zinc anodes for prop shaft | Ditto above, except I check it more often when diving/snorkelling. If it is disappearing then it is probably time to check the engine zinc. These are easier to find. I carry 2 spares. |
| rocker cover gaskets | |
| oil | I carry only enough to do one change plus an extra litre for topping up since our little Volvo will use half a litre in the 100 hours between oil changes. You can buy good oil almost anywhere but some places won't let you dispose of it! I buy oil only from places that will take back the used oil. |
| transmission fluid | Carry some if this is different from the engine oil. |

Table 11 - Engine Spares for Self-Sufficiency

| Spares | Comments |
|---|---|
| water pump | More than $300 for our Volvo™ 2003!! We quit right here! |
| alternator & spare brushes | Part numbers for all of these items could be put in the ships log if you don't have a parts manual. |
| voltage regulator | |
| starter motor & spare brushes | |
| starter brushes | |
| fuel injector | |
| engine mounts | |
| head gasket set | |
| cutlass bearing | For the prop shaft. |

This full set will be expensive! You may need assistance installing some of the items but at least you won't need to wait to get the parts.

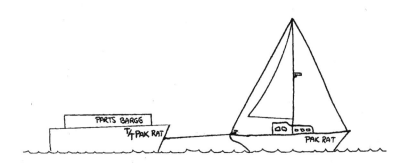

**Storing all your spare parts can be tricky.**

# Ground Tackle - The Ultimate Insurance

Man! This anchorage has the best holding!

Should you get insurance for your boat? Yes! Absolutely! We have always had the best insurance we can get on *Two-Step* but it isn't all through an insurance company. We have always taken the best precautions we can to avoid problems in the first place. When you think about it, getting money back in compensation for a disaster is not nearly so appealing as avoiding the disaster in the first place. Good sturdy equipment and the knowledge to use it effectively are the ultimate insurance.

## Choosing Ground Tackle

Ground tackle is one area where we spared no expense when equipping *Two-Step* and if the following list looks excessive it's worth considering that in almost 4 years of full-time cruising, our boat has never suffered damage at anchor and has never dragged more than a few feet. In that time we have weathered winds up to 60 knots at anchor and have used 3 anchors **at once** (along with most of the chain and 5/8" rode) on 6 separate occasions.

I should point out that *Two-Step* is 37 feet LOA and displaces 19,000 lbs. Most people size ground tackle based on the displacement and size or windage of the vessel but it is not a precise science. I prefer to err on the large size. Anyway here's the list for our boat:

Table 12 - Ground Tackle for Classic 37 Two-Step

| Ground Tackle | Comments |
|---|---|
| 45 lb. CQR | This is always on the 140' chain. |
| 25 lb. CQR | Our secondary anchor. |
| 25 lb. Danforth type | Alternative anchor - good in sand. |
| 25 lb. Fisherman | Good in weeds. |
| 200' rode 5/8" twist | |
| 100' rode 5/8" twist | We have two of these. |
| 200' rode 1/2" braid | |
| 140' 3/8" chain | This weighs 1.7lb per foot or 238lb total |
| 25' 3/8" chain | |
| 10' 3/8" chain | |
| Simpson Lawrence SL555 manual windlass | A windlass is almost a necessity with a lot of chain. |
| sounding lead | |
| 20' anchor snubber | See diagram of chain snubber. |
| assorted shackles | |
| rotating shackle | To attach an all-chain rode to the anchor to prevent twists. |

The big CQR is our primary anchor and lives on the bow roller attached by a rotating shackle to the 140' piece of chain. We often use a second anchor -- maybe 50% of the time. We decide which of our other anchors to use based on conditions- CQR in mud, Danforth in sand and Fisherman in grass or weeds. Then we shackle either the 10' or 25' piece of chain to it before connecting the rope.

# Windlasses

I consider an anchor windlass to be a necessity if you have an all chain rode. I don't think you can handle the weight of the chain by hand. For instance, lifting our 45lb anchor off the bottom in 40 feet of water means lifting 40 feet of chain plus the anchor straight up. That's 45lbs plus 40 by 1.7lb per foot for the chain... 45 + 68 = 109 pounds!!

Even hauling an anchor with just 20 feet of chain can get tiresome. But I think the best reason to consider a windlass is the safety factor when setting the anchor, not raising it. Resetting the anchor is much easier with a windlass. If it's a simple matter to haul up the anchor and try again I know I'm much more likely to do it if I'm not totally satisfied. Many times I have pulled up our anchor and dropped it again just 20 feet away. Either I misjudged a crowded anchorage and we wound up to close to another boat, or just felt uncomfortable as boats swung back and forth after we had anchored. It's great to know you can easily pull the hook and try again.

## Anchoring Strategy

Over the years I have worked out the following anchoring strategy and have found that I sleep better if I follow it carefully.

1)   Select a place to anchor at a safe distance from other boats, shoreline, reefs and other obstacles. Consider depth (at *low* tide) as well as the type of bottom, protection from swell <u>and</u> weather forecast. Allow room to set sufficient scope.

2)   Place the anchor by heading up into the wind and slowing right down to a standstill. Then lower the anchor until it sits on the bottom, and reverse to drop back with the wind to help you. Let out rode slowly as you drop back on the hook. When most of your planned scope is out, set it in the bottom by tugging forcefully on the rode in reverse gear.

*Sheryl checks the anchor. Note the flukes are entirely set in the sand and at least 30 feet of chain is lying on the sand - not pulling up to the boat. This is quite well set.*

3)   If there is a strong current I usually set a second anchor in the opposite direction so we sit on one in the flood tide, and the other for the ebb. We often row the second anchor out with the dinghy. I put the anchor and chain in the dinghy and Sheryl minds the bag of rode on the foredeck, letting it out as I row (or motor) to where we want the second hook.

4)   Then, if possible, swim down to look at the anchors (this works better in the tropics than say Antarctica) and force them in by hand if necessary.

5)  Tidy up. I use a snubber with our all-chain rode to absorb shocks. (A snubber can be just a length of line with several half hitches to attach to the chain. But *Two-Step* uses a custom-made snubber. See diagram below) I also put chafe protection on rodes where they go through chocks and take bearings on nearby objects so I can tell if we're dragging.

6)  Admire your handiwork. Think pessimistically of any weak links in your anchoring set-up. Imagine it's dark, you can't see the shoreline anymore, the wind has changed around and squalls are gusting around you. Are you still confident? If not, FIX IT NOW. Have a nice sleep.

7)  Wake up in the night anyway!! Get up every once in a while and check your bearings to see if you've moved. I've seen the most beautiful starlit panoramas

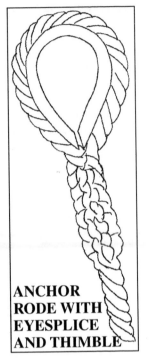

**ANCHOR RODE WITH EYESPLICE AND THIMBLE**

on my midnight sorties to the foredeck. A carpet of stars overhead, the shoreline and other boats silhouetted in the distance -- even storm winds tugging the boat back and forth against her anchors are beautiful sights if you've paid up your insurance.

**DETAIL OF ANCHOR CHAIN SNUBBER**

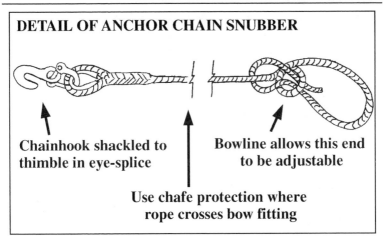

Chainhook shackled to
thimble in eye-splice

Bowline allows this end
to be adjustable

Use chafe protection where
rope crosses bow fitting

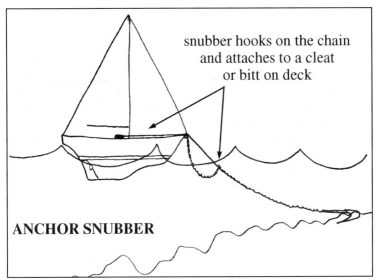

snubber hooks on the chain
and attaches to a cleat
or bitt on deck

**ANCHOR SNUBBER**

## The Electronic Anchor Watch

I have found that a great way to get a good discussion going with cruising sailors is to tell an anchoring horror story! In our favourite story, we anchored right at dusk in a bay in the Hudson river. I set the anchor, took bearings on two shore-side lights that would remain visible all night (I hoped!), and set the Loran anchor watch alarm to beep if it detected our position moving more than 100 feet. Before bed, the Loran alarm had already gone off so I rushed on deck to check. With everything looking

OK, I went back below and sat for a while watching the Loran position display. Although we were sitting almost motionless in the river, the Loran indicated we were moving 50 and sixty feet every few seconds. Obviously the Loran system errors would require an increase in the anchor watch radius just to handle signal variation. By the time we turned in, I had increased the swinging radius to 200 feet and the alarm only chirped once every half hour or so. Still, we were nervous and took turns doing anchor watch.

So, what happened at 2 a.m. you might ask? Yes, the alarm beeped and kept on beeping. Were we heading for Staten Island on the ebb current? No, we were exactly where we had been all night, as we found from a hurried trip on deck. One of the Loran stations had gone off the air and that was the last time I have ever used the Loran Anchor Watch feature!

*Two-Step seeks shelter from an approaching storm in a small and very protected anchorage in the Bahamas. We set our main anchor and chain, plus two lighter anchors on rope rodes and wait. With the three anchors set we don't even budge when the tide turns.*

**Table 13 - Recommended Anchor Weight Versus Boat Size**

## Plow

| Plow | Boat length in Feet (10–60) |
|------|------------------------------|
| 20 lb | ▓ ~15–27 |
| 27 lb | ▓ ~22–33 |
| 35 lb | ▓ ~30–38 |
| 45 lb | ▓ ~37–45 |
| 60 lb | ▓ ~45–52 |
| 80 lb | ▓ ~52–60 |
| 120 lb | ▓ ~55–60 |

## High Strength "Danforth" Type

| Type | Boat length in Feet (10–60) |
|------|------------------------------|
| 8 lb | ▓ ~15–27 |
| 12 lb | ▓ ~22–33 |
| 20 lb | ▓ ~30–38 |
| 35 lb | ▓ ~38–47 |
| 60 lb | ▓ ~47–55 |
| 90 lb | ▓ ~55–60 |

## Yachtsman

| Yachtsman | Boat length in Feet (10–60) |
|-----------|------------------------------|
| 15 lb | ▓ ~10–20 |
| 25 lb | ▓ ~20–28 |
| 38 lb | ▓ ~28–37 |
| 54 lb | ▓ ~37–45 |
| 75 lb | ▓ ~45–52 |
| 127 lb | ▓ ~52–58 |
| 199 lb | ▓ ~58–60 |

*Table courtesy of Kingston Anchors - Kingston Ontario. Suggested anchor sizes are provided as a general guide and are based on the American Boat and Yacht Council design guidelines. Heavy displacement hulls or those with high windage should select the next size larger.*

## The Nav Station

# Position-finding Equipment

Whether we are approaching Bimini after a Gulf Stream crossing or sighting the Azores on a transatlantic passage, landfall is usually the most emotional and nerve-wracking point of the journey on board *Two-Step*. I worry about navigation as we approach a landfall. Have I calculated the Gulf Stream drift accurately? Is our track really snaking confidently towards the Azores as we have plotted?

When we sailed from the Azores to Madeira there was a light mist for the last 2 days and the horizon was indistinct -- maybe 2 miles visibility. It was a nervous few hours approaching the island even though there are no off-lying shoals so we **knew** we would see the shore before we got into trouble. The rational knowledge that everything was OK, was small comfort as we strained our eyes to the horizon for a glimpse of Madeira. Then the horizon seemed to darken a little and finally the steep rocky sides of the island loomed out of the mist at about 3 miles. Exactly where it should be. Incidentally, not all islands are where they should be! Some remote islands are charted up to 2 miles away from where they really are due to inaccuracies in olden day surveys. Faith in the modern GPS with 100 meter accuracy could be disastrous in such situations.

Figuring out where you are and plotting a safe course to the next destination is what navigation is all about. There are a wide variety of technologies, old and new, to help figure out where you are. On board *Two-Step* we use a GPS for fixing our position out of sight of land. It is an incredible improvement over the old Satnav system we had on our first transatlantic passage that gave a fix whenever a satellite flew over -- intervals of 20 minutes up to three hours. We also carry a sextant and tables and practice with it occasionally as insurance. If there is a discrepancy between the sextant and the electronic methods, the sextant is disregarded.

For coastal piloting, we use conventional plotting on a chart and take two and three bearing fixes using a hand-bearing compass. We usually leave the GPS on but only glance at it out of curiosity or if we can't recognize any landmarks to get a fix.

Whatever methods we use to determine it, we record the position in the log book and plot it on the chart at least every 4 hours, more often if we are close to land. In between fixes, the log contains all information to determine our "dead reckoning" position

## GPS and the Sextant

GPS (Global Positioning System) is an obvious choice in new technology for any sailor since it gives accurate fixes at any time, anywhere. With the price of the systems so low, there is almost no reason not to have one on board.

GPS systems are so cheap now that it makes sense to carry two units. Where our single SatNav unit cost $1100 in 1990, we got two GPS for just $500 in 1997. I installed a built-in unit in the Nav station and we leave it on most of the time at sea. Our little Garmin handheld is a backup and can be used on deck as we make a landfall. Both units are 12 channel and that seems to mean they get a fix much quicker than the 1 channel unit we tried first.

We recommend one of each, handheld and built-in. The built-in unit is cheap to run since it doesn't chew through batteries and is not likely to be dropped. The handheld is a cheap backup and won't be affected by any problem with the ships electrical system.

A small group of traditionalists has resisted modern electronics, claiming possible electronic problems and the potential for governments to turn the systems off, as reasons to stick with celestial navigation.

*It was good enough for Christopher Columbus and so it's good enough for me!*

The flaw in this theory is that he didn't have a choice! In fact, Columbus didn't even have a sextant to check his latitude! The Astrolabe was in common use at the time, and was much less accurate than the sextant (invented in the 1700's). If someone had approached him with an accurate timepiece and offered to sell him celestial tables as well, I'm sure he would have leapt at the chance to improve his navigational accuracy with the latest technology.

We will **consider** any new technology that can improve our navigation. However we don't discard the old technology if losing it would impair our navigation. For example, computer charting systems might be a nice idea but it would be foolhardy not to have paper charts as well since they never say *"system fatal error -- please reboot."* We like hard copy.

## Radar

Radar is another technology that can help a yachtsman fix his position. (Why is it that yachtsman's positions are always getting broken in the first place??) Before GPS, radar could be a help getting a fix since it could determine an accurate range to a shoreline but this is less important with GPS providing accurate fixes full-time and worldwide. On a foggy or misty day (such as when we approached Madeira) the ability to "see" the coast and other yachts has seemed appealing. But since we have done most of our sailing in fog-free climates we have never taken the plunge. During our 3-year Atlantic cruise we only sailed in fog on five occasions. The weight of the radome high up the mast, plus the cost of a unit, have also been factors in our decision.

### Loran-C and RDF

Other position finding equipment, such as an RDF (radio direction finder), and Loran-C are not selling nearly as well these days as they used to! The GPS can do it all -- but we are not throwing away our old Loran unit. It still works fine. And if I had a RDF I would keep it too!

### Magnetic Compasses

The compass is still the mainstay navigational instrument, hundreds of years after its invention. A good binnacle compass is essential. It is also important that this points north! It should be checked against another compass and if there is any possibility that it is being affected by any nearby magnetic field (other than the earth's poles!), it must be corrected. To do a quick check, sail directly towards a distant object, and compare the heading given by the ships compass, to the bearing given by a hand-bearing compass. Stand up so the hand-bearing compass is well away from anything that could conceivably be magnetic.

Our hand-bearing compass is the small "puck" type with a faint radioactive glow inside that enables it to be seen at night. It is a much more accurate method of taking a bearing on something than trying to sight over the main compass. We have even used it as a replacement for the main compass.

On a passage home to Canada from the Caribbean, I noticed a bubble in the top of the compass dome and oil leaking out around the base. Sure enough the bubble grew and grew until the compass card was only barely covered by oil. I took a look inside to find there was a leak in the diaphragm in the bottom of the compass. I tried numerous repairs before finally coating the membrane in epoxy to reinforce and waterproof it. Tied to the dock in Nassau, I reassembled it and filled it with mineral oil. Sure enough it was pointing north, and agreed with the hand-bearing compass.

Heading out of Nassau Harbour, towards the Berry Islands I realized I had a new problem! After coming onto a new heading it took almost 20 seconds for the compass to catch up! So it turns out compasses are filled with a very light mineral oil -- not the type you can buy in the pharmacy. We relied on the hand-bearing compass all the way to back to Canada.

## Knot Log & Depth Sounder

Accurate plotting would be very difficult without a knot log. And there can be no better aid to tuning the sails than an accurate speed log -- if trimming the sails can pick up even ½ knot, I want to know! It could save almost 2 days on an Atlantic crossing at *Two-Step's* 5 knot average.

Incidentally, the knot log must be calibrated to show true speed for use in plotting. We kept arriving everywhere late until we discovered we were actually going almost ¾ knot less than indicated.

A quick check can be done by running in a straight line for 15 minutes or more and comparing distance run from a GPS or Loran-C with the log reading. This must be done in calm water -- obviously any current will distort the log reading.

A depth sounder is also an indispensable aid to navigation. My only complaint with our sounder is that its depth alarm, guaranteed to beep if you venture into shallow water, will also beep if the water is more than 150 feet deep! I think it just reads the strongest echo it can get and, if there is no bottom at all, it will accept a weak echo bounced off a thermocline near the surface instead.

This means we can't just leave it on all the time since even in the middle of Lake Ontario it will frequently sound the alarm. If you're in the market for a new one, check that its alarm won't be fooled by very deep water -- it couldn't be that hard!

On the topic of depth, a lead line is a great piece of gear. We have a small one (given to us as a gift by Bob and Mary on *Polar Bear*) that we use in the dinghy. It is marked with coloured ribbons made from spinnaker cloth at 2 foot increments and has just a 4 oz. lead sinker as a weight. We sometimes use it to check out an anchorage in advance and also to scout routes when we're gunkholing. A great idea!

Table 14 - Navigation Equipment

| Navigation Equipment | Comments |
|---|---|
| GPS built-in unit | Doesn't use AA batteries! |
| GPS handheld unit | Get a real multi-channel one. The alternative is a one-channel receiver that multiplexes between channels but takes much longer to get a fix. |
| Sextant | Practice with it once in a while. |
| Radar | More use these days for collision avoidance than for getting a fix. |
| Loran | |
| Radio Direction Finder | |
| Magnetic compass | |
| Hand bearing compass | |
| Knot log / depth sounder | |
| Binoculars | |
| Clock | |
| Wind speed/direction | |
| Charts | |
| Cruising guides | |
| Ship's log book | |
| Plotter or parallel rules | We find the plotter much easier to use than parallel rules. (This is a rectangular plastic device with a rotating compass rose on it) |
| Pencils,sharpener,eraser | |

# Communications Gear

Besides a VHF radio (we consider this necessary) we also have a HAM radio on board. Definitely a lot of fun, HAM has been a great morale booster for us on long passages. Even just listening in on the various nets is entertaining and can be very informative. Weather information, contacts with cruising friends and even contacts back home are all great reasons to consider becoming a HAM.

I first got interested in HAM in the Bahamas and got an American HAM licence (**N3IFE**) when we returned to Florida, before crossing the Atlantic. Since I am a Canadian, I have now obtained a Canadian licence as well (**VE0SEA**). Having taken both exams I think there is not much difference. As of 1997 both countries require proficiency in Morse code to get the licence needed to transmit on the long-range HAM bands. Many people find this a problem but practicing with Morse code training tapes will help get you through.

An alternative to HAM for long-range communications is a Marine "single-sideband" radio. A marine SSB unit, for use on the marine bands, requires a special licence but there is no need to learn Morse code. The radios are more expensive than HAM but easier to operate -- sort of like a long-range VHF.

*Using the HAM radio as a receiver for weatherfax signals. With a program like "PC HF Facsimile" for the computer and a connector between radio headphone jack and computer serial port we suddenly have a weatherfax receiver.*

Either a HAM or Marine SSB set will require a special antenna. We have insulated our backstay by cutting it and putting two "Norseman" type insulators in -- one six feet off the deck and the other near the masthead -- and now use it as an antenna. You will need a "tuner" and other gear as well. And in order to produce a strong signal, an excellent ground is essential. For fibreglass and wood vessels, this means at least a large copper grounding plate (like a Dynaplate™) near the base of the antenna. For even better performance, experts recommend copper screening under the back deck (beneath the insulated backstay) to act as a counterpoise. Ham radio is a gadgeteer's paradise!!

If you don't want to invest the money in a HAM or Marine SSB radio, consider an all-band short-wave receiver. A small unit that can receive the frequencies under 30 megahertz will allow you to listen in on short-wave broadcasts from around the world. When we're feeling homesick we sometimes tune in to Radio Canada International to hear programs from home.

The public stations broadcast in AM mode but marine SSB stations and most HAM transmissions are on "sideband" -- so make sure the receiver can receive sideband. Not all can.

# Email Onboard

Having used Email in my job since 1982 I was keen to see if it could work while cruising. Email is what is known as a "store and forward" system. The basic concept is perfectly suited for cruisers! Unlike faxes and telephones that must be connected all the time for you to receive anything, email messages will be stored by your email "provider" and then when you check them, they are forwarded in a batch to your computer! Perfect for sailors who just want to switch the system on every few days.

But how could we actually get Email on *Two-Step*? After much experimentation (and a fair bit of money on phone calls) I have a system that works well for us and is quite economical. In 1997 I investigated options for satellite communications, cellular phone connections and the PinOak Digital system (which actually uses Marine HF radio with a special modem. All these systems have a place on the water, but not on Two-Step. For big boats (or ships), big budget worldwide commun- ications the satellite systems are perfect. You get high speed connections from anywhere in the world but weight and expense are high. Cellular phones work best for anyone who stays near the coast in a specific area where they have an agreement with a cell-phone service provider. Outside that area it gets complicated and expensive. In Europe the cell- phone system is different so an American phone wouldn't work. And at sea there is no coverage. Marine HF systems such as PinOak are the best option for smaller cruising boats who need email offshore. The system is relatively affordable and compact but email will still cost a lot if you send and receive a lot of messages. This may change in the future as these systems mature but in summer 1997 when we met Peter on *Sandeeks*, he was trying to train his family at home to write short emails and use abreviations since he was paying per character sent and received.

*Im fin Arrived Azors today Ruf passage but fast Sunny Here 3*
*+ days then on urop Luv u Mum*

My solution was to get an older computer (so I didn't have to worry about drowning it) a regular modem and an America Online Internet account. Our "486" notebook has an internal modem and a good battery pack. I carry it ashore and hook it up to a phone line in a bar, or post office or phone centre. Then I dial the local AOL access number and automatically upload all our outgoing email and collect what's waiting. This means I have either a local call or a cheap call to the nearest access number. The cost is quite reasonable. The cheapest AOL account provides more than enough internet time for these quick email connections, and the phone calls are cheap too. Even downloading 15 emails including a photograph of a new niece was just a few dollars and that was with the nearest access number in Lisbon when we were sitting in Peter's Cafe Sport in the Azores!

Obviously we can't use this system at sea but I'm not sure I even need Email at sea. If you do, and don't mind the cost, the HF systems are the way to go until global cellular phones become affordable.

*A HAM enthusiast at anchor in the southern Bahamas. Note the complex rigging off the bow to allow his antenna to have the most effective shape.*

## Weather Information

*Two-Step* swung at her anchor off a deserted Bahamian cay and we had just returned from a walk on the beach. There was no one around for probably 3 miles in any direction; the nearest settlement 6 miles away. We had come back onboard to get the weather so I turned on the computer and tuned the radio for our weatherfax channel. In less than 10 minutes we were looking at a satellite photograph of the planet that had been taken only 1 hour previously!! It seemed incongruous with our remoteness to be able to get such a picture. Back on deck there was still no sign of another soul in our isolated paradise.

Weatherfax and Navtext are the two weather systems in common use today. Both can be stand-alone systems purchased as another box for the nav station or as a software package and connector to run on a computer -- and connect to the radio. If you have a computer aboard this is the obvious way to go. More fun for the gadgeteers and lots more fun learning about the weather. Especially with the fax, there is a fair bit to learn about weather and fax maps before they make any sense at all. Don't plan on just plugging it in before a major passage without learning to read them first. I keep Alan Watts fine book <u>Reading the Weather: Modern Techniques for Yachtsmen</u> on board as a reference for interpreting fax maps. Even though I have already read it cover to cover twice, there's still lots to learn.

A barometer is still a useful tool to have, it looks pretty on the bulkhead and it's interesting to see just how low the pressure gets in a bad storm. We have never been surprised to see it fall though! We always knew in advance through either a VHF weather report if close to shore, or a HAM or Marine SSB report if offshore. But I guess if our radios all died we could still use the barometer to forecast the short-term weather.

# More Gadgets

You can always find someone who recommends a particular gadget. This does not persuade me to rush out and add it to *Two-Step's* nav station. The cost of that radar I haven't yet got, represents 2 months of cruising at our typical budget! And the new Inmarsat-C satellite transceiver would equal maybe 4 months of sailing. Don't give up or postpone your dream cruise just to get more gadgets -- but HEY -- if you have the money, space and a burning desire to support the electronics industry, a whole universe of stuff awaits!

# Plumbing

*Paul works on the "head". Not his favourite job!*

There surely is no less glamorous part of the boat than the plumbing and the heads. Certainly on board Two-Step, working on the head rates right up there with going aloft at sea, both in terms of overall desirability and the coefficient of nauseousness. At this point, it is tempting to recount a plumbing horror story but I will resist. As I mentioned in the previous chapter, anchoring horror stories are a great way to encourage lively Happy Hour conversation. Plumbing stories, however, are a sure way to kill off conversation and, if told at all, must be carefully phrased to avoid ruining everyone's appetite.

## Holding Tanks and Y-Valves

One issue that must be dealt with is "holding tanks". Many boats that have a holding tank do not have a way of discharging overboard since this is illegal in some areas. Those without a holding tank should consider one if planning a cruise to areas where their use is mandatory.

The Great Lakes of Canada and the USA have long had tough legislation requiring a holding tank so we built *Two-Step* with this in mind (our home port is on Lake Ontario). Waste all goes into a holding tank (no "Y" valve) that can be pumped out through a deck fitting where facilities exist -- or overboard via a macerator pump (see diagram).

The common alternative is a "Y" valve between the head and the tank but we see two problems with this. Firstly, this is not legal in many areas although if you talk sweetly and fly a foreign flag you might have a reprieve. Secondly, there is no option as to when to pump out.

We have appreciated the use of the head when the boat is hauled out for a few days and we're working on her, still living on board. Also, we don't like the idea of discharging in anchorages. If we want to anchor in an idyllic place for a few days, we'll use the holding tank and pump out in open water. A friend told me how one day he was swimming under his boat when someone on board... oh yes -- no head horror stories!

The only disadvantage to the system is the added complexity of the macerator pump, but we feel it's worth it.

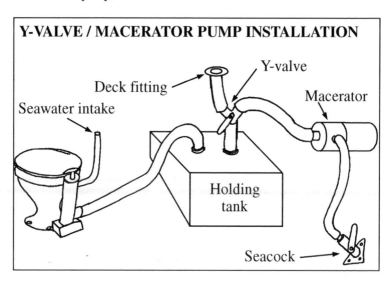

## Fresh water pumps

We do not have a pressurized water system on board, and while I don't advocate everyone chucking their pressure systems for long-distance cruising, it is worth adding a manual pump as a backup. Most people find they also save water. We like the foot pumps, especially under way. With one hand to hold on and one for brushing teeth I can still dispense the exact amount of water I need -- not a drop more. A small victory maybe, but these things assume a larger importance if you have to carry your drinking water from a well on a remote island! Also, foot pumps are quieter -- none of the irritating noise of the water pressure pumps. We once spent an evening aboard a boat whose pump cycled on every 10 minutes. We jumped out of our skins every time. The lights dimmed with the power drain and we wondered how these nice folks could enjoy a quiet anchorage. Other friends, Janis and Ila on *Simmerdim* got a shock the first time they turned on the tap when motoring with the autopilot on. Interference from the pump caused the autopilot to turn the wheel hard over. Every time the pump came on, the boat deviated wildly from her heading until Janis fixed it.

# Maintenance

*"Doing routine preventative maintenance is more fun than
emergency repairs... especially when the heads are involved"*

Besides checking for leaks, worn fittings and cracked hoses, the
head system must be de-limed regularly. A calcium deposit forms on
saltwater passageways and will restrict the flow until finally causing
clogs. In less than 1 year of living aboard in the tropics this had built up
to 1/8" thick at some points in the head discharge hose. Some cruisers
pump a cup or two of vinegar through the system every week but I find I
still have to disassemble the pump and hoses every year or so to clean
everything. I flex the hoses back and forth to dislodge the build-up then
shake it out. An alternative to vinegar would be CLR™, available in
hardware stores to remove scale from plumbing fittings.

Table 15 - Plumbing Spares

| Plumbing Spares | Comments |
|---|---|
| head rebuild kit | |
| galley pump rebuild kit | Keep part numbers for all rebuild kits. |
| bilge pump rebuild kit | |
| elec. pump rebuild kit | |
| macerator rebuild kit | Macerator pump is used to empty holding tank overboard when offshore and away from pump-out facilities. |
| various hose clamps | |
| Teflon tape | For sealing pipe threads (caulking compound can be used except for drinking water applications). |
| hose | Various pieces of hose for misc repairs. |
| hose connectors | For joining hoses, emergency repairs etc. I carry a selection of 1/2, 3/4, 1 and 1.5 inch barbs, connectors T fittings and adaptors. |
| vinegar to de-lime pieces | A spare gallon would not be too much. Note vinegar can also be used to clean wet epoxy off your hands instead of toxic acetone. Pickling vinegar is best. |
| bungs | To plug thru-hulls in an emergency. These are conical pieces of wood that can be jammed in a hole. |

# Summary

- There must be a way to discharge the head overboard when away from areas with pumpout facilities.

- Waterways tend to produce rock-like calcium carbonate deposits. We remove toilet hoses and flex them back and forth to break up calcium every six months in the tropics.

- Head pump should be de-limed regularly. Some people recommend a quart of vinegar or some CLR™ left to sit in the pump/piping every couple of weeks. I service the pump of my Lavac™ head every six months.

- DO ROUTINE MAINTENANCE - this is much more pleasant than emergency repairs to the heads - don't ask how I know!

- Any anti-siphon "vented loop" fittings that handle saltwater must be checked and de-limed regularly.

- Consider a manual water pump in case electric system fails.

# Are You Sinking?
# The Case for a Bilge Pump Alarm

Would it be worth $20 to know you were sinking? Or maybe I should ask, wouldn't it be worth a mere $20 to know the second there is any water in your bilges so you can take action? (Please answer yes so we can go on!)

The answer is a bilge pump alarm! I installed one on *Two-Step*, following an incident I would prefer not to relate, and have never regretted it. This is an alarm beeper that is triggered whenever the float switch for the electric bilge pump comes on. If you don't have an electric bilge pump, here's the excuse you've been waiting for to install one.

Any 12-volt electronic alarm will do fine providing it is loud enough to hear it where you want it, and it doesn't draw so much power that the bilge pump plus the alarm will trip the fuse in the control switch. One amp is probably fine. Connect it to the manual side of the control switch. This ought to be the same as connecting it to the output side of the float switch.

Now whenever the bilge pump comes on, even if just for a few seconds, everyone knows. I've learned that *Two-Step* takes on a litre of water every hour through the anchor hawse pipe if she is pounding to windward so I knew immediately the day I forgot to put the hawse plug in after raising anchor - the alarm was on every couple of minutes!

## CONNECTING A BILGE PUMP ALARM

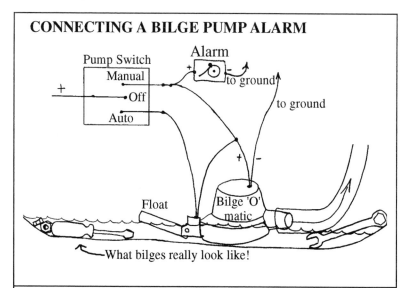

What bilges really look like!

**Note:** If you have one of the newer automatic pumps that incorporate the float switch (such as the Rule™ "Computerized" series) you will need to install a separate float switch to trigger the alarm. More work but still worth the peace of mind.

An alternative version of an alarm, that would act independently of the pump can be fashioned from an inexpensive smoke detector. Electronics consultant Janis Priedkalns of Current Solutions, recommends connecting a wire from either side of the smoke sensor, and running them down to the bilge. Connect each wire to a conductive rod (or some other sort of probe) and fasten the two probes an inch apart, and a couple of inches above the normal level of the bilge water. They will cause the alarm to go off if the water rises to submerge the tips of the probes.

# The Redundant Rig - Insurance Aloft

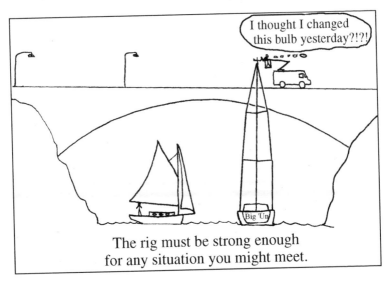

The rig must be strong enough
for any situation you might meet.

Can we count on the mast staying up? That was the question we asked ourselves when we were planning our first offshore cruise. In searching for the answer, we came up with two potential strategies:

**1**  Ensure no single component can cause the mast to fall.

**OR**

**2**  Ensure that no fitting that could bring the mast down, ever fails.

Strategy 1 involves planning a rig that has no single point of failure. For example, having an inner forestay is one way to insure a forestay failure wouldn't bring down the mast. We chose this option when building *Two-Step*. She has double spreaders and we rigged fore and aft lower shrouds to the lower set, and an inner forestay with running backstays to the upper set. The result is a very well supported rig, and if a racer would accuse us of having unnecessary weight and windage aloft, I say at least I am confident in the rig.

Of course, we had the option to do all this since we built the boat ourselves. Upgrading existing rigging is easier for most boats than adding shrouds or changing the whole rig.

Strategy 2 involves taking measures to make sure no single point of failure, ever fails. This is the practical approach for existing rigs that have been designed with one or more fittings that could cause the mast to fall if they failed. An example would be a rig with only one chain plate for each port and starboard shrouds. This chain plate is a potential point of failure for the whole rig and it must not fail. All fittings in this category must be very carefully inspected and replaced or upgraded if there is any suspicion they might fail. If a turnbuckle is hard to turn it should be disassembled and checked for galling (when the screw fuses together with the threaded part -- both parts must usually be replaced). Leaks around a chain plate might be a sign that the chain plate is moving under load.

For most sailors outfitting their boat for cruising, the best strategy is to evaluate the rig, and repair and upgrade as necessary. One practical possibility for some boats is to add a removable inner forestay. This eliminates one point of failure and also allows a staysail to be flown.

Evaluating and upgrading the rig is a very important step especially if offshore passaging is planned. Like choosing and using the proper ground tackle, it is one way to buy insurance for the cruise.

## Adding an Inner Forestay

Adding an inner forestay is one way to increase both the strength and safety of the rig, as well as allowing more sail combinations to be flown. Many voyagers who added one say they wanted a hank-on sail available in case of a problem with the roller furled jib.

Since we built *Two-Step*, she has had a inner forestay, rigged from the upper spreaders down to the deck 5 feet abaft the forestay. This yielded a very small staysail, and in the summer of 1997 just before our third transatlantic passage, we decided to re-rig it higher, attaching the upper end just below the mast-head. We wanted to be able to fly a second sail downwind, and the old staysail was just too small to be worth flying in less than 25 knots of wind. The new jib has roughly twice the area of the old staysail. Of course we can still fly the old jib on the new stay if we need to.

The new rig has been a great success. We ran under two jibs with the wind on the quarter for over a week en route to the Azores. One jib was poled out with our downwind pole, the other with the sheet through a snatchblock at the end of the mainboom. We swung the boom out all the way, put a preventer on and ran for days with just the two jibs.

An added advantage of this rig is that having the two jibs moves the center of effort forward for sailing downwind. This makes most boats easier to steer. Our wind-pilot took us effortlessly through some quite large following seas, Two-Step being led along by the two jibs.

*Running under two headsails. This is great downwind since the centre of effort is well forward. Both jibs are poled out so it is quite stable.*

The attachments of the stay to the mast and deck will be the most daunting parts of this job. If you aren't comfortable doing this project yourself, a rigger could offer assistance or advice.

I designed a bracket to be bolted or riveted to the mast near the head (see diagram below). This was made from 3/32" stainless steel with 3/16" stainless used for the tang to attach the jibstay. I made a model of the shape of the front of our mast out of wood and cardboard. This was used as a template to get the correct bend. This is a good sturdy design and only cost us $150.

The chainplate attachment for the foredeck is the other difficult part of this project. It is essential to tie the deck fitting down to something solid underneath. The forces of a sail on a stay will pull up the foredeck if it isn't very well reinforced. One option is to rig a turnbuckle and wire from the deck on down, transfering the load of the inner forestay down to the hull. A second option is to build a partial bulkhead directly underneath the deck where the stay will be attached. In a fiberglass yacht, this could be 1/2-3/4" plywood with epoxy and glass bonding it to the deck. Again, if you aren't comfortable with this kind of work it might be best to seek assistance from an expert.

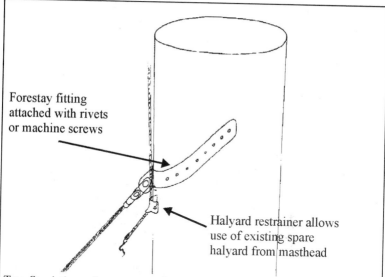

Forestay fitting
attached with rivets
or machine screws

Halyard restrainer allows
use of existing spare
halyard from masthead

*Two-Step's inner forestay attaches 2 feet down from the masthead. The fitting was custom made from 3/32 by 1.5 inch stainless and attached to the mast with machine screws. We insulated the fitting from the mast with 2 layers of electrical tape to prevent corrosion.*

We used a halyard restrainer to redirect our spare halyard. As it comes out from the masthead it goes straight down 2 feet and then through the restrainer. This saved us from having to install a new halyard box in the mast. Another alternative would be to add a new external halyard.

The project was not as difficult as I had expected and has provided tremendous benefits. It was definitely worth the trouble and expense to improve our downwind passaging.

# Are Your Sails Ready for Cruising?

One glorious daysail in Florida's Indian river came to an abrupt end for us when the halyard tore the head off our roller furled jib. We had been enjoying an east wind that cut across the waterway, giving us a nice beam reach in flat calm water! Although the river is quite wide, it is shallow enough that much of the waterway is dredged in this area. The trees bordering the route often have pelicans roosting in them and these prehistoric birds, combined with the quiet nature of the area, are such a contrast to the huge space shuttle building at Cape Canaveral that peers over Merritt Island. And occasionally the shuttle itself that looms in the distance.

Previous passages we'd made through this area had been with a headwind. The channel is too narrow for tacking so we'd had to motor. The beam wind this time through was a bonus and we were having a beautiful sail! Then, just as we were coming up to our anchorage for the night, the stainless steel ring at the head of the jib tore through the webbing holding it onto the sail.

After we had pulled the jib down and anchored for the night I looked at the torn webbing. I hadn't thought about it before, but when the sail is furled the UV protection strip on the back edge of the sail covers everything **but** the head and the tack of the sail. Sure enough, the webbing at the tack was deteriorating as well.

Talking to the sailmaker a few days later he pointed out that the webbing was polypropylene instead of nylon -- much less resistant to the sun. The Dacron of the sail and even the thread used to attach the perished webbing were both fine.

Offshore sailing adds new factors to the equation. Besides absorbing the basic wear and tear of cruising, the sail plan for an offshore passage must be able to drive the boat in a wider variety of weather conditions. The coastal sailor can usually avoid heavy weather but does not have this option if caught offshore.

For example, a mainsail with only two reef points will likely reef down to 65% of its full size. This may be enough for coastal sailing but is probably too much sail for winds over 30 knots -- a condition that likely will be encountered at some point on a long passage. Adding a third reef point or storm trysail would allow the boat to continue sailing between 30 and 40 knots.

An extended cruise makes heavy demands on the sails! If your plans include heading south, the same sun that makes the tropics such an inviting destination has a lot of extra power to destroy your sails. When this is combined with the increased use of the boat, a single season of tropical cruising equates to a decade of occasional use in northern climes.

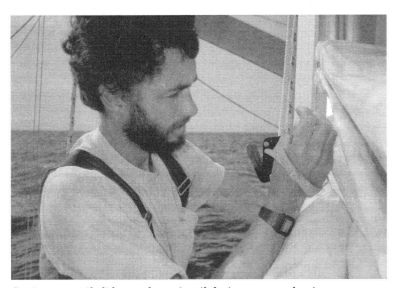

*Sewing new sail slides on the mainsail during a transatlantic passage.*

# Ditty Bag - Sail Repair and Maintenance

Table 16 - Ditty Bag - Sail Repair and Maintenance

| Spares & Tools | Comments |
|---|---|
| sailmakers palm | We have two. Left-hand for Paul; small right-hand version for Sheryl. |
| various needles | |
| sail tape | This is a spinnaker cloth with adhesive on the back. It will attach over a hole and should then be sewn on since the adhesive isn't that great. 2-3" wide good for small repairs |
| sail repair cloth | Adhesive cloth as above but available in 18" widths for larger repairs. |
| sail thread | A special waxed thread. |
| scraps of sailcloth | |
| sail slides | In one year we broke 5-6 of the plastic slides for our mainsail. |

# Rigging Maintenance and Spares

The sails are the engine that drives our boat. The first time I *really* understood this was when we set sail for Bermuda from Ft. Lauderdale in 1990. Of course I had enjoyed sailing *Two-Step* many miles prior to this, but this was to be our first real passage "offshore". The direct distance is 800 nautical miles - about 2 times our range under power alone. We would not be able to depend on the motor to save us if we lost the use of the sails.

That passage profoundly changed our attitude. Where before we had been used to sailing on lakes and waterways and knowing we could motor back home, or call for assistance on the VHF, now we would be on our own. Starting right then, I began a routine of checking the mast and rigging from top to bottom before any passage, or at least every six months.

I go aloft and examine the standing rigging -- all end fittings and all points where wires touch anything such as where shrouds go over the spreaders. I also look at the halyard exits and check for chafe on the halyards.

Back on deck I finish checking the standing rigging, looking at the lower terminals, cotter pins and split pins. I look at the boom gooseneck fitting, the downwind pole and check over blocks and running rigging for signs of chafe. This checking over procedure usually involves looking at things closely and squirting a little lubricant/rust inhibitor (I use Boeing T9™) into blocks and onto fittings that need protection from the salt. For example, I find my traveller car and downwind pole release fitting both need regular lubrication.

As with any maintenance tasks, it is important to "listen to" the rigging. The sounds of the winches and blocks, the difficulty of pulling on a line can all be hints as to whether a problem is developing. Investigate those hints! On two different occasions I have found a reefing line 1/3 chafed through, and a problem in the gooseneck fitting by looking for the source of a new noise. These didn't become disasters because I found them first.

Staying on a particular point of sail can chafe a line or stress a fitting that hasn't given any trouble until then. Even after we had been living aboard for 2 years, and had sailed 12,000 miles, I was still surprised by the amount of wear and tear an ocean passage can have. Our passage from Brazil to Grenada was 2000 miles entirely downwind and at one point we did not adjust the sails for 4 days. In that 2 weeks we did more down wind sailing than *Two-Step* had done in her whole life and new squeaks appeared, lines and sails chafed in new places!

# Summary

- The sun is the worst enemy of modern sails. Check sails for wear regularly.

- Consider adding to sail inventory or modifying sails for heavy weather conditions if going offshore.

- Check standing rigging regularly. Carefully check problem areas where wire goes over spreaders and at all terminals.

- Check halyards for chafe or "meat-hooks" at wire/rope splices.

- Be vigilant!! INVESTIGATE potential problems.

    - listen for "squeaks"

    - feel if any line gets harder to pull

# Running Rigging Spares

Table 17 - Running Rigging Spares

| Spares | Comments |
|---|---|
| various fids | For splicing 2-in-1 braided line, I carry 1/4, 3/8 and 1/2 inch fids to cover all the line we have onboard (the 1/2 fid works OK for 5/8 as well). |
| diagram of braid splice | I can't seem to memorize this splice so I keep it right in the rigging kit. |
| reference text | e.g. The Marlinspike Sailor by Hervey Garrett Smith or other knot and ropework guide. |
| razor knife | I use an Exacto™ knife for cutting line. |
| needles | For a proper whipping (see Figure 3 on page 119) and also for sail repair. |
| masking tape | For temporary seizing during splicing or whipping. |
| lighter | To melt the ends of synthetic ropes after whipping. |
| marking pen | To mark measurements. |
| whipping twine | |
| spare thimbles (1/2, 5/8) | Useful mainly for anchor line (see diagram on page 91). |

Table 18 - Standing Rigging Spares

| Spares | Comments |
|---|---|
| cotter pins | In case you drop one overboard - at least one of each size onboard. |
| misc. split pins | We carry enough 1/8, 3/32 to replace all onboard. |
| various shackles | |
| lanolin | To lubricate turnbuckles. |
| rigging tape | |

Figure 3 - A Proper Whipping

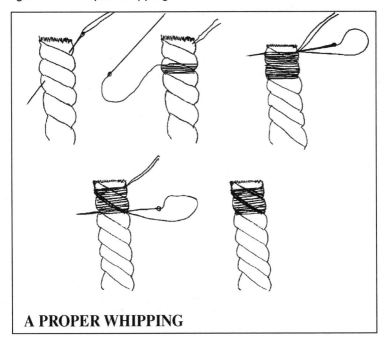

**A PROPER WHIPPING**

Step 1   - Pass needle through rope under whipping.
Step 2   - Wrap whipping twine tightly around rope.
Step 3   - Pass needle through rope to finish wrapping.
Step 4   - Bind wraps together along shallow spots between strands.
             For braid just do 3 or 4 cross loops.
Step 5   - Pass needle through rope twice to finish off.

### Extra Spares for Complete Self-sufficiency

     Norseman type fittings are a do-it-yourself alternative to swaged wire fittings. Consider a couple of these plus a piece of wire that could be used to fashion a spare shroud or stay or as a "jury rig". Since many rigging failures occur right at a swage fitting, the wire can be re-terminated a little shorter and connected to the old chain plate using spare shackles or chain. (See Figure 4 on page 120)

| Spares | Comments |
|--------|----------|
| Norseman fittings | A eye or two for each wire size onboard. |
| spare Norseman cones | These should not be reused once the fitting has been under load. |
| rigging wire | We carry 55 feet of 8mm 1x19 wire to replace a broken shroud or stay. |

Figure 4 - Norseman-type fitting to repair rigging wire

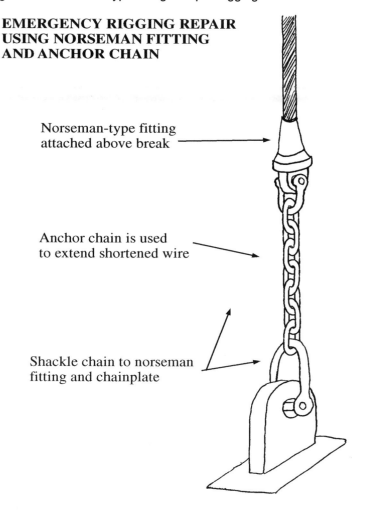

**EMERGENCY RIGGING REPAIR USING NORSEMAN FITTING AND ANCHOR CHAIN**

Norseman-type fitting attached above break

Anchor chain is used to extend shortened wire

Shackle chain to norseman fitting and chainplate

# Stoves and Stove Fuel

When we were outfitting *Two-Step* we took special care that the galley would be a safe and comfortable place to prepare meals of the quality we were used to at home. We didn't want to be roughing it when we lived aboard.

*Stove safety features include a solenoid to turn off the gas back at the tank, a sniffer with sensor under the stove to detect gas leaks, and a bar in front of the stove protect the cook. Each of the burners has an automatic shutoff if the flame goes out.*

The stove we chose has an oven and broiler in addition to the 2 burners on the top, and has been a delight to cook with. The oven is rarely used on passages but most of our time is spent at anchor and it is appreciated then.

Some stoves are not equipped with a protective bar in front of them but this is a necessity for cooking under way. (See"Cooking at Sea" on page 223)

Consider the following safety features for the stove.

- Gimbaled stove for use under way. (Multi-hull owners claim this is not necessary on their boats!)
- Adjustable pot retainers to keep things on the stove.
- Thermocouple at each burner to turn off gas if flame goes out.

- Protective bar so cook cannot fall onto stove.
- Strap for cook to lean against allowing use of both hands for cooking.
- Solenoid at propane tank to allow remote shut off.
- Bilge sniffer to detect fumes in the bilge.
- Lots of handholds.

# Alternative fuels

Although propane/butane gas is the most popular option for stove fuel, it is not the only choice. There are some excellent kerosene stoves for cruising boats and this fuel has the advantage of being easier and safer to store on board. The disadvantage is these stoves are not so convenient, usually requiring priming with alcohol to get them lit, and have more of an odour than gas, although that depends on the quality of the kerosene.

Diesel stoves are similar to kerosene in their need for priming (usually with alcohol) so they are less convenient than gas. They need a chimney or smoke head to vent the fumes outside, but the fuel will be the cheapest of any stove fuel, and it is safe.

Natural Gas, called CNG, is another safe fuel since it is lighter than air and will not collect in the bilges. Availability is a big problem, however, and it is also much bulkier than propane.

Alcohol is a popular alternative to propane, and is relatively easy to buy and to store. It does not burn as hot as the other fuels, and because the flame is almost invisible, there have been accidents lighting the stoves. Also, I am not aware of alcohol ovens, and at least on board *Two-Step*, the oven is a necessary creature comfort.

If you detect some bias here, a propane favouritism, you are correct! I will therefore devote the remainder of this section to hints for the propane equipped cruising boat.

# Propane off the beaten track

One of the biggest advantages of using propane as a cooking fuel is its widespread availability. We've seen it used in all the remote islands we've visited and have always been able to buy it BUT it has sometimes taken a little ingenuity and persistence.

The first problem is getting to the supplier. Most taxis and buses won't carry gas cylinders so if you find a refill station close to the waterfront, it's a good time to fill up -- even if you're not right empty. We carry two 11 lb. cylinders so we don't run out all at once. This also means a full cylinder is only 26 lbs. (15 lbs. empty weight + 11 lbs. of gas) and can be carried some distance. The 20 lbs. cans last longer but are heavier to carry. An 11 lb. cylinder lasts us about 1 month of living aboard for the two of us. That includes baking once in a while and using the stove to heat water since we don't have an engine water heater.

Once you've got to a place to buy gas you can face your next challenge. Many small propane vendors in the islands use the gravity feed method and have got only a large cylinder of propane and a hose to connect your tank. In one small Bahamian Out Island, I helped up-end a 100 lb. cylinder and held it balanced precariously on a splintered old table as the gas slowly dribbled down into our tank. To speed the flow we had to keep disconnecting the rig, venting the extra pressure from our tank and starting over again.

It was here I learned a subtle difference between tank valves available for the common North American tanks. Some have a small bleed screw you can use to vent pressure and avoid the situation above. (This is in addition to the standard pressure release valve that all American tanks have) Tanks I purchased in Canada do not have this screw - the one I got in Florida has it - maybe it's a law. I recommend having the valve with the pressure release screw if you plan to travel off the beaten path. You can have the valve replaced if your existing tanks don't have it.

In Europe there does not appear to be a universal standard. Cylinders seem to be different in each country and even the fuel is different from North America. Butane is much more common than propane but there is no problem using butane in a system made for propane. The gas pressure is lower and will safely work in a propane installation. DO NOT USE **PROPANE** IN A SYSTEM MADE FOR **BUTANE**!!!

In Portugal, Spain and many other countries, people trade in their empty tanks for full ones rather than having their own tanks refilled. This means there are large factory-style filling stations rather than the small local stations common in Canada and the USA. On the two occasions we visited these places they were able to find the proper adapters to fill our cylinders directly. The problem is that these factories are few and far between.

When we stayed in Gibraltar there was no filling station in the whole country! Customs forbade carrying the cylinders across the border to Spain since there had been instances of smuggling goods in empty gas cylinders. I came up with the following alternative. I made an adapter to connect my cylinder to a small CampGaz cylinder. This is another "exchange" system that holds about 6 lbs. of butane but is readily available all around Europe including Gibraltar. This way I could fill our cans from CampGaz cylinders.

Note that the following procedure must be done outside, away from the boat, and away from sparks or open flames. Any gas fuel is highly explosive and must be handled with extreme care!

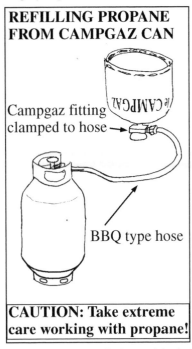

**REFILLING PROPANE FROM CAMPGAZ CAN**

Campgaz fitting clamped to hose →

BBQ type hose

**CAUTION: Take extreme care working with propane!**

I bought a CampGaz cylinder and used the adapter to empty it into my cylinder by connecting the two cylinders together, hanging the CampGaz one upside down and opening both valves. Again this benefits from having the release valve on the American cylinder to speed up the filling process. It can take hours to drain down without the valve - minutes with it. From then on I could just trade my CampGaz cylinder in on a new one whenever we needed more.

I made this adapter by cutting the barbecue end off a propane BBQ hose fitting. This left me with a 4-foot hose and connector to the standard North American gas cylinder. In Europe the CampGaz connectors are fairly common. I purchased one and clamped it to the open end of the BBQ hose with a hose clamp.

## Propane Hints:

- BE CAREFUL!! Propane is very explosive!
- A gas "sniffer" is a good idea.
- Butane can be used in a propane system.
- Propane **cannot** be used in a butane system!
- Check for system leaks once in a while (see below).
- Have tanks with a pressure release bleed screw if cruising to the islands or further afield.

# Checking for Propane Leaks

Every week or so when living aboard, I do a simple check for leaks in our propane system. This involves letting propane into the hosing to the stove, turning off the valve at the tank and seeing if the system can hold pressure. Since we don't have a pressure gauge, I include this simple test:

1. Turn on the solenoid to allow gas into the system. Then turn off the solenoid or valve at the cylinder.
2. Try to light the stove. The burner should ignite for just a second using up the residual gas in the system.
3. Turn off the burner again.
4. Turn on the solenoid to allow gas into the system then turn it off again and turn off the valve at the tank for good measure. You have trapped some gas in the hose.
5. Now leave the system for a few hours (I leave it overnight) with the pressure in the hose.
6. Try the test later and there should still be enough gas to light the burner again for a second or so. If not, there is a leak! Do not turn the solenoid on - you're just trying to see what was left in the hose! [1]

The second, and more involved test I do is oriented more towards troubleshooting.

1. Put a squirt of dish-washing detergent on a kitchen sponge or cloth and add a little water. Squeeze it out and try to get a little heap of bubbles - just like playing in the tub!
2. Put some bubbles around any connections in the propane system as if you were molding clay around it. Do this anywhere fittings attach together. E.g. either side of the regulator and at the tank connection.
3. When the bubbles have covered over the joint between two fittings carefully observe for a few seconds to see if any gas is escaping from the system into the bubbles. If it is, the bubbles will grow, inflated by the leaking gas - otherwise they will just sit still until they pop. I even use this whenever I connect a new cylinder to the system to make sure everything is OK. If there is any doubt, pile some more suds on.

---

[1] An alternative to lighting the stove is to install a pressure gauge next to the tank. Check the gauge after the system has sat overnight with gas in the line.

4.  Clean up with paper towels afterward: the result is a clean system as well as peace-of-mind.

I use the first test to check the overall integrity of the system every week or so. Whenever I connect a fresh tank to the system, I use the second "bubble test" to make sure there isn't a leak at the connection. I would also use the "bubble test" if a leak showed up with the first test.

# Steering and Self-Steering

A yacht sailing short-handed on long passages must be capable of steering herself! I cannot imagine what it would be like to steer by hand for days with only 2 or 3 people to share the work. In fact, I think that may be a good way to invent a new form of self-steering -- head off on a long passage without it!

Joshua Slocum was able to get the *Spray* to steer herself by cleverly setting the sails. Solo circumnavigator Yves Jelinas had enough time to think about it during a non-stop circumnavigation (beautifully filmed in *"Jean du Sud Around the World"*) that he invented a new system, Cap Horn self-steering, which he is now manufacturing.

Luckily, the sailor outfitting a cruising boat doesn't have to build his own! There are a wide variety to choose from but the two main categories are wind-vane types or electronic pilots.

The wind-vane pilot will work from light winds right up to very heavy conditions. Modern vanes are dependable, powerful, quiet and do not rely on battery power to work. Many ocean cruisers have a wind-vane aboard for serious passagemaking.

Electronic autopilots work in a wide range off conditions from calms up to moderate-heavy winds. A built-in pilot strong and quick enough to rival a wind-vane in heavy conditions will be as expensive or more so than a wind-vane. It also relies on battery power and is much more difficult to repair at sea. Almost all ocean cruisers have at least a light duty electronic pilot aboard. An increasing number have a belowdecks electronic pilot, and have beefed up the battery and charging systems to keep it fed on long passages.

# Wind-Vane Self-Steering

*Looking over the stern at the windvane paddle in the water. The whole paddle and arm assembly swings from side to side pulling on the control lines shackled on above. It swings like a pendulum, being directed by the vane and control settings on the fixed mechanism above. Note the remote control lines running forward from the small control wheel. This sets the course relative to the wind by aligning the vane into the wind.*

The idea of a wind-vane steerer is to adjust the heading of the boat so that it is constant to the wind. The power to do this comes from the wind and the flow of water past the yacht.

Most units have a relatively small vane that sits in clear air at the transom. This moves if the relative wind direction changes -- if the boat is heading steadily, the vane will sit in one position. If the boat shifts off course the vane will be blown around to a new position and it is this movement that will be used to steer the boat back on course. The vane "senses" the relative wind direction.

The problem is that the wind over the vane does not have enough power to steer most yachts. It needs an amplifier! As the vane swings around it is used to steer a small balanced rudder that hangs in the water beneath the unit. This is where the power comes from. The rudder is rigged to swing from side to side and if it is turned slightly to port, it will swing to the port side.

This is like holding a paddle in the water over the side of a canoe. A small turn away from the boat and the paddle is pulled away from you. Turn it back in and the paddle is forced back against the side of

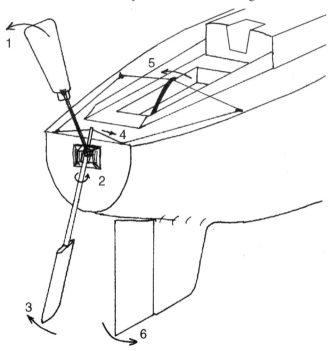

Figure 5 - Pendulum-type wind-vane.

the canoe. Don't try this for too long or everyone else will stop paddling and start splashing you with their paddles!

Anyway, most wind-vane self steering systems use a small rudder of some kind to amplify the signal they get from the wind vane itself. The boat drifts off course a little, the vane moves over in response to the relative wind shift 1), and in doing so, turns the small rudder 2). The small rudder (being mounted on a pendulum) swings around 3) and *this* movement has enough force in it to be used to turn the boat. In the WindPilot™ and Monitor™ systems for example, lines connected to each side of the tiny rudder 4) run through pulleys and connect to the tiller 5) so that these lines are used to steer the ship 6) by the main rudder.

Advantages of wind-vane systems include that they can steer a boat in a variety of conditions ranging up to very heavy weather -- without using battery power to do it. They are easy to repair and, with some spare parts, very dependable. They even provide a basis for a jury rigged steering system if the main rudder is out of action.

One disadvantage is that they do not work in a calm, since they require wind moving over the vane to know which way to go. However, this can be overcome by connecting a small tillerpilot to steer the windvane. This is an inexpensive way to add an autopilot to a boat that already has a vane.

## *Two-Step* gets a Windvane

In 1997 we added a WindPilot™ model windvane to *Two-Step*. Having sailed over 25,000 miles without one, the change has been a revelation! She handles so nicely in the big waves that used to be a real strain for the Autohelm™ 3000. Sailing downwind used to be a difficult point of sail since large corrections are required to keep a steady course. The Autohelm was just not fast enough, but the WindPilot handles the boat with quiet power. The vane moves back and forth following the wind and the pendulum sizzles through the water, pulling the lines to steer.

An added benefit is the ability of the servo-pendulum style vanes such as the Monitor™ and our WindPilot, to correct the yawing of a boat in large seas. This happens because of the motion of the pendulum as it hangs down over the transom.

In normal operation, if the yacht veers off course to port, the vane directs the pendulum to swing to port. That pendulum motion transmits through the control lines to the rudder as a correction back to starboard. Similarly if the yacht veers off course to starboard, the vane directs the pendulum also to swing to starboard. That pendulum motion transmits through the control lines to the rudder as a correction back to port to get the yacht back on course.

Notice that the pendulum moves to the opposite side of the boat compared to the turn it is inducing. The pendulum swinging to port induces a turn to starboard and vice versa. This may seem counter-productive, but in fact it creates a very important feature of these systems. It will reduce the yawing of a yacht!

Running downwind in large seas is normally a very demanding point of sail. Waves approach the boat from astern and try to broach her - pushing the stern ahead faster than the bow and trying to turn her broadside to the waves. This yawing motion demands fast reactions on the helm and is often too much for a small autopilot. The advantage of a pendulum windvane (such as our WindPilot) is that the yawing motion of the boat actually causes the pendulum to correct the course automatically! As the stern slews to port the pendulum is thrown to starboard and this automatically means the system will begin a turn to port. In summary, the yawing of the boat is fed back into the system as a correction to the course by the pendulum. If all the above seems too complicated, just spend a few days at sea in the cockpit watching a windvane in action and you may even come to understand it! Trust me, it works.

# Electronic Autopilots

Electronic autopilots can work in calms as well as windy days and appear to be the obvious high-tech alternative to wind-vanes. But they are not without problems of their own. Their chief shortcoming relates to their use of power. When the wind and seas are up, so is the effort at the helm and that extra force the pilot must use will translate directly to more amps drawn from the battery. Some pilots draw more than 2-3 amps almost continuously in a heavy sea.

A pilot that draws fewer amps may not have the power to turn the rudder quickly in a heavy sea or if the boat is a little overcanvassed. This will work nicely in light to moderate conditions and lose control just when you really need help steering.

The stronger electronic autopilot that can handle any conditions may draw so much power that the engine needs to be run 3 or more hours per day to supply it with electricity.

*Two-Step* has a small Autohelm™ 3000 unit that mounts in the cockpit and drives via a belt and drum connected to the wheel itself. This unit is really too small for our 37' boat but we have managed to coax it (with numerous repairs) twice across the Atlantic. The larger autopilots that mount below decks are the better choice for heavy going but of course these cost more in both dollars and amps consumed under way. Many cruisers use a small unit like ours to steer the boat in light air and under power, and use a wind-vane for most offshore sailing.

A big advantage of an electronic pilot is the ability to hold a compass course, and to do it in a flat calm if necessary. Most electronic pilots also allow a tiny wind vane to be plugged in to allow the unit to hold a course relative to the wind -- close-hauled for instance.

Note that any self steering system, electrical or mechanical will benefit from having the sails correctly trimmed to balance the helm. There will be less effort at the wheel and less turbulence with the rudder closer to centre.

# Steering Systems

Before we set sail on a long passage, I crawl into the tiny access space over our fuel tank and take a look at the steering system. This generally entails pulling enough gear out of the cockpit locker to get the access hatch open, and then finding a relatively comfortable place to lie amongst the remaining stuff (anchor rode is good; fisherman anchor is uncomfortable) as I peer in. Sheryl turns the wheel back and forth and I check for any play in the linkages. It is a very good feeling to see it move smoothly back and forth. I spray a little Boeing T9™ here and there and wiggle back out.

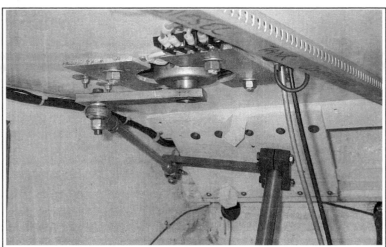

*Two-Step's steering system below decks. The ship's wheel turns the arm in the foreground and single link connects that to the tiller arm on the rudder post in the back of the picture.*

Besides regular maintenance and inspections, there is not much to do about a steering system in preparation for a long cruise. There must be no doubt about its integrity, of course!

When we set sail from the Canary Islands for Brazil, I had some doubts about our largest jib. It was getting tired, but I didn't want to repair it there. However, it's a different matter with a rudder. You can't exactly say:

*Well, the rudder seems a bit loose but it's only an equatorial crossing, not like sailing in the northern ocean. There you really need your rudder!!*

If there is any question about the rudder, it *must* be addressed before setting sail.

The rudder takes a real beating on passages. When we arrived in the Azores on our first transatlantic passage, we were shocked to see the number of broken rudders littering the docks at Horta Marina as sailors from all nations worked to rebuild them. It was the same situation when we returned there on our second transatlantic. It pays to check!

One clever idea, still on my to-do list, is putting a ½ inch hole in the aft edge of the rudder to allow an easy jury rig in the event of a steering system failure. A quick trip over the side (during a calm period) would allow lines to be tied to it, and the disconnected rudder could be controlled from on deck. It would be more effective than rigging the head door as a rudder plus would allow greater privacy in the head on the trip back to harbour.

## Summary

- Consider self-steering for any offshore yacht, especially for short-handed crews.
- Wind-vanes conserve battery power and can handle rough conditions and downwind sailing. They are mechanically simple and repairable.
- Electronic autopilots can handle the boat if there is no wind, and they can steer a compass course. But it must be strong enough for heavy seas if it is used full-time. The electronics will be harder to fix than a mechanical wind-vane unit.
- Maintain the ship's steering gear -- not many sailors really want to just "go where the wind blows them".

# Safety Equipment

There is a fundamental difference between a life raft and a sea anchor. The same distinction exists between a lifejacket and a safety-harness, and between an EPIRB and a radar detector.

Although they are all safety equipment, the first items - the life raft, lifejacket and EPIRB - are all designed to save sailors who need rescuing. Now this is an admirable goal, and if I were floating around without a boat, I would sincerely appreciate all three of these things. There are testimonials for all these items from people whose lives were saved. Steve Callahan floated across the Atlantic in a life raft - 76 days chronicled in *Adrift* - and there are other stories of people who survived in life rafts even longer.

Reading the accounts of the perils they faced on the sea in something little bigger than a truck tire, it's amazing they lived to tell their tales.

Strangely enough, there must be something reassuring about a life raft because there are numerous occasions where people have abandoned their boat in favour of a raft, have died, and their boat was found weeks later, still afloat (this happened in the Fastnet race of 1979)! Possibly the raft represents salvation from the storm in a figurative sense, although unless the yacht is actually disappearing beneath the waves or afire, a raft is surely less seaworthy.

The EPIRB seems an even more direct salvation! Like something out of Star Trek, a call for help including the name and position of the yacht, bounces off a satellite and is relayed to the rescue parties (at least in theory). Then the shipwrecked sailor can hope to have only a few days in a life raft, drinking water from his hand-operated desalinator and waiting for the helicopter to arrive.

But the problem with all this is the heavy dependence on another party, the rescuer! The self-sufficient sailor must avoid this. Besides the fact that any number of things could go wrong with the rescue scenario -- it's too stormy or remote for immediate rescue; the life raft doesn't survive the storm; the EPIRB does not work or rescue parties are tired of chasing false alarms -- it means the skipper must put his faith in an outside party for something so important! It is essential that the captain and crew do all they can to save themselves. Seamanship demands it!

Here's where the safety devices in the second group comes in. Equipment such as a sea anchor, safety harness and radar detector will help sailors to *avoid* needing rescue in the first place! The boat and crew that are prepared for all situations are obviously less likely to get into trouble.

Within this category are devices that can help repair damage, and aid in recovery from problems at sea. This includes tools to effect emergency repairs such as underwater epoxy and a collision mat to staunch the flow of water through a hole.

This is not to say that a well found cruising boat doesn't need a life raft and EPIRB. Just that good seamanship requires everything possible be done to avoid trouble in the first place, that the crew do everything they can to recover from emergency situations and finally that activating an EPIRB and climbing into a life raft be done as a last resort. If you abandon ship, you must give up the most valuable resource you have - the yacht - and this must not be done lightly!

Table 19 - Example of preventive measures vs. repair and rescue for various problems at sea.

| Problem | Prevention | Repair | Rescue |
|---------|-----------|--------|--------|
| collision | watchkeeping<br>radar reflector<br>radar<br>radar detector | collision mat<br>watertight<br>bulkhead | life raft<br>EPIRB |
| fire | vapour alarm | fire extinguisher | raft etc. |
| MOB | life harness | lifejacket | lifesling |
| pitchpole | sea anchor or drogue | everything! | raft? |

# Prevention

### Watchkeeping

Good seamanship, careful navigation and conscientious watch-keeping are major factors preventing problems at sea.

With lots of time at sea between Florida and Bermuda on our first offshore passage, we had plenty of opportunity to consider how we could handle any problems. On that 8-day passage we saw roughly one ship per day (excluding all the traffic close to Florida) -- obviously a collision at sea was a real possibility. By estimating the distance at which we could see a ship (maybe 5-7 miles in good visibility) and our closing speed (*Two-Step*'s 6 knots + their 15 knots) we calculated that we would see a ship at least 15 minutes before it could reach us. Therefore, we decided to do a thorough scan of the horizon every 10 minutes for ships. In practice we usually see ships more than 20 minutes before they reach us and have had lots of time to alter course if we're on a collision bearing. We have never had a close call with a ship at sea.

---

Distance to horizon = $1.17\sqrt{\text{height in feet}}$

**e.g.**

Two - Step to horizon = $1.17\sqrt{9}$ = 3.5 miles

Horizon to ship's lights = $1.17\sqrt{20}$ = 5.2 miles

Total distance = 3.5 +5.2 = 8.7 nautical miles

Therefore a ship's light that was 20 feet above the water would be visible a maximum of 8.7 miles away -- with my eye 9 feet off the water as I stood in the cockpit. Assuming a clear night and a strong light!

---

### Adding a Radar Detector

In 1997 we added a device I have wanted for a long time; a radar detector. The C.A.R.D. unit from Survival Safety Engineering is a well built and very cleverly designed unit made especially for boats. It has a 4 point compass display that shows the relative bearing of the radar unit being detected. There is an audible alarm as well as the LED display. Any ship running their radar will be detected - in some cases before they could be seen over the horizon. (note that not all ships run their radar - but most do, especially in fog or reduced visibility)

I spoke with Bob Morris, a cruising sailor himself and President of Survival Safety Engineering before we installed the unit. He recommended the C.A.R.D. as part of a complete system including a radar unit. The radar would be used for reduced visibility (and navigation), and the C.A.R.D. run all the time.

Unlike radar, it draws so little power I cannot see any difference in my ammeter when it is turned on! So we just leave it on all the time - an extra pair of eyes to help the person on watch and extra insurance against a collision at sea.

### Life Harnesses/Jacklines

Jacklines and safety harnesses are an essential and inexpensive safety item to have on board. The temptation is not to wear them (studies show this reduces their effectiveness dramatically!!) and I admit to having ventured forward a few times without wearing mine. To counter this, we got nice ones that fit well -- like a vest with a solid fabric back --

and have adjusted one for each of us. Sheryl stitched the shoulder straps so they would always be right and we labelled them .

Besides running the jacklines from bow to stern on each side deck (see "Deck Layout" on page 50), I put a sturdy U-bolt near the companionway so we can clip on as we come out of the cabin and move freely in the cockpit. I also spliced on a longer lanyard (6 feet as opposed to 5) so we can go below to pour a cup of tea or grab a tool from the toolbox without unclipping. Now our life harnesses are so comfortable, we put them on and forget about them.

### Heaving To / Sea Anchor

Good ground tackle has already been discussed in "Ground Tackle - The Ultimate Insurance" on page 89 but it should be mentioned that it is safety equipment as well.

A sea anchor is in the same category and could help in the event of being caught out in a real storm. Much has been written recently about the value of heaving to in a storm, and a sea anchor will allow even modern vessels, sometimes unwilling to heave-to, to rest quietly, slowly sliding downwind in their own protective slick of calm water.

We learned the value of heaving to when we crossed the Atlantic from Bermuda to the Azores. We spent one terrible night in sustained winds of 45 knots, with gusts of 52.

We'd made a poor gamble on a weather window and, less than one day out from Bermuda, the wind and sea began to rapidly increase. We sailed on under much reduced canvas until the wind was a steady 35 knots. With the last of the light fading from the dark storm sky, we found ourselves sailing in a black cocoon. Huge wave crests hissed up out of the dark, all that long night, visible only at the last second in the faint glow of our tiny masthead light, nearly fifty feet above the decks. The wind screamed in the rigging and, finally, exhausted, we decided to heave to. We unrolled a scrap of our jib and backed it. Then we locked the rudder over. The improvement in the boat's motion was amazing as compared to crashing along under sail!

Since then we have decided to heave-to on numerous occasions -- mostly just for a rest or to wait for daylight to enter an inlet -- but it still surprises us how comfortable it is.

*Heaving to can be a comfortable alternative to sailing in very rough conditions, especially since **Two-Step** tends to be a wet boat.*

### Bilge Alarm

I mention the bilge alarm as a preventative safety feature, mainly because there have been numerous instances where sailors have been surprised to find their boat sinking. They came down from on deck to find the cabin awash and were unable to save the yacht from sinking because they weren't able to find the leak with all the water everywhere.

In most cases of a boat taking on water, it is not the catastrophic collision and gaping hole that all sailors fear, but a fitting or hose come adrift and letting water in. The bilge alarm will give immediate warning of a problem and allow time to fix it. For more information, see page 108.

# Repair

In the event of a problem, the resourcefulness of the crew and the resources of the yacht will be put to the test. I include a list of some suggested items for use in repairing a major disaster -- taking on water. I include water tight bulkheads in that list although obviously this is something that must be built in advance.

An open mind and a willingness to experiment (sentiments that will likely be encouraged by a situation such as sinking) are the best tools to tackle any problem. Thinking problems through in the comfort of a quiet anchorage, and purchasing a few special items (such as underwater epoxy) will improve the odds of handling a problem. Use this list as a starting point -- imagine various disasters befalling you, and add items that will help you recover! (When I find myself getting depressed with this game I go back with renewed zeal to ways of preventing the problem in the first place!!)

- fire extinguishers
- collision mat and various bungs to fit through-hulls
- high capacity bilge pump
- underwater epoxy
- watertight bulkheads
- a comprehensive tool kit
- replacement VHF antenna

# Rescue

The best advice I have ever heard for abandoning ship is to *step up into the life raft*. Only when everything else has been tried and the ship is actually going beneath the waves, is it time to get into the raft.

The following rescue-oriented safety items include items commonly carried by most offshore sailors. At the bottom of the list things get expensive and some sailors we know have preferred to invest in safety equipment to keep the yacht afloat rather than pay the $3,000 to $5,000 dollar cost of a good life raft.

- lifejackets
- practice MOB drill
- MOB pole/drogue/strobe connected together
- Man Overboard recovery system (e.g. Lifesling™)
- flares
- personal strobes
- handheld VHF in waterproof case
- SSB or HAM radio
- EPIRB
- life raft

Any opportunity to practice with safety items will be a good idea. For example, the marine store in our home town of Port Credit holds an annual flare night with our local Power and Sail Squadron where people can try firing off their newly expired flares. Experts are on hand to help and everyone who tries it will definitely be better prepared to use the flares in the event of an emergency. Any chance to try out emergency equipment will make it more effective -- we also go to the life raft service centre to see our life raft unpacked, and practice retrieving a lifejacket once in a while as well.

### Abandon Ship Bag

As you may have guessed by now, our general attitude is that, if you have to get into a life raft, your chances of survival are slim. We prefer to put our efforts into keeping *Two-Step* afloat rather than concentrating on surviving the wrath of the ocean in a little rubber life raft. However, we do take precautions.

We have our 4-man life raft, which we keep lashed to the deck in a fiberglass case, checked and repacked once a year of voyaging. We watch the process being carried out, to be sure it is done properly and to make ourselves familiar with the contents and set-up. Conditions are likely to be pretty bad in the event of leaving the mother ship, so we don't want to be sitting, decks-awash in the dark, trying to read the instructions with a flashlight!

On all passages, we keep our Avon dinghy inflated and lashed on deck as well to serve as a second life platform - one that is so familiar to us we could off-load it blindfolded.

We also pack an abandon ship bag (also called a survival bag) to supplement the supplies in our life raft. We stow it in one of the cockpit lockers within easy reach next to our dive bags which contain our wet suits - good for preventing hypothermia. We make sure these bags stay on top during the course of a passage. Our brightly coloured duffel bag is easy to see and we don't pack it so full that it is difficult to carry. The youngest or least strong crew member should be able to lift it and our dive bag. All the contents of our abandon ship bag are individually packed in waterproof bags to keep them dry.

Table 20 - Abandon Ship Bag

| Contents | Comments |
| --- | --- |
| Handheld VHF radio and batteries | From our research of survival at sea, the stories are countless of victims watching ship after ship pass them by unnoticed. In our experiences at sea, we found ships depended on radar more than visual watches, **but always had their radios on.** |

| Contents | Comments |
|---|---|
| | A female voice on the radio gets a response every time. If you're near a shipping lane, we feel this is the most important item in your survival bag. |
| EPIRB | |
| Flares & flare gun | |
| Waterproof flashlight and batteries | |
| Fishing kit | This includes hand-lines, extra hooks, sinkers, and lures. We also keep our spear on deck so we can grab it as well. |
| Filleting knife | Sheryl's mother bought us one of those "does-everything" knives that is a filleting knife, sharpening stone, line cutter, and set of pliers all in one fold-out contraption. |
| Filleting board | So you have a hard surface to clean the fish without damaging the raft. |
| Swiss army knife | |
| Dinghy repair kit and pump | |
| Can opener | |
| Canned goods | Foods low in sodium and more carbo-hydrates than fats. Protein foods need more water to metabolize. We pack canned beans, and fruits and vegetables high in water content. Dehydration is more of a problem than protein deficiency. |
| Non-fat dry milk | In packets. To supply calcium. |
| Vitamins | Multi-vitamins |
| Important documents | Photocopies of our ship's papers and our passports |
| Chart | Overall chart of the area we're cruising in a waterproof case. |
| First aid kit | Including sunblock and seasickness pills |
| Sponge | For collecting rain and dew |
| Water | There are water rations and a solar still in our life raft but we keep two 5-gallon jerry jugs of fresh water lashed on deck to take with us if we abandon ship. Be sure they are no more than 3/4 full so that they float! |

# Getting Spares along the Way

As you travel, you will need to replenish your stock of marine supplies and spare parts. We are firm believers in supporting the local businesses in the places we visit but often you will find yourself in a remote area where the specialized supplies you need are not available. In this case we recommend carrying a West Marine catalog on board and ordering what you need through their International Orders department. Experienced cruisers who understand what it's like to be in your situation are on call to assist you. The West Marine catalog also contains a lot of indepth information on marine systems and supplies and is a useful reference guide.

**West Marine**
Order 24 hours a day, 7 days a week
By phone:      1-800-BOATING (262-8464)  US and Canada
               408-728-4430
By Fax:        408-761-4421  US and Canada
               408-761-4020  International
By E-mail:     wmarinternat@earthlink.net
By Snail Mail: West Marine
               PO Box 50070
               Watsonville, CA 95077-5070
               USA

# Part 4 : Provisioning

# How to Provision

Provisioning for a cruise can be a daunting prospect. The fear of being far from home and discovering that you haven't packed enough food or are missing essential items can add unnecessary anxiety to a voyage.

Fear not! No matter what length of cruise you are planning - a week, a month, a year - you can develop a specific strategy for what you need, how you're going to use it and when.

When Paul and I started long-distance cruising aboard *Two-Step*, we read every book and magazine article on provisioning that we could find. Some provided a list of standard items and tips on storing fresh vegetables but, as had to be expected, reflected the tastes, budgets and cruising styles of the authors. We were looking for *a good system* to help us determine *our* needs.

So we made a lot of notes, did some experiments, adapted methods used by other cruisers and, with a little trial and error, came up with a reliable system for keeping our boat well-stocked in all conditions. We have now travelled over 30,000 miles on *Two-Step* since we began cruising in 1989, have crossed the Atlantic three times, have weathered the doldrums and the Bermuda Triangle, and have survived the adventures of shopping in local markets around the world. We rarely find ourselves short of supplies. With our lockers full of our favourite foods and supplies, we are free to linger in remote places. Delays due to poor weather no longer concern us. *The more precisely we provision to meet our needs, the more relaxed and enjoyable our cruising life becomes.*

Careful planning pays off in the long run. Besides, it's fun! Even if you're gazing out your window at a snowdrift, you can start planning your cruising inventory now.

# The Shard System for Successful Provisioning

A well provisioned boat is a joy to be aboard! The six steps outlined on this page are the heart of our provisioning system. We then cover each step comprehensively in the upcoming chapters.

1.   **Start a provisioning binder.** Set up a notebook or binder and begin recording the foods, household goods and boat supplies you use on a regular basis. Record useful information beside each item on your list such as consumption rate, the most convenient or economical size, preferred brand etc. (See "Starting a Provisioning Binder" on page 147 and "Tip 3 - Recording Your Food and Supply Usage" on page 151)

2.   **Identify *your* parameters for provisioning.** Characteristics of your boat, crew and cruise will determine *what* to provision and *how much* to stow. (See "The 10 Parameters of Provisioning" on page 153)

3.   **Create menu plans.** Menu plans will remind you of details, streamline supplies for maximum use of storage space, let you relax more while travelling, and help prevent life threatening situations when you are cruising in remote places or on an ocean passage. (See "Creating Menu Plans" on page 161)

4.   **Make the shopping process hassle-free.** Hassle-free shopping outings result in more efficient provisioning since you are in a better frame of mind and therefore less likely to overlook important items or to impulse buy. Storage space is valuable so you want to be sure you are filling it with supplies you will need and use. (See "Hassle-free Shopping" on page 167)

5.   **Practice the art of good stowage**. If supplies are not carefully stowed, they will break. Not only is this a waste of money, it means they are not available when you need them. (See "The Art of Good Stowage" on Page 213)

6.   **Maintain inventory.** In tropical climates, fresh foods can quickly go bad. Bottles can break when the seas get rough and infrequently used items can get lost in the bottom of lockers. Checking bins and lockers regularly means you know what you have, and haven't got. Then, when it's time to provision, you won't be caught short or buy things you already have. (See "Maintaining Inventory" on page 207)

Preparing well to provision your boat takes a little time but you can carry out the steps in bits and pieces. It's worth the effort since it saves money and reduces frustration. But best of all, the end result will be an efficiently stocked boat that contains supplies and food items that suit *your* cruising style since the system is based on your established routines and personal preferences. Your tastes and priorities may change during the course of your cruise, in the same way they do over time at home, but this method allows you to keep pace with the changes and still maintain a reliable list of supplies.

Read on for more details on making this system work for you!

# Starting a Provisioning Binder

Several months before our first major cruise, we started tracking our food and supply uses at home. This was the first step in designing a custom provisions list based on our individual needs and preferences.

We used a three-ring binder with alphabetical index tabs which now contains complete and thorough lists of all our regular supplies. We entered items alphabetically in our binder every time we went grocery shopping and as we used things around the house and boat. (See Table 21 below)

Over time, we developed a custom inventory of food items, cleaning and maintenance products, household goods and first aid supplies. We made notes beside each entry on how quickly we used things up, in what seasons we tended to eat more of certain foods and the changes in consumption rates of various products when guests stayed for a while.

This book is now our bible for provisioning. We consult it every time we go shopping to remind us of things we need. It is the foundation for our cruising inventory and provides reliable guidelines for how long we can cruise in isolation based on the supplies we have on board at the time.

Table 21 - Sample of page recording items and rate of use.

| Item | Size | Notes |
| --- | --- | --- |
| butter | 1 lb. | - use 2 lb./mo. when baking |
| batteries | D cell | - use for flashlight only/6 mo. |
| bathroom cleaner | 650 ml | - use in 5-6 months |

Of course, when living aboard the boat, our regular eating habits and supply usage change somewhat due to factors such as the availability of certain products, our increased appetites due to physical activity and the basic galley equipment we have on *Two-Step*. However, we have found that our favourite foods at home are still the foundation of our provisions list for the boat.

As we travel, we discover new foods when we explore local markets and sample exotic cuisine in the ports we visit. In Spain, we developed a fondness for custard apples; in the Azores, two local women showed us how to prepare a delicious octopus stew; and in Brazil, a village boy introduced us to a refreshing bottled drink made from the fruit

*Fresh air and exercise increase appetites.*

of the cashew tree. We make notes in our binder of any new "finds" and take them into consideration for future provisioning.

Sometimes, we have to make substitutions or learn to live without products we enjoy at home when they are not available in the areas we are cruising. It was quite a shock to discover that peanut butter is only a staple in North America and difficult to find (or outrageously expensive) in most other countries. When my mother learned this, she shipped us four huge jars of our favourite salt-free, sugar-free brand to Bermuda to get us across the Atlantic and sustain us for a while in Europe. Now there is a big note in our provisioning binder to stock up on peanut butter when we're going foreign!

We also take note of any changes we make in our regular routine while cruising. For example, we're real meat and potatoes people on shore but in many places around the world good meat is hard to find, expensive, or difficult to store. So when we are cruising, we are happier eating more stir-fries, stews and vegetarian meals (which are better for us anyway.)

Like many first-time cruisers, we initially made the mistake of loading the boat with canned goods we would never eat at home because books we had read said they stored well on a boat. If you don't eat canned corned beef or baked beans now, don't put them on the boat. Serving a crew food they hate will make them mutinous. On the other hand, nothing cheers up a wet miserable crew on a rainy night like a delicious meal of their favourite food or a surprise pack of a snack they love.

*Preparing foods that everyone enjoys prevents mutiny.*

Building a list of food items and supplies you use regularly and annotating it with notes on how frequently you restock them, takes only a little time and starts you on the road to custom provisioning.

*Go with what you know!*

There are probably many things on your grocery list that you know how often to buy. For example, we know, without a doubt, that we go through 4 litres of milk every week whether living afloat or ashore. Start with the information that you know, and build from there. Any items you are uncertain about, make a point to observe and record your consumption rate in your provisioning notebook. (See Tip 3, page 151)

Of course, if you are planning a short-term cruise or cruising in an area where shopping is easy, you won't need such indepth records to plan your meals. But the longer and further you travel, the more helpful this kind of detailed information becomes.

When Paul and I were building *Two-Step* and our Atlantic cruise was a far-off dream, designing our stores list became an uplifting project after busy days at work. We'd quickly forget the stresses at the office as we added items to our provisioning binder and discussed the supplies we'd need for an ocean passage or a winter in the tropics.

Fuel your imagination as you create a master list of foods and supplies important to *you*!

Tip 3 - Recording Your Food and Supply Usage

## Recording Your Food and Supply Usage

A good way to begin a custom provisions list for your cruise is to set up a notebook or binder to record the supplies you use regularly.

Whenever you shop for food, household items or marine supplies, add the items to your book so you will have a master list of the common supplies you depend on.

The next step is to record the rate at which you consume them. This way, you will know how long things will last during your voyage and how often you will need to replace them.

A laundry marker and masking tape are useful tools to help you record the consumption rate of each item on your master list. Whenever you open a new tube of toothpaste, write that day's date on it with the laundry marker. When it's all used up, record the number of weeks it took to finish it. Repeat the process a few times to get an average. For items that you can't or don't want to write on, such as paper towels, write the date on a piece of masking tape and stick it inside a nearby cupboard door.

Every couple of weeks, go through a cupboard in your kitchen, storage room, or the lockers in your boat to remind yourself of items that you don't buy regularly but like to have on hand. Certain spices, soup mixes, and cleaning products fit into this category for us. Add them to your lists and estimate how often you'll have to replace them if you are planning a long-term cruise.

These records are invaluable when provisioning for your cruise since they reflect *your* personal needs and preferences.

# Provisioning Parameters

When we set sail for our first long-distance voyage from Lake Ontario to the Bahamas in 1989, we felt overwhelmed. Our average cruises had been one-week vacations on the lake. On those trips, if we overlooked anything, we could stop at a marina and usually find what we needed in town.

Now we were planning a one-year sabbatical (that later stretched into a three-year odyssey that took us across the Atlantic twice). We didn't realize yet, how reliable the information in our Provisioning Binder was and felt uncertain about how to properly prepare. How much stuff should we take for that length of time? What things would we need when living on the boat full-time that we didn't think of when just summer sailing? What products and food items that we relied on, were only available in Canada?

We asked the experts. We went to slide shows. We read books. The advice was conflicting and confusing. So we took *everything*! Or so it seemed. The day we left, we could hardly move through the boat with all the un-stowed bags, boxes and packages we had piled in the cabin. There wasn't room left in the lockers but we kept bringing wheel-barrow loads down the dock - just in case! The waterline sank and with a ceremonious farewell we heaved off into the horizon.

We had way too many clothes. They took up precious storage space. We'd bought canned goods we'd never tried and didn't like. They took up precious storage space *and* added unnecessary weight to our already burdened vessel. To survive, we ended up shipping home a large box of clothes, textbooks and other unnecessary gear that we'd hastily packed (this cost $105!!) and gave some things away just to make the boat liveable again.

With time and experience, we learned to identify common factors that determined what provisions we required for a specific length of time or for a specific cruise. We call these factors the 10 Parameters of Provisioning. They help answer the questions of "what to take" and "how much" by clarifying our needs. They prevent us from loading the boat with a lot of unnecessary supplies and make it easy to create menu plans that are practical for the conditions we will be facing on our voyage.

## *The 10 Parameters of Provisioning*

1.  **The Length of the Cruise** - For a one month cruise, supplies will be needed for breakfast, lunch, dinner and snacks for roughly 30 days. Even if several restaurant meals are planned, we recommend provisioning as if every meal will be eaten on board so you have the freedom to change your mind.

2.  **Opportunities for Reprovisioning** - If you are going to be offshore or cruising in a remote area for several weeks where you won't have a chance to re-stock supplies, this will have a dramatic effect on how you provision. Attention to detail becomes imperative and good back-up supplies necessary. For offshore passages, we carry at least an extra month's worth of supplies in case of a serious delay. The common rule among cruisers is to provision for 50% more time than you plan to be away. This is a good guideline but use your best judgement. Imagine the worst scenario possible and plan accordingly - it could save your life! Consider too the quality and selection offered by local merchants in the distant ports you will be visiting. Prices and selection are usually better in large mainland cities so it is a good idea to stock up before sailing to isolated places.

3.  **The Number of People** - This determines the portions and amounts of various supplies. If guests will be joining you for part of your cruise, take this into consideration. What appears to be a good stock of supplies can vanish at an alarming rate with a couple of extra people on board. Stock up for lots of casual entertaining. Something we hadn't anticipated when we first began cruising was the regularity of evening get-togethers with fellow cruisers. Prepare for lots of Happy Hours!

4.  **The Appetite Level of Your Crew** - Cruising is an active lifestyle and with all the fresh air and exercise - sailing, swimming, diving and exploring - appetite level increases, so plan slightly larger portions than at home. On the opposite side of the coin, appetites tend to dwindle when passage-making due to inactivity, interrupted sleep patterns, seasickness or anxiety. If you are taking on crew or having visitors on board, keep in mind that younger people generally have more voracious appetites than older people.

5. **Personal Tastes and Diet Restrictions** - Everyone has their favourite foods. Eating is a pleasure and a comfort so plan tasty nutritious meals that everyone is sure to enjoy. We keep a good supply of everyone's special treats on hand - they can be valuable morale boosters on a bad day! Also, it is important to identify any dietary restrictions your crew members may have so you can plan meals that are safe for everyone to consume. We have relatives who are severely allergic to peanuts so when they join us on a cruise, peanuts, peanut butter and cooking with peanut oil are right out.

6. **Climate and Conditions** - The foods you enjoy in a tropical climate will differ from those you crave when the weather turns cold so plan menus accordingly. Also, if you anticipate rough conditions you will want to stock up on foods that are easy to prepare.

**The crew is disappointed to see Vichyssoise
and frozen Daquiris for lunch the third day running.**

7. **Storage Space** - Storage space determines how often you need to re-stock supplies. The more cargo your boat can carry, the more you can stock up and take advantage of good deals when you find them. Be careful not to overload the boat though, and be careful how you distribute weight when loading on supplies. Keeping heavy items down low and out of the ends of the boat improves performance and safety in rough conditions. We learned the hard way. *Two-Step* handles a rough sea much better since we stopped loading up the forward locker under the bunk with so much pop and beer. (How could we resist beer at $5.99 per case of 24?)

8. **Galley Equipment** - The type of galley equipment you have will affect the type of foods you can prepare and how you can store them. We have a two-burner propane stove with an oven and broiler so we can cook in the same style as we do at home - broiled fish, roast turkey, etc., but on our first long-term cruise we did not have refrigeration. Our ice-box was well insulated and could stay cold for about 10 days before we needed to load up the ice again so we were in good shape for most passages. However, the further afield we travelled, the harder it was to buy ice so we had to learn how to store and preserve foods like our grandmothers did. It was fun and we ate well but we had to provision much differently than we do now that we have a fridge and freezer.

9. **The Cook(s)** - Paul and I both love to cook which shows in our provisions list - exotic spices, special sauces, numerous ingredients for baking, and a wide variety of meats, pastas and grains. How much the cook or cooks enjoy cooking will affect the types of meals you plan and what supplies you take on board. Paul has a rule that he doesn't like to spend much more time preparing dinner than it takes to eat it so he designs meals that are simple and easy to prepare.

10. **Budget** - The bottom line. Buy the most essential supplies first, at the best price you can find. If it looks as if you will be over budget, adjustments can be made on the more frivolous items at the end of your list. On our Atlantic cruise from 1989 to 1992 we spent $200 U.S. to $250 U.S. per month on food including wine and beer which we drink moderately. On our recent cruise from the Chesapeake Bay across the Atlantic to the Portuguese islands of the Azores (1997) we still averaged about $250 U.S. per month.

These 10 Provisioning Parameters help determine provisioning needs so you can plan more efficiently and economically. Every crew and every cruise is different. Provisioning well adds greatly to the success and enjoyment of your voyage.

# Provisioning Parameters

Photocopy for your own use. Also available on disk. See the Appendix.

Worksheet 3 - Provisioning Parameters

## 1. The Length of Your Cruise: _____

## 2. Opportunities for Reprovisioning:

Can you reprovision along the way? _____

If yes, where? _____

Location of stop #1: _____

Location of stop #2: _____

Location of stop #3: _____

Location of stop #4: _____

Average time between stops: _____

What will be expensive or hard to find in our next provi-

sioning stop, that we should stock up on now? _____

_____

_____

## 3. Number of People: _____

Are guests visiting during your cruise? _____

If yes, how many and for how long? _____

_____

_____

## 4. Appetite Level of Your Crew:

Normal:_____ High:_____Low: _____

Notes: _____

_____

_____

## 5. Personal Tastes and Diet Restrictions:

Favourite Foods or Special Requests: _____

_____

_____

_____

Diet Restrictions or Dislikes: _____

_____

_____

## 6. Climate and Conditions:

Meals for:  hot weather_____cold weather _____

rough weather_____  other  _____

Notes: _____

_____

## 7. Storage Space:

How many lockers or bins are available for provisions? \_\_\_\_

What items get priority for storage space on board?

_____

_____

_____

Can you fulfill your cruising goals with the storage space

you currently have? _____

If not, what changes or compromises can you make and still

be happy on board?_____

_____

_____

## 8. Galley Equipment:

Will you be able to prepare meals the same way you do at

home?  If not, what are your limitations?_____

_____

_____

_____

Solutions:_____

## 9. The Cook(s):

Who is going to cook? _____

Does he/she/they like cooking? _____

Does he/she/they get seasick? _____

Notes: _____

_____

_____


## 10. Budget:

Provisioning budget for your cruise?: $ _____

Priority items on your list: _____

_____

_____

Areas where you can cut back, if necessary: _____

_____

_____


*Sail Away! A Guide to*
*Outfitting and Provisioning for Cruising*
© 1998 by Paul and Sheryl Shard

# Creating Menu Plans

Once you have identified your provisioning parameters, the next step is to create menu plans. Menu plans are the most detailed level of provisioning preparation and the foundation of provisioning success. Since storage space on a boat is limited, it is necessary to have some sort of plan for how every item on board is going to be used. Menu plans provide that information for your food supplies. They help you to get ideas on paper so you bring only the supplies you need. Then, you don't waste space or add unnecessary weight to the boat.

Efficient purchasing saves you money too. On our first trip down the Intracoastal Waterway, we really got hooked on southern cooking, especially after a scrumptious feast at Mrs. Wilkes' Boarding House, a famous restaurant in Savannah, Georgia. We bought Mrs. Wilkes' cookbook and stocked the boat with canned mustard greens, yams, and succotash (a milky mixture of corn and lima beans) but after a few weeks we got tired of southern fried chicken and sweet potato soufflé. We carried those canned yams and greens around for a year and finally got rid of them in Europe. (Yes, they crossed the Atlantic!)

Menu plans prevent you from having to interrupt an enjoyable cruise because you run short of some necessary supply. Sailing out of your way to purchase it is not always easy, especially if you are doing wilderness cruising.

Another thing that menu plans give you control over is nutrition. Maintaining proper nutrition is very important on a boat especially on long-term cruises where physical demands are great and bodies need to be strong and healthy. Sometimes it's hard to find the quality of fresh foods that we are used to at home, so taking the time to design nutritious cruising meals in creative ways can prevent ill health. We follow Canada's Food Guide and have included a copy in the book with a sample menu plan. (See page 164)

When cruising in remote areas or sailing across oceans, menu plans are a safety tool - they prevent starvation! Even though we have been cruising full-time for more than 5 years now and are pretty relaxed about provisioning, I still make detailed menu plans for all offshore passages - just to be sure!

Otherwise, our menu plans are pretty general and yours probably will be too if you have a lot of experience cooking and meal planning. For example, we have learned from experience that we eat chicken a couple of times a week, beef one or two times, pasta once a week, at least, and seafood the rest of the time. So I make sure that we have supplies - fresh, canned or frozen - to do that.

If you haven't done a lot of meal planning or are just feeling a bit uncertain about applying your experience to living on a boat, detailed menu plans will give you confidence that you have thought of everything you need.

We mostly rely on the information recorded in our Provisioning Binder now and load the boat with all the supplies we need to take us through to our next provisioning stop. Initially, however, I made a detailed menu plan for a two week cruise - a manageable time period - and then doubled, tripled or quadrupled it, depending on how long we were going to be away from suppliers. A few adjustments were necessary here and there but it was a very reliable system. We always had enough supplies on board for the time we were planning to be away. Different spices, sauces and vegetable combinations create different meals, so even though we were repeating menus, we weren't eating the same thing every two weeks.

*Flexibility is the key to cruising success!*

People are often leery of menu plans because they hate the idea of regimentation. So do we. Just because we plan spaghetti on Tuesday and grilled steaks on Wednesday on our menu plan, doesn't mean we have to do it! The menu plan just gets us started so we have something to work with. Flexibility is important for successful cruising so you can meet the demands of weather, seasickness, unexpected guests, your mood that day, or whatever.

I don't know about you, but I find deciding what to make for dinner every night can be a drag. If I spend a little time making up menu plans, then the decisions are made. I can relax as we travel since I know I have everything on board I need and I actually *try* some of those new recipes I've torn out of magazines! Detailed menu plans are also useful when you want to streamline your supplies for weekend cruises or to increase performance by keeping cargo weight down.

Table 22 - EXAMPLE OF MENU PLAN

| MEAL | Ingredients |
|---|---|
| Breakfast<br>**Toasted bagel with<br>   peanut butter**<br>**Banana**<br>**Orange juice**<br>**Café au lait** | -2 bagels<br>-peanut butter<br>-2 bananas<br>-2 orange juice in juice boxes<br>-ground coffee, coffee filter<br>-milk and sugar |
| Morning Snack<br>**Granola bar**<br>**Tea** | -2 granola bars<br>-tea bags, milk and sugar |
| Lunch<br>**Tuna sandwiches**<br>**Carrot sticks**<br>**Fruit punch** | -12 slices of bread (6 sandwiches)<br>-butter, mayo<br>-seasoned salt<br>-2 tins of tuna<br>-1 stick of celery, chopped<br>-lettuce<br>-2 carrots, cut into sticks<br>-4 juice boxes, fruit punch |
| Afternoon Snack<br>**Cheese popcorn**<br>**Beer, Iced Tea** | -popcorn and oil, parmesan cheese<br>-beer, iced tea mix |
| Dinner<br>**Stir-fried chicken**<br>**Green salad**<br>**White wine**<br>**Peppermint tea** | -2 chicken breasts<br>-garlic, onions, carrots, celery, ginger, rice<br>-Soya sauce, cooking oil<br>-lettuce, cucumber, salad dressing<br>-white wine, peppermint tea |
| Evening Snack<br>**Hot chocolate** | -hot chocolate mix, milk |

Notes:   - Kevin and Cristina arrive in Nassau at 1000 for 3 days.
        - Lunch under sail.
        - Have 2-3 extra drinks per person for thirst during day.

Table 23- Canada's Food Guide

| | |
|---|---|
| **Grain Products**<br><br>**5-12**<br><br>servings per day | 1 slice bread<br>30 g of cold cereal<br>175 ml (¾ cup) of hot cereal<br>125 ml (½ cup) rice or pasta<br>½ bagel, bun or pita |
| **Vegetables / Fruits**<br><br>**5-10**<br><br>servings per day | 1 medium size vegetable or fruit<br>125 ml (½ cup) fresh, frozen or canned<br>   vegetables or fruit<br>250 ml (1 cup) of salad<br>250 ml (½ cup) of juice |
| **Milk Products**<br><br>Children 4-9yr:  2-3 servings<br>Youth 10-16yr:  3-4 servings<br>Adults:          2-4 servings<br>Pregnant & Breast-feeding<br>Women:          3-4 servings | 250 ml (1 cup) of milk<br>50 g (3" x 1" x 1") cheese<br>50 g (2 slices) cheese slices<br>175 g (¾ cup) yogurt |
| **Meat & Alternatives**<br><br>**2-3**<br><br>servings per day | 50-100 g of meat, fish or poultry<br>50-100 g canned fish<br>1-2 eggs<br>125-250 ml (½ to 1 cup) beans<br>100 g tofu<br>30 ml (2 tbsp.) peanut butter |

## Different People Need Different Amounts of Food

The amount of food you need every day from the 4 food groups and other foods depends on your age, body size, activity level, whether you are male or female and if you are pregnant or breast-feeding. That's why the food guide gives a lower and higher number of servings for each food group. For example, young children can choose the lower number of servings, while male teenagers can go for the higher number. Most other people can choose servings somewhere in between.

Taste and enjoyment can also come from other foods and beverages that are not part of the 4 food groups. Some of these are higher in fat or calories, so use these foods in moderation.

We have provided a blank menu plan so you can design meals that *you* enjoy. (See next page.) This form is also available on computer disk so you can easily create and store your personalized menu plans on your computer. See Appendix.

Happy planning!

### Steps for Creating Menu Plans

1.   Identify the characteristics of your crew and cruise that will determine your provisioning needs by using the 10 Parameters of Provisioning and Worksheet 3 (page 157) as a guide.

2.   Create a chart or use the blank one provided in Worksheet 4 (page 166) to outline meals and snacks required for your cruise. List all the ingredients needed so shopping is easy.

3.   Check Canada's Food Guide (on page 164) to see that you have chosen food from all food groups and adjust menus accordingly.

4.   Get ready for hassle-free shopping!

# Menu Plan

Photocopy for your own use. Also on disk. See Appendix.

Worksheet 4 - Menu Plan

| MEAL | Ingredients |
|---|---|
| Breakfast: | |
| Morning Snack | |
| Lunch | |
| Afternoon snack | |
| Dinner | |
| Evening Snack | |

Notes:

# Hassle-free Shopping

We don't particularly enjoy shopping so we prefer to do a major provisioning three or four times per year. Then we can shop less frequently and spend more time sailing, diving and sightseeing! The focus of our cruising life is having the freedom to travel to remote places. Because of this, we are not bothered by the slower speed we get with a fully loaded boat except when passage-making. If your pleasure is performance cruising, you'll probably opt for shopping more often and keeping the boat light for maximum speed.

When our stores are running low (we always keep a minimum of one month's worth of supplies on board when cruising full-time), we plan a stop in a major port where the selection and prices are good. Then we load the boat with basic supplies such as flour, rice, canned and packaged foods, beverages, medicines, cleaning products, etc. Later, as we cruise along, we only have to shop occasionally for fresh meats and produce. Usually we can do this by walking to a local market which we consider a pleasant outing rather than a chore.

### A Well Organized Shopping List

The first step towards hassle-free shopping is to create a good shopping list from the information in your menu plans and from notes in your provisioning binder. The importance of this is often overlooked. The way we see it, a well organized shopping list serves three purposes:

1.  **It ensures that you don't forget necessary supplies when you go shopping.** If you are going to be at sea for a while you cannot afford to overlook essential items. If you are doing a major provisioning en route, you will probably have to hire a taxi or rent a car to get supplies back to the boat. Frequent trips to the grocery stores and chandleries get expensive. A thorough list can save you time and money by reducing the running around you do.

2.  **It provides a clear view on the big picture as you work your way through the task of provisioning.** As you wade through a cabin filled with grocery bags and start wrestling packages, jars, and boxes into lockers, it's easy to lose track of what you have and haven't got. Keeping a good list and crossing items off as you purchase them, gives you perspective on what you've achieved and what's still left to do. Crossing stuff off lists is tremendously

satisfying too, especially when you're working on a big job like provisioning for a long-term cruise.

3.    **It becomes the foundation of your inventory list.** If you keep a well organized shopping list, it is easy to turn it into an inventory list since it is a record of what you have just brought on board. The only missing information is the location where you will stow items on the boat. This is easy to record as you put stores away in lockers. (See section on Maintaining Inventory, page 207)

When we're doing a major provisioning we spend a lot of time preparing our shopping list. First we do an inventory of the supplies we have on board to make sure we don't put things on our list that we already have. Then, we go through our Provisioning Binder and menu plans to determine the amounts we need for the length of time until we next provision.

We divide our shopping list into about 5 or 6 separate pages and list items under categories that roughly fit the way products are organized in the stores.

We save our lists in our Provisioning Binder for future reference and over the years have developed a standard list that reflects our tastes and style of cruising.

We also make a point of trading lists with fellow cruisers. We have got lots of new ideas by seeing how other sailors provision and vice versa. You never stop learning!

Once again, getting everything down on paper will save you time, money and effort. It will reduce the chaos and anxiety that the chore of provisioning can create so when you sail off into the sunset you will enjoy a feeling of confidence, security and freedom.

### A Basic Shopping List

The following is a checklist of basic food items and non-edible supplies to consider for your shopping list. At the end of this section in the chapter titled Provisioning Lists starting on page 175, we have included detailed annotated lists which show specific items we keep on *Two-Step* and how we use them.

Figure 6 - Shopping List for Non-edible Supplies.

| | |
|---|---|
| Abrasive cleanser (Comet™) | Lighter refill (butane) |
| Air freshener | Matches (waterproofed) |
| All-purpose spray cleaner (Fantastik™) | Mouse and roach traps |
| | Napkins |
| Aluminum foil | Oven cleaner |
| Ammonia | Paper plates and cups |
| Bleach | Paper towels |
| Brass cleaner | Plastic bags (storage bags, |
| Broom | resealable Ziploc™ bags, |
| Candles (birthday, dinner, | garbage bags) |
| emergency) | Plastic wrap |
| Clothes pins | Pot scrubbers |
| Dish detergent | Soap (bars or liquid) |
| Facial tissues | Sponges |
| Fabric softener | Toothpicks |
| Head chemical | Toilet paper |
| Laundry detergent | Wax paper |
| Lighter (for stove) | Whisk and dust pan |

Figure 7 - Shopping List for Basic Food Items

Baking powder and soda*
Bean sprouts seeds*
Beverages (juices, pop, alcohol)
Biscuit mix*
Bread crumbs*
Bouillon cubes
Butter or margarine
Cake mixes*
Cereals
Cheeses
Cocoa, chocolate chips and baking chocolate*
Coconut*
Coffee and tea
Cornstarch*
Crackers
Eggs (fresh, powdered)
Fish (fresh, canned, frozen)
Flour
Fruits (fresh, dried, canned)
Herbs and spices
Honey and molasses*
Jams and Jellies
Ketchup
Lemon juice (reconstituted)
Mayonnaise
Meat (fresh, canned, frozen, dried)
Milk and cream (fresh, canned, long-life UHT, powdered)
Mustard
Nuts
Oatmeal (regular and instant)
Oil (cooking, salad)
Olives, cocktail onions
Pancake mix
Pasta (macaroni, spaghetti, noodle mixes, etc.)
Peanut butter
Pickles
Relish
Rice (regular and mixes)
Salad dressing
Salt and Pepper
Sauces (canned, dry mixes)
Shortening*
Snack foods (popcorn, potato chips, pretzels, etc.)
Soups (canned, dry mixes)
Soya sauce
Sugar
Syrup
Vegetables (fresh, canned, dried)
Vinegar
Yeast (canned or packages)*
Yogurt culture*

\*    We only keep these items on board for long-term cruising. For weekend cruising or trips of 1-2 weeks, we rely on complete mixes or don't bother baking.

### Getting to the Stores

Armed with your list, the next step is finding a convenient way to get to the stores. If you are provisioning in your home port, you probably have access to a car, which makes shopping a whole lot easier. You also have the advantage of knowing where the stores are, who has the best selection, and where you can get the best prices.

Transportation is always a bit of a problem when you are provisioning en route so it pays to ask local sailors or those who cruise the area frequently, where the best place to stop and shop is. You are looking for a town where there is a variety of stores and marine suppliers easily accessible to the boat. Cruising guides often provide this kind of information as well.

As a general rule, we find the most convenient way to do a major provisioning is to go into a large port and stay at a marina that offers a courtesy car or shuttle service for shopping. (This service is rarely found outside North America.) The second best option is to go to a marina and rent a car which gives you more freedom but is usually more expensive. Often, you can arrange to share a rental car with other cruisers which saves you some money and is fun to do. If there is a grocery store within walking distance, it's economical to walk there and take a cab back.

*The job of provisioning is easier when the boat is at a dock.*

Although we love being at anchor whenever possible, we find it's hard on our nerves to provision when we're swinging on the hook. Loading supplies into the dinghy, worrying about them getting wet, unloading them again onto the boat and having no room to move around while we're stowing supplies really gets us down. Since our cruising motto is, "Keep it fun for everyone!", we budget for marina stops at provisioning time. Cleaning and preparing the boat is easier with water hook-up and hose. Rolling a cart load of supplies right down to the boat and having a dock to hold supplies until we're ready to transfer them below decks, makes the job of packing a lot nicer.

However, it is not always possible, convenient or affordable to stay at a marina. We then try to find an anchorage near a town with a dinghy dock that has grocery and hardware stores within walking distance. We take our back packs, canvas tote bags and the folding shopping cart we carry on board, and head for town. It's a good idea to recycle plastic grocery bags and carry them along. In several cities, we were astonished to find that they only had paper grocery bags which are impossible to carry if you have more than two bags of groceries per person.

When grocery stores are not within easy walking distance, we ask the locals where the best stores are and if the stores provide transportation for sailors provisioning their boats. This is a common practice in port towns where merchants are anxious for business and want to provide good customer service to the cruising community. So ask around first before you hire a taxi.

Some small towns are quite innovative about this. In Cobourg, on Lake Ontario, the Chamber of Commerce provides free bicycles with carriers so visiting boaters can get to town and shop, and the Cobourg IGA provides free folding shopping carts so you can load up with groceries and get them back to the boat easily. The North Carolina Maritime Museum in Beaufort, , has a courtesy car that sailors can sign out for 2 hours to do shopping. All they ask is that you fill it with gas. The River Forest Marina in Belhaven, South Carolina, provides courtesy golf carts for transportation to town. Charge 'em up and away you go!

## Shopping

If you're planning to do a major provisioning all in one go, talk to the store manager about volume discounts. We have received 5-10% discounts if we purchase more that $200 worth of groceries at one time. Not all stores will do this, but it doesn't hurt to ask.

As I mentioned in an earlier section, we divide our master shopping list into about five or six pages. If we don't have a lot of time, we each take a separate grocery cart, split up the pages of our list and head for different ends of the store. We race to see who can finish shopping first, crossing items off as we go and don't stop until the carts are filled.

Once, we were rushing to provision at the Publix in Fort Lauderdale. We had a weather window to catch for a comfortable sail across the Gulf Stream to the Bahamas where we were going to spend the winter. Paul was madly clearing a shelf of canned soups and loading them into an enormous shopping cart. As he did, a wide-eyed little boy watched in amazement.

*"Mommy, why is that man buying all that soup?"*

*"Oh, he probably owns a restaurant."*

Whenever Paul opened a can of soup after that, he would make a joke about his restaurant's *soupe du jour* .

But, ideally, it is better to shop a little bit at a time so the job is not so overwhelming. You may not get volume discounts by shopping this way, but you'll have the time to shop around and will probably save more money in the end. Also, since you won't be in such a panic, you'll be less likely to waste your money on items you buy on impulse. Stowing supplies is much more pleasant as well when you are going to be in port for awhile and can do a little bit of shopping everyday.

When we're in a rush, and try to do all our provisioning in one go, our boat looks like one of those photos in a magazine article on provisioning - boxes, bags, crates of produce and supplies everywhere. This is supposedly the dream picture of heading off on a great voyage. But really, it's not much fun.

When the boat is loaded with all that stuff, we can't get at the lockers to stow our supplies because there are so many things piled on top of them! Every time we try to put something away, we have to move everything else. It's irritating and exhausting so we tend to just stuff things any old where just to get them out of the way. Then things aren't properly stowed, they break, and we can never find anything because we were too tired to do inventory when we put them away - a sure recipe for a cranky crew.

So we recommend provisioning gradually. You stay in a better frame of mind, feel more organized and do a better job. If we have a few days in port, we start with page one of our master shopping list and buy all our canned goods first - a good selection of canned meat, fruit and vegetables to hold us over when fresh supplies are not available. They are the heaviest supplies and the most bulky to store so it's good to get them under control first. Then we go for a walk, go sightseeing or just relax for the rest of the day.

Over the next few days, we work through the other pages of our list, watching what we've spent and making adjustments to fit our budget. The very last thing we purchase is perishables - fresh fruits, vegetables, bread, and meat so they will last as long as possible on the journey.

When we set sail, we are not so tired and feel much more in control because shopping has been hassle-free.

# Provisioning Lists

In this section you will find detailed lists of the provisions we keep on *Two-Step*. We have categorized them for easy reference and have included notes on how we use particular goods. This way, you can determine if they would be useful to you too.

The supplies we carry reflect our personal tastes and cruising style. We present these lists only to give you an idea of the items and procedures involved in provisioning a boat. They are not "required items". We carry a lot of baking supplies because we enjoy cooking; maybe you don't. We have a lot of storage space and like to keep our boat well stocked. Perhaps you would prefer to travel light so would carry less and provision more often. Or maybe you have enough power to run a big freezer, microwave oven and a bread maker which would make your provision list quite different from ours.

We offer these lists as a starting point only, and encourage you to add and subtract from them to suit your own needs. When we started cruising, other sailors did the same for us and it made the job easier. If you have access to a computer, these lists are available on a 3.5 inch disk for use on IBM-PC. Then it's easy to make changes. The lists print out on standard 8 ½ X 11 inch paper so you can insert them into a standard binder and create a inventory manual designed for your boat. (See Appendix for more information.)

## Baking Items

We do a lot more baking when we are cruising than when we are living ashore. There are several reasons for this. We like fresh wholesome foods like multiple grain breads and raisin bran muffins as part of our diet, but they are not always available in the ports we are sailing to. We both enjoy preparing delicious meals and we have more time to experiment and create when we're living on the boat. Also, everyone needs treats once in a while to celebrate a special occasion or satisfy a craving and it's nice to have the ingredients on board to whip up an angel cake or make a tray of cookies.

For cruises of one or two weeks in length, we recommend using complete mixes whenever possible to reduce the number of ingredients you have to pack and take home again. Mixes offer convenience so are also great for passage-making when you want freshness without too much fuss.

For a list of baking utensils and tools, see the section on Cooking At Sea on pg. 207.

Table 24 - Baking Items

| Baking Items | Uses |
|---|---|
| baking powder | - raising agent for pancakes, biscuits |
| baking soda | - raising agent for pancakes, biscuits |
| batter mix | - coating for deep fried seafood. |
| Bisquick™ | - convenient for tea biscuits and pancakes. |
| bouillon cubes:<br>    beef<br>    chicken | - base for soup, add flavour to gravies. |
| bread crumbs: | - (see Grains) |
| butter | - (see Dairy Products) |
| candied fruit | - for fruit cakes, chewy bars. |
| cake mixes | - a variety for special occasions. |
| chocolate:<br>    chips<br>    baking squares<br>    sauce | - cookies, energy bars, dessert topping. |

| Baking Items continued | Uses |
|---|---|
| cocoa powder | - used in cakes and for hot chocolate. |
| cooking wine | - adds flavour and zest to sauces. I save wine that we don't enjoy drinking or that has been uncorked for too long. |
| cooking sherry | - as above. Great in soups, stir-fries and seafood sauces. |
| corn meal | - (see Grains) |
| corn starch | - for thickening sauces & gravies. |
| corn syrup | - making candy and energy bars. |
| cracker meal | - makes crisp coating for fish, etc. |
| cream of tartar | - raising agent used in some recipes. |
| dried fruits | - e.g. raisins (see Fruits and Vegetables) |
| flour | - (see Grains) |
| gelatine | - needed for jellied salads, some dips and glazes. |
| graham crackers and crumbs | - good energy food snack, crumbs make good base for key lime pie and other treats. |
| graham pie shells | - convenient and store easily. Storage: refrigeration is not required but, if stored in a cool place, they won't go stale as quickly. |
| herbs & spices: basil bay leaves Bay Spice BBQ seasoning bouquet garni Cajun seasoning cayenne pepper celery salt chili powder chives cinnamon coriander curry powder cumin dill garlic pepper garlic powder | - herbs and spices add character to foods and are fun to collect as you travel. As you can see, we love to cook with them! For short-term cruises just bring along a couple of your favourites. Storage: Keep in tightly sealed jars or plastic containers. Herbs and spices can lose their "zing" in the humid air and some, like cayenne pepper and paprika, can harbour insects. |

| Baking Items continued | Uses |
|---|---|
| Greek seasoning<br>ginger<br>Italian seasoning<br>mustard powder<br>nutmeg<br>onion powder<br>oregano<br>paprika<br>parsley flakes<br>pepper<br>peppercorns<br>red pepper flakes<br>saffron<br>salt<br>seasoning salt<br>tarragon<br>thyme | |
| icing | - canned, ready-made icing is convenient for occasional cakes and is easy to store. |
| Jell-O mixes | - Jell-O makes a nice healthful dessert that is easy to digest. If we're recovering from seasickness and still feeling a little off, Jell-O seems to fill the gap without too much distress. |
| maraschino cherries | - for cocktails and as a dessert garnish. |
| marshmallows | - to garnish hot chocolate and to roast at beach party bonfires. |
| meat tenderizer | - good meat is not always easy to find. Meat tenderizer makes budget cuts taste better. In the Caribbean, it is common practice to rub meat with the juice of a papaya to tenderize it. The enzyme in the juice breaks down tough connective tissues in the meat and is what is used in commercial meat tenderizers. |
| molasses | - mineral-packed sweetener for breads and other baked goods. |
| muffin cups | - paper liners for muffin pans, are attractive on muffins and cupcakes, make clean-up easier. |
| nuts: | - good snack, adds crunch to canned |

| Baking Items continued | Uses |
|---|---|
| almond slivers<br>pecans<br>sunflower seeds<br>walnuts | vegetables and fresh salads, also a nice topping for casseroles. They keep better if you buy with shells on. |
| pie fillings | - convenient for pie making, fruit crumbles or dessert topping. |
| pie shells | - ready-made, easy to whip up a pie. <u>Storage:</u> usually have to be frozen. |
| pastry mix | - if you don't want to store pie shells but still want convenience for making pies, pasties and other pastry items. |
| pudding mix | - pleasant way to get calcium. |
| shortening:<br>  vegetable | - to grease bread pans, use in baked goods, and occasionally for deep-fried treats like donuts, French fries, onion rings, cracked conch and other breaded seafood. |
| sugar:<br>  brown<br>  confectioners<br>  white | - a basic staple; used for baking, tea and coffee, porridge, etc. |
| vegetable dyes | - for colouring icing and Easter eggs. |
| vegetable oil | (see Soups, Sauces & Condiments) |
| vinegar | (see Soups, Sauces & Condiments) |
| yeast | - for yeast breads and coffee cakes. Use 2 lb. yeast per year if bake bread or coffee cake twice a week. <u>Storage:</u> Best to buy in a resealable can or individual foil packs. The individual packages are convenient and keep longer since the yeast is not exposed to the air until you use it. However, they create more garbage and the packages are not bio-degradable because they have a plastic coating. Packages or cans of yeast are good for 2 years if stored unopened. |

# Beverages

It is important to get plenty of fluids throughout the day when you are living on your boat. Fluid loss through perspiration increases when you are out in the fresh air and getting lots of physical activity.

Sometimes the symptoms of dehydration are subtle, especially if the weather is cool and you don't *feel* sweaty or thirsty, but you will notice the effects in your mood and energy level. If I'm feeling tired and irritable for no apparent reason, I know that I am probably dehydrated. A big glass of water can instantly re-energize me and I'm my normal self again. For more information about water (minimum rations, purification, storing and conserving) see page 231.

Of course, in hot weather the danger of dehydration is even greater, so be sure to have lots of beverages on board. Water is best, followed by fruit and vegetable juices since they hydrate the body well. Soups are a good choice anytime but are especially revitalising for cold weather sailing. Tea, coffee, and alcohol are diuretics which stimulate the kidneys to *pass* water instead of restoring it. Sailors are susceptible to kidney stones because they are often dehydrated, a result of trying to conserve drinking water and general fluid loss from physical activity. See the Medical Section for the Golden Rule for preventing dehydration.

Table 25 - Beverages

| Beverages | |
|---|---|
| alcoholic beverages<br>  beer<br>  liquor<br>  wine | For entertaining or with a meal, it is nice to have these aboard, so stow the ones you enjoy and use in moderation. Boxed wine stows and keeps well. |
| coffee:<br>  regular, ground<br>  decaf., ground<br>  regular, instant<br>  decaf., instant | |
| Horlicks™ | Malt drink mix similar to Ovaltine™ which is high in calcium. Soothing at bedtime. |
| hot chocolate mix | Envelopes good for passages, don't get hard in damp air. |
| fruit drinks:<br>  canned/bottled<br>  concentrates:<br>    bottled<br>    frozen<br>    powdered mixes | |
| iced tea mix | powdered mix or canned |
| milk | see Dairy section. |
| soft drinks | |
| tea:<br>  regular<br>  decaf<br>  herbal | |
| water | see section on Water, page 231 |

# Dairy

Canada's Food Guide recommends 2 - 4 servings of milk products per day for adults, 3 - 4 servings for pregnant and breast-feeding women, 3 - 4 servings for youth age 10 to 16, and 2 - 3 servings for children age 4 to 6. (See Canada's Food Guide, page 164)

### Milk

Fresh milk is often difficult to find in remote areas and difficult to store for long periods. We find that long-life (UHT) milk in 1 litre tetra-bricks is a great alternative. The boxes pack neatly in lockers and the milk lasts for at least 8 months without refrigeration. Once it is opened, it is best to refrigerate it, but before we had refrigeration on *Two-Step*, we found it would last for 36 hours in the tropics sitting on the countertop. You can tell when it has gone off by its sour smell, just like fresh milk. Long-life (UHT) milk has a slightly "baked" taste that we don't mind since we just use it to make yogurt and sauces, in baking, and in tea and coffee. When chilled, it tastes okay on cereal.

We also keep small cans of evaporated milk on board for use in tea and coffee. As a replacement for whole milk, mix equal parts of evaporated milk and water.

On occasions, we have been able to buy long-life (UHT) coffee cream which is a treat when you've been in the wilderness for a while. Thick Danish cream is available in cans and is a nice addition to a dessert if you are feeling sinful. If you stir in a teaspoonful of lemon juice into this thick cream and mix it up, it makes a wonderful substitute for sour cream.

We also keep a supply of non-fat dry milk powder on board which we buy in individual envelopes. It keeps better in the envelopes because we only use it occasionally. If we had to open a large box, it would absorb moisture from the air and go stale before we could use it up. We mix non-fat dry milk into bread dough and baking items for extra calcium and to make low fat yogurt if we're in an area where we can't purchase yogurt. (See recipe on page 185). We also store several envelopes in our abandon ship bag. In most island nations in the Caribbean, you can buy full cream powdered milk which has a much better flavour. If you mix it and leave it in the fridge overnight, it tastes better the next day.

### Cheese

Hard cheeses keep well without refrigeration if wrapped in cheese cloth which has been soaked in cider vinegar and wrung out so it is damp but not dripping. It can then be sealed in Ziploc™ bags and stored in a cool place for a couple of months. The vinegar prevents mold from forming.

To store it for longer periods, I prepare the cheese as above, but instead of putting it in plastic bags, I dip each wrapped piece of cheese into melted paraffin wax. This seals in the vinegar and cheese cloth. Before dipping these tidy packages in the melted wax, I tie some string around each bundle to keep the cheese cloth in place and to give me something to hold on to when I lower each bundle into the melted wax. I dip each piece of cheese about four times to seal it with several thin layers of wax. When the wax has cooled and hardened, I put the sealed pieces of cheese into a large jar or Ziploc™ bag and store them in a cool locker where they won't be crushed. After several months, mold may start to form but it can be cut off and the cheese still used. Cheeses that are already waxed, such as gouda, are great!

If you can buy cheese in vacuum packed packages at the supermarket, you don't have to go through the above procedure since the vacuum seal protects the cheese from molds. We also found canned brie and camembert cheeses that keep for months without refrigeration although it was recommended on the package. Of course, whenever we can, we buy fresh cheese from local markets.

### Eggs

We have kept eggs purchased in North American grocery stores for 2 months without refrigeration. Farm-fresh eggs that have never been refrigerated will keep even longer. Eggs go bad when their shells dry out and become thin which allows air to get at the yolk. There are several ways to prevent this: coat the shells with petroleum jelly or vegetable shortening, or simply turn the eggs every day which coats the shells from the inside and keeps the yolk suspended in the middle of the shell.

We find the latter method the easiest. We buy several cartons of eggs and just turn the cartons over every day or every other day. In the out islands of the Caribbean and Bahamas, eggs bought from the grocery stores were sometimes so super chilled they were almost frozen. They went off in a couple of days, even when stored in our fridge! Fresh eggs have a firm rounded white. The older they get, the "runnier" the white becomes and are then better used for baking only. When eggs go bad, you know it immediately - they are a dark sloppy mess when you break them open and they stink! Powdered eggs are a nice option for use in baking since the packages store compactly and require no maintenance. Camping stores are a good source for these and other dried foods.

We plan one egg per person per day when provisioning. This accounts for eggs used in baking as well.

### *Butter*

We prefer butter over margarine and, when possible, buy canned butter which keeps for 3 to 4 months when stored in a cool locker, preferably against the hull. Margarine in plastic tubs keeps the same length of time, stored in the same way. When canned butter is not available, I preserve fresh butter myself.

Start by sterilizing enough glass jars, following the hint below. When the jars are cool, I pack them with cubes of butter and then fill the jars with a cooled brine solution (dissolve 5 tablespoons of coarse salt in a litre of boiling water and let cool), then screw the lids on tight. I put each jar in a clean sock to protect it from breaking and store them all in a cool locker.

When we're ready to use the butter, we dump the brine solution and give the butter a fresh water rinse. It's delicious!

Whenever we can buy fresh dairy products, we do, and use the alternatives mentioned above when fresh ones are not available.

Tip 4 - Sterilizing Jars for Preserving

| **Sterilizing Jars for Canning and Preserving** |
| --- |
| I sterilize glass canning jars by dipping them into boiling fresh water for about 5 minutes. I put a trivet (a rack used for cooling cookies will do) on the bottom of our big seafood pot so the jars don't make direct contact with the heat -- they could crack, otherwise. I remove the jars from the pot with sterilized tongs and let them cool under a clean dish towel or paper towels. To sterilize the lids, I just dip them into boiling water for several seconds so the rubber seals don't melt, and let them cool on a clean dish towel or paper towel. |

Table 26 - Dairy

| Dairy | |
|---|---|
| butter:<br>  canned<br>  fresh | |
| cheese:<br>  cheddar<br>  mozzarella<br>  canned brie<br>  camembert<br>  cheese food | |
| cream cheese | |
| cream:<br>  fresh<br>  long-life<br>  canned | |
| eggs:<br>  fresh<br>  powdered | |
| milk:<br>  evaporated<br>  fresh<br>  long-life (UHT)<br>  powdered<br>  sweet-condensed | - we plan 3-4 litres per week. |
| sour cream | |
| whip cream:<br>  fresh<br>  spray canned | |
| yogurt | - snacks, dips and sauces. If we're in a country where we can't buy it, I've learned an easy way to make it. Recipe follows. |
| yogurt culture | - only carry it if we can't buy yogurt. |

# How to Make Yogurt

Yogurt is a versatile food to have on board. It's filling and nutritious and goes down well if you're feeling a little queasy. It's a quick breakfast topped with fruit and granola, a soothing mid-day snack, a tangy base for vegetable dips and a healthful substitute for mayonnaise in sandwich fillings and salad dressings.

Since we use it so much and it's not always available, I've learned this simple method to make it myself. To make yogurt on a boat, it is best to be in a calm anchorage or at a dock which is well protected from wakes since sudden motion affects it adversely. Having said that, I have successfully made yogurt on offshore passages. On our 20 day passage from the Canary Islands to Brazil, I made at least a dozen batches with powdered skim milk when *Two-Step*'s motion was steady and gentle.

Yogurt likes a steady temperature too, about 110 degrees, which is why I make it in a wide mouth thermos. Some cruisers are successful at making yogurt in a heavy pot that they wrap in a towel and put out in the sun. I've never tried it, because the thermos is so reliable at maintaining a constant temperature.

I prefer to use non-fat dry milk for making yogurt. Fresh milk contains an enzyme which requires it be scalded at 180°F and then cooled to 110°F before making yogurt. Dry milk doesn't have the enzyme so you can skip this step and avoid the mess of burnt milk!

Using non-fat dry milk, I simply fill our wide mouth thermos, one third to one half full, with the milk powder. Meanwhile, I heat some water in a pot on the stove until it reaches 110°F (I initially measured the temperature with a candy thermometer but now can tell by feel - very hot to the skin but not scalding.) Then pour it over the milk powder until it almost reaches the top - about 1/2 inch below the fill line on the thermos. If the milk is too hot it will kill the living organisms that activate the yogurt; if it is too cold, less than 105°F, they won't do the necessary work either.

I then add a tablespoon of fresh yogurt from my last batch as a starter, or powdered yogurt culture which I buy in little foil packages from the health food store (follow package directions on package for amount). It is important not to add too much starter. If the bacilli are crowded, the yogurt will be watery and sour.

I gently stir the mixture, screw on the thermos lid, and let it sit undisturbed for 7 or 8 hours. I usually make it in the evening and leave it sitting behind the stove overnight so it's ready in the morning.

The yogurt will keep for a week in the fridge. When we didn't have refrigeration, we would use it all in one day and make a new batch at night. If we didn't feel like having yogurt for a few days, we would use powdered yogurt culture to start the next batch when we felt like it again. I stock up on lots of yogurt culture because sometimes fresh yogurt collects other organisms from the air which create unpleasant tastes or odours in the next batch if used as a starter. Making yogurt on board adds variety to cruising cuisine and increases your sense of self-sufficiency afloat. Who needs a dairy!

# Fruits and Vegetables

Canada's Food Guide recommends 5 - 10 servings of vegetables and fruits per day. (See page 164)

When Paul and I were researching storage techniques for our first major cruise, we were surprised at how many fresh fruits and vegetables you could store long-term without refrigeration. Our grandmothers, who grew up without refrigeration, laughed at our astonishment. How quickly new generations lose knowledge!

At that time we had a large well-insulated ice box but, since we were planning long passages and cruises to remote areas, we thought we would have to rely on canned foods when the stuff in the ice box ran out. What a delight to learn that we could be away from civilization for a month or more and still be eating fresh produce. Canned meats take on flavour and texture when you add them to a stir-fry full of tender-crisp vegetables or a stew laden with fresh carrots, potatoes, onions and peppers. Apples are still crunchy and flavourful after weeks at sea. We now have a refrigerator and freezer but still store most of our produce supply in the old way to leave more space in the fridge for fresh meats, drinks and delicate vegetables like lettuce.

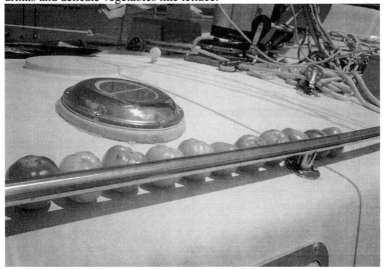

Careful preparation before setting sail and judicious monitoring of the produce while travelling is the secret to maintaining your supply. When shopping buy firm, unbruised, nearly ripe vegetables and fruits. Try to buy them the day you set sail if you can. That way they will last as long as possible.

Before bringing the produce on board, check over thoroughly for insects. Cockroaches hide easily in leafy vegetables such as lettuce and cabbage, or fruits such as bananas. Get rid of any cardboard boxes or paper grocery bags which can harbour insect eggs before climbing aboard as well.

The general rule for storing produce is to give it lots of ventilation, keep it as cool as possible, keep it dry, keep it from bouncing around, and keep it out of the light. On *Two-Step,* we store our produce in open weave plastic baskets in the quarter berth near our companionway stairs. It's cool, dark, well ventilated and accessible to the galley. Wicker baskets can harbour insects. The plastic ones are easy to clean and are durable. Some sailors store their produce in net hammocks but they have never worked for us. There doesn't seem to be a space for them to swing freely on *Two-Step* and if something goes bad, it drips on to the bunk below. The food is well ventilated but generally gets too much light in the places we can hang them so goes off faster.

We bleach wash most of our fruits and vegetables (see instructions below) if we're going to be storing them for long periods to kill molds on the skin. Then we let them dry in the sun. Exceptions to this are root vegetables such as potatoes and carrots which store better with a little earth clinging to them. We don't bleach wash lettuce or cabbage either to keep them as dry as possible. Then we stack them into our plastic baskets with the hard fruits like green apples on the bottom and the more fragile ones like plums on top to prevent bruising. I have read so often not to store onions and garlic with potatoes because the gas given off from onions or garlic makes the potatoes sprout. I store them in separate baskets but they are still all together in the confines of the quarter berth. So far I haven't had any trouble. Bleach washing isn't necessary if you can frequently replenish your produce supply en route.

---

### Tip 5 - Bleach Washing Fruits and Vegetables

Bleach washing fruits and vegetables to be stored for long periods retards the growth of mold on the skins which results in rot.

First check the produce over for insects and shake out any hitch-hikers. Dunk the fruit or vegetables into about 2 litres, (½ gallon) of fresh water to which 25 ml (1 tbsp.) of household chlorine bleach has been added. Rub the skins gently and then dry with a clean cloth or paper towels. Sun drying on the deck is also effective and gives you time to do other things. Just be sure that it's a calm day so your newly washed produce doesn't go rolling over the side! When the fruits and vegetables are thoroughly dry stow them carefully below decks.

It is very important to pick over your fruits and vegetables every day or two to catch any food ripening or going bad. If one lime goes moldy, the mold can quickly spread to the rest of your supply. I am especially careful when the climate is hot. When foods are ready to use, I work them into my menu plans for the day to get best use of our supply.

We do keep a stock of canned fruits and vegetables on board as back up. They also provide an easy way to get our daily fruit and vegetable requirements if it is too rough to be scrubbing potatoes or slicing melon. Canned produce has been picked at its height of freshness and is often more nutritious than the under-ripe fruits and vegetables that have been trucked across the country to the grocery stores. Try to use the liquid in the cans for maximum nutrition. Dried fruits are also convenient and make good snacks.

| Fruits and Vegetables | |
|---|---|
| apples | - green apples last the longest, about two months in hot weather, longer if it's cool. Bleach wash. |
| apricots | - keep only a week or two in hot weather and bruise easily. Bleach wash. Dried ones are good snacks. |
| asparagus | - we buy fresh when it's available and use right away. Canned asparagus tips are a treat once and a while and are useful as a garnish for canapés. |
| avocados | - buy in different stages of ripeness and bleach wash. When they are dry, wrap each one in a paper towel. Place the softer ones on top of the least ripe ones. May keep 3 weeks if the weather is cool. |
| bananas | - buy at various stages of ripeness so they don't go all at once. Check CAREFULLY for insects. Bleach wash. |
| beans:<br>  baked<br>  black beans<br>  garbanzo<br>  green<br>  kidney<br>  refried | - fresh green beans keep 4 to 7 days and we use them as soon as we buy them. Other beans we buy in cans. Dried beans are cheaper, lightweight and store more compactly but take time, water and stove fuel to prepare. |
| bean sprouts | - see Tip 6 on growing bean sprouts (page 194) |
| beets | - canned beets are a colourful addition to salads. |
| broccoli | - doesn't keep more than a couple of days so we buy only in port. |
| capers | - garnish for fish and canapés, use in sauces. |
| carrots | - farm fresh carrots with earth still clinging to them keep longest, about 2 weeks in hot climates if you leave the dirt on them. If you can only buy them in a plastic bag, remove them from the bag and wrap the carrots loosely in a couple of paper towels. Check for black spots every couple of days. If you find any, cut them off and use the carrot that day. |

| Fruits and Vegetables | |
|---|---|
| cabbage | - buy firm cabbages with the outer leaves intact. Check CAREFULLY for insects. Keep them very dry. Remove outer leaves when they dry out or start to rot. Never cut into the cabbage; just peel off the leaves as you need them. Trim the stems if they start to go soft. They are cheap, readily available, and store well. They keep 2-3 weeks in hot climates and 2-3 months if it's cool. Great for coleslaw, stir-fries and stews. When the lettuce runs out, cabbage makes a good base for salads. |
| cauliflower | - only lasts a few days so we only buy in port. |
| celery | - it is often hard to find good quality celery in the islands. We like it as a snack, in salads and stir-fries. We keep it stored in a plastic bag. It only lasts a few days without refrigeration, a week or more in the fridge. |
| chick peas | - also called garbanzo beans |
| coleslaw | - available in cans and tubs when you don't feel like making your own. |
| corn | - canned corn tastes great and stays crisp. Makes a good ingredient in salads too. In most places around the world you can't buy fresh sweet corn which we enjoy, only cow feed. |
| cucumber | - buy dark firm ones, bleach wash and keep out of the light when storing. Turn every few days and check for soft spots. Can last up to two weeks. |
| eggplant | - also called aubergine in some countries. Bleach wash and remove stem if it will pull away on its own. Lasts about a week. |
| fruit cocktail | - easy dessert or snack on watch. |
| garlic | - we love it and use it in something every day - curries, vinaigrettes, gravies, etc. It lasts 4 to 6 months if you buy large bulbs and keep them very dry so they don't go moldy. A braid of garlic stores well. Bulbs with small cloves dry out too quickly. Garlic stands up to a lot of abuse and stacks well. |
| grapes | - usually expensive since difficult to ship. Buy only if firm and unbruised. Bleach wash and |

| Fruits and Vegetables | |
|---|---|
| | hang to dry. |
| grapefruit | - thin-skinned and heavy with juice are the best way to buy them. Bleach wash and stack in baskets. Canned sections are great for salads, desserts or at breakfast. |
| lemons | - buy thick-skinned and slightly green. Bleach wash and wrap in aluminum foil when dry to prevent mold spreading when they start to over-ripen. Will last about a month. |
| lettuce | - stores best in the refrigerator. Take leaf lettuce apart, wash it and wrap in a tea towel and store in a plastic bag. Tightly packed iceberg lettuce with outer leaves intact or romaine lettuce lasts 10 to 14 days without refrigeration if well ventilated (but goes rather limp.) Trim the stalks if they start to darken. |
| limes | - see lemons. Last 4 to 6 weeks and are still good when they go brown and hard. |
| mangoes | - you can pick these when they are hard and under-ripe and they will gradually ripen on board. Bleach wash. They only last a week. |
| melons | - watermelon is only good to store when you know you'll have a crowd to feed. They go bad before the two of us can eat one. Small melons are packed with vitamins and are a refreshing snack or dessert. Bleach wash and store only one layer deep. |
| mixed veg | - buy canned or frozen. |
| mushrooms | - fresh are hard to keep. We keep canned or dried ones to add to sauces and stews. |
| onions | - squeeze onions before buying to make sure they are firm and dry. Remove loose outer skin and stack in a basket. They last for months. |
| oranges | - see grapefruit. Quality ones last 4-6 weeks. |
| papaya | - also known as pawpaw. Lasts about 1 week. |
| peaches | - Bleach wash. Last about 1 week. Canned are delicious and we use them a lot. |
| pears | - ripe pears keep only for a few days so eat right away. Hard pears with ripen slowly and can store for a month. Canned pears make a good |

| Fruits and Vegetables | |
|---|---|
| | snack or dessert. |
| peas | - fresh peas only last a few days. We prefer frozen or dried peas for voyaging. |
| peppers | - come in green, red, yellow, hot and mild varieties. Dried versions are handy. Fresh ones last only a week or two if kept well ventilated. Still good for cooking when they shrivel if there is no rot. |
| pimento | - canned or bottled pimento is a nice garnish. |
| pineapple | - if bought under-ripe they will keep a couple of weeks. They are ready to eat when a leaf pulls out easily. Bleach wash and CHECK CAFEFULLY FOR INSECTS in the leaves. |
| plums | - buy firm but not too under-ripe. Last a few days. |
| potatoes fresh canned flakes | - Nicely rounded potatoes with a little earth clinging to them last about 2 months. New potatoes and irregularly shaped ones don't seem to keep as long. We stack them in a basket and check over them every few days. If sprouts form we cut them off. Canned potatoes are good if the weather is too rough to start peeling or chopping fresh ones. We also keep potato flakes on board for a convenient topping for shepherds pie or to thicken sauces or stews. |
| potato salad | - canned potato salad is convenient on passages. |
| prunes | - good snack and a natural laxative. |
| pumpkin | - we always keep a can on board for pumpkin pie on Thanksgiving. Makes interesting sauce if spiced. |
| squash | - bleach wash. Will keep several months. |
| strawberries | - buy fresh as a treat. Canned are nice as a dessert topping. |
| sweet potatoes | - used a lot in the islands and southern cooking. Available canned. Fresh ones store and last like regular potatoes. |
| tomatoes | - buy green and they will ripen along the way. Bleach wash and store carefully to avoid bruising. When they start to ripen, wrap them in |

| Fruits and Vegetables | |
|---|---|
| | paper towels for greater protection. Last 3 weeks in hot weather, more if it's cool. |
| turnip | - last 3 months in the tropics. We know this because we don't really like them, and avoided eating the one we bought until it went bad. Apparently they're good in soups and stews. |
| zucchini | - also called courgette in some countries. Treat the same as cucumbers. A canned version in tomato sauce is delicious. |

## Tip 6 - Growing Bean Sprouts

We eat a lot of salads but when we've been at sea for a couple of weeks the lettuce goes limp. That's when I rely on bean sprouts. No matter where we are, we can produce fresh greens! Bean sprouts can provide up to one third of your daily requirement of vitamin C and add fibre to your diet.

Sprouting is easy to do. I use 1 litre (1 quart) Mason jars with a piece of window screen or cheese cloth cut to fit under the canning ring. This provides ventilation to the sprouts so they don't rot and acts as a sieve when you rinse the seeds daily with fresh water.

Soak 25 ml (1 tbsp.) of seeds or 60 ml (¼ cup) of beans in 250 ml (1 cup) of fresh water overnight. In the morning, pour off the water and save for making soup or gravy. Rinse the seeds or beans with a little fresh water and turn the jar on its side in a bowl (I use a plastic basin) so it can continue to drain. Rinse the sprouts once or twice a day and you will have salad greens by the third or fourth day depending on the climate. When we sailed to Brazil, the sprouts grew in a day at the equator!

When the sprouts are ready, I leave them in the sun for a few hours until they turn green. This increases the vitamin content. Then I store them in the fridge or we eat them right away.

I keep two jars going and stagger the starting dates so there are always sprouts ready for eating. Sometimes I mix the seeds for variety in flavour and texture.

We sprout alfalfa, chia, radish and mustard seeds as well as dried mung beans, chick peas (also called garbanzo beans) and lentils. There are many others. Check at the health food store where you purchase the seeds. The seeds store for a year, sometimes more, if kept dry.

Use the sprouts in salads, stir-fries and in sandwiches.

# Grains

Breads, cereals and pasta are all high in fibre which aids digestion and helps eliminate wastes from the body. They are an excellent source of carbohydrates which supply much needed energy for active cruisers. Canada's Food Guide recommends 5 - 12 servings per day of grain products. (See page 164)

Grain products must be purchased carefully since they tend to harbour insects and should be sealed tightly in cannisters when stowed on board. I throw 4-5 bay leaves into the cannisters as well which, for some reason, is an effective means of protecting grains from vermin. In four years of cruising to Europe, South America, the Caribbean and Bahamas, we have never had weevils.

It is best to purchase flour, oats, bran and noodles in sealed packages rather than from bulk bins, if possible. I buy 2 or 5 lb. bags of flour so I don't have large amounts open at one time. I double-wrap unopened bags in clean grocery bags in which I have placed 4-5 bay leaves and then seal them closed with masking tape and label them. I have stored all-purpose flour for a year this way but prefer to buy it more often than that. Other flours such as whole wheat and rye spoil more quickly, so for long-term storage it's best to refrigerate or freeze them.

Table 27 - Breads, Cereals and Pastas.

| Grains | |
|---|---|
| bran | - use in bran muffins. |
| bread | - we buy fresh bread when it's available, otherwise we bake it ourselves. (See recipe on page 198) The day we're leaving on a passage, we buy bread with preservatives in it so it will last 1-2 wks. |
| bread crumbs: plain seasoned | - toppings for casseroles, coatings for fish and seafood. Purchase in resealable cardboard cannisters when available or double-bag them and seal tightly. |
| breakfast cereal: Cheerios™ shredded wheat granola sm. variety packs | - variety packs are good for passages -- no dishes! |
| corn meal | - coating for seafood, for making cornbread |

| Grains | |
|---|---|
| | and cornmeal muffins, for coating bread pans or pressure cooker when baking bread. |
| couscous | |
| crackers | |
| flour | - mostly for baking bread but for other baked goods like cakes and cookies. A 5 lb. bag makes 6 to 8 loaves of bread. See bread recipe on page 198. |
| noodle mixes:<br>  alfredo carbonara<br>  butter and herb<br>  chives<br>  parmesan<br>  stroganoff | - they store well and add variety to meals. Top with chopped cooked meat or vegetables for dinner. |
| oats:<br>  instant<br>  rolled | - for making porridge and oatmeal cookies. |
| pasta:<br>  egg noodles<br>  fettuccini<br>  macaroni<br>  rotini<br>  spaghetti | |
| Red River cereal | |
| rice:<br>  brown<br>  long grain<br>  wild<br>  mixes | |
| tabouli mix | |
| taco shells | |
| tortillas | |
| pita bread | |

Figure 8 - Sheryl Shard's On Board Bread Recipe

# Sheryl Shard's On Board Bread

2 cups very warm water (90° -100°F) or 2/3 cup seawater + 1/3
    cup fresh
2 Tbsp. (2 packets) active dry yeast
1/8 cup honey
2 tsp. salt (if you don't use seawater)
5 cups all-purpose or bread flour
1-2 cups additional flour

In a large bowl, mix the first 3 ingredients, stirring gently until yeast is dissolved. Let stand 5 minutes. Add salt and 5 cups of flour and mix well. Add 1-2 cups more flour until no longer sticky. If the air is humid you may need to add even more flour.

Knead on a floured surface until smooth and elastic, about 10 minutes. Place in a lightly greased bowl and cover with a damp tea towel. Let rise in a warm draft-free place until double in size, about 40 to 60 minutes.

Punch down the dough and knead for 2 minutes. Divide into 2 loaves and let rise in lightly greased and floured bread pans for another 40 to 60 minutes. Preheat oven to 350°F.

Bake until golden brown, about 25 to 30 minutes. Jab each loaf with a toothpick; if it comes out clean the bread is done. Remove loaves from pans. Let cool 15 minutes before cutting.

# Meat, Fish and Poultry

We eat less meat when we are cruising than when we are living ashore. Good quality fresh meat is hard to find in some places or is so expensive we just treat ourselves once in a while. Chicken seems to be cheap and affordable in the Caribbean and is available frozen so we learned a lot of recipes for chicken!

Canada's Food Guide recommends 2-3 servings of meat and alternatives such as beans, tofu or peanut butter per day. (see page 164)

Table 28 - Meat, Fish and Poultry.

| Meat, Fish and Poultry | |
|---|---|
| anchovy paste | - adds flavour to Caesar salads. |
| bacon<br>  canned<br>  packaged<br>  bacon bits | - we first found Celebrity canned bacon in 1990. Inside was a pound of sliced bacon wrapped in wax paper. We ate the last can 2 years later ... still fine! For our 1997 cruise I ordered it from Black Fly Provisioners in Annapolis MD  **www.blkfly.com** or 800-631-3338 |
| beef<br>  canned chunks<br>  canned chili<br>  canned curry<br>  canned slices<br>  canned stew<br>  canned mince<br>  fresh ground<br>  fresh steaks<br>  fresh roast<br>  frozen hamburgers | - we only keep a few meals-in-cans like chili, curries and stews for storms. Otherwise, we prefer to prepare meals from scratch using fresh vegetables to spice up the canned stuff. e.g. Canned stewed steak, canned mushrooms plus fresh onions and green peppers form the basis for a great stroganoff! |
| chicken:<br>  in white sauce<br>  canned chunks<br>  canned whole<br>  fresh<br>  frozen<br>  spread | chicken in sauce is a good ready-to-eat meal if you're in a hurry or in rough weather. Its available canned, in jars and foil pouches. |
| crab meat:<br>  canned | - nice for crab cakes, salads and seafood Newburg. |

| Meat, Fish and Poultry | |
|---|---|
| ham:<br>  canned<br>  flaked<br>  spread | |
| hot dogs:<br>  canned<br>  frozen | |
| meat pies:<br>  canned<br>  frozen | - great for passages |
| oysters:<br>  canned smoked | - use on canapés. |
| paté:<br>  canned<br>  packaged | - use on crackers, canapés or for sandwiches. |
| pork:<br>  fresh chops<br>  frozen chops<br>  fresh roast | |
| salmon:<br>  canned<br>  frozen | |
| sardines:<br>  canned<br>  frozen | - serve with crackers. Barbeque large ones. |
| seafood<br>  fresh | - Look for local seafood on sale in fish markets and from fishermen. We catch conch, lobster and fish ourselves where possible.. |
| shrimp:<br>  canned | - use in salads, dips, or in seafood dishes. |
| tuna:<br>  canned | |

# Soups, Sauces and Condiments

Soups are an easy meal to prepare and we enjoy them even when we are sailing in the tropics. There's nothing like fresh conch chowder when you feel like a simple meal at sunset. Home-made soups are best and we often make chicken soup the day after a roast chicken dinner, adding fresh vegetables and noodles from our stores. Canned chicken or beef stock speeds the process and adds flavour to gravies as well. When underway, nothing beats the convenience of canned or dried soups. We prefer canned soups which taste fresher to us and they do not require so much water as dried, but dried soups stow more compactly and don't add the weight and bulk that canned soups do. Soup warms the body on a cold beat to windward and is quick and hearty fare. We always keep a variety of instant soups that you mix in a cup with hot water for night watches or if it's too rough to cook. Canned cream soups also make easy sauces to dress up a meatloaf or to pour over pasta with a little meat and some steamed vegetables.

Sauces of all kinds give a lift to a meal, adding flavour and colour. Condiments do the same thing so we keep a good selection in the galley cupboard.

Table 29 - Soups, Sauces and Condiments.

| Soups, Sauces and Condiments | |
|---|---|
| Angostura Bitters | - flavours fruit drinks and cocktails. |
| barbecue sauce | - we use our propane barbecue a lot. It keeps the heat out of the boat. Ready-made barbecue sauce adds a zing to meat, fish and poultry. |
| chocolate sauce | - (see Baking Items) |
| chutney<br>    Sher's apple | - curried chicken is one of our favourite cruising dinners served with chopped fruit and a spicy chutney. Chutney is expensive to buy though, so on a rainy day motoring down the Intracoastal Waterway to Savannah, Georgia, I developed a recipe for apple chutney that is easy to make underway and costs a tenth of the price of store bought chutney. (See recipe on page 204) |
| cocktail onions | |

| Soups, Sauces and Condiments | |
|---|---|
| gravy<br>   powdered mixes<br>   canned | home-made is best but these are great in a pinch or to add variety at sea. |
| honey | |
| horseradish | |
| hot sauce | |
| jams and jellies | |
| ketchup | |
| lemon concentrate | |
| lime concentrate | |
| maple syrup | |
| Marmite | |
| mayonnaise | |
| mint sauce | |
| molasses | |
| mustard | |
| oil:<br>   olive oil<br>   vegetable oil | - used mostly for cooking and as bases for salad dressings. |
| olives<br>   green<br>   black<br>   stuffed | - olives dress up a salad or a plate of hors d'oeuvres or make a good snack all on their own. |
| peanut butter | - stock up if you are leaving North America! |
| pickles | - good with sandwiches or when you need to crunch on something. |
| relish | |
| salsa | |
| sauce mixes | e.g. Béarnaise, Hollandaise, peppercorn |
| soup:<br>   instant<br>   mixes<br>   canned | - we keep a variety of soups for convenience |
| spaghetti sauce | |
| steak sauce | |
| tomato paste | |
| tomato sauce | |
| vinegar:<br>   balsamic | - we enjoy lots of fresh salads with vinaigrette dressings so keep lots of |

| Soups, Sauces and Condiments | |
|---|---|
| cider<br>pickling<br>regular<br>wine | different vinegars on board. We also keep a good supply of white vinegar and pickling vinegar for cleaning purposes. It is great for washing down mildewed surfaces, makes a good clothes rinse when added to rinse water and. If you are doing projects with epoxy and happen to get some on your skin, pickling vinegar is safer for removing it than acetone. |

*It's amazing what you can find in cans!*

# Sheryl's Apple Chutney

2 seeded chopped lemons
2 chopped cloves of garlic
1.5 kg (3 ½ lb.) firm apples
1 kg (2 lb.) bag of brown sugar
375 g (12 oz.) of seeded raisins. i.e. half a 750 g bag
500 mL (2 cups) finely chopped or shredded ginger root
15 mL (3 tsp.) salt
2 mL (½ tsp.) cayenne pepper
1 litre (1 quart) cider vinegar
4 chopped red peppers, seeds and membranes removed

Peel, core and chop apples. Peel and chop ginger and lemons. Simmer all ingredients in a large pot until the fruit is tender and the liquid is reduced to the consistency of thick syrup. On the hot flame of our propane stove it takes a couple of hours. If the chutney starts to bubble too vigorously, I turn the burner off for a few minutes, then start again.

When ready, put in hot sterilized jars (see page 184 for instructions on sterilizing jars) and seal them. Put each jar in a clean gym sock to prevent it from breaking and stow in a locker or cupboard.

Makes about 16 half pint or 250 mL jars of chutney. If you want fewer jars, the recipe divides in half easily.

# Snacks

When we started cruising full-time, one thing we under-estimated was the amount of entertaining we would do when travelling. As a voyager flying a foreign flag, you are intriguing to the locals and people seek you out. Often when we pull into a port or anchorage, someone interesting drops by and we end up inviting them for a drink or a meal. Cruising sailors are a sociable bunch and there are always dock parties, pot luck suppers and happy hours to participate in. Preparing hors d'oeuvres is now a part of day to day life on *Two-Step*! Our stores list contains a good supply of mixed nuts, cocktail nibbles like olives and pickled onions, crackers and patés so we can always put something together quickly for a social occasion.

When you are cruising you are doing a lot more physical activity so snacking for your health is important to provide fuel to your body. In hot weather salty snacks can help prevent salt deficiency. This is one time when you don't have to cut back on salt. Snacks keep you going at sea when the weather is rough and you cannot prepare a proper meal. This is also easier on the digestion. (See the section on menu plans for examples of the way we use snack foods.)

Try to plan a variety of nutritious snacks but, face it, we all love junk food once in a while and if you are out at sea craving a chocolate bar, life can be miserable if there isn't one on board. Try to have a few treats stashed away. Its good for morale.

Table 30 - Snacks

| Snacks | |
|---|---|
| chocolate bars | - we buy bags of small ones at Halloween. |
| corn chips | |
| crackers | - (see grains) |
| cookies | |
| dried fruits | - e.g. raisins, apricots. |
| granola bars | - good for snacks and breakfast on the run. |
| mixed nuts | |
| party snacks | - e.g. cheese balls, pretzels |
| popcorn | - great for having on board since cheap and compact. For variety we sprinkle with parmesan cheese or cajun seasoning or curry powder. |
| potato chips | |
| trail mix | |

# Part 5 : Maintaining Inventory

# Organizing the Space Below

> *"All concepts of order, from the simplest system of closet arrangement to the most complex rocket technology, share one essential characteristic: an organizing principle. The idea behind the organizing principle is that any practical system always contains an essential priority around which all other components group themselves. ...If you determine what purpose you want to achieve, practical solutions will flow fairly easily.*

> Stephanie Winston
> ***Getting Organized***

What is your main reason for going cruising? Is it because you want the personal challenge of getting your boat across an ocean? Or is it to explore remote places you can only get to by boat? Or perhaps you love living in the outdoors and enjoy the sense of freedom that comes from travelling with the winds.

Whatever your reason, it's important to organize your boat to fit your own desires and goals. For example, our principle of organization is that we cruise to travel to remote places where we can stay at anchor for long periods of time. Self-sufficiency is our focal point which means we have to have lots of storage space for long-term provisioning yet maintain comfortable living quarters. We don't care that our sailing speed is reduced by all the cargo we're carrying since we enjoy the freedom that it provides.

Our English friend, Keith, who at age 73 completed a two-year circumnavigation in his Nicolson 32, *Happy Girl A*, has a very different principle of organization. He loves passage-making and performance sailing. Keeping weight down is a priority so he does smaller provisionings more often. His storage priority is for his large sail inventory. Personal comfort is not such a concern and we always tease him because he has streamlined life on board so much that he doesn't allow crew members to have pillows. They have to use their one allotted duffel bag for a pillow too! He teases us about all the space we "waste" storing "great bloody cauldrons" (my extensive collection of pots and pans).

Keith loves the sport of sailing. One of his biggest reasons for cruising is the feeling of the boat sailing well. While a two-year circumnavigation wouldn't be enough time for Paul and me to savour out-of-the-way places in the way we enjoy, it was perfect for Keith. Yet, all of us love cruising and have been doing it for a long time. Keith would be unhappy in our heavy-laden vessel with minimal sail inventory and we would be unhappy in his prize-winning pillowless racing-cruiser.

(Note: Last Christmas, 1997, we got a letter from Keith who is now well into his 70's. His happy news was that he had recently gotten married. Congratulations Keith and Betty! *Happy Girl* has been sold but Keith is still active in the sailing community giving excellent slide presentations about his circumnavigation.)

If you are feeling irritated and uncomfortable with the space on your boat, chances are you need to define your cruising goals more clearly and make changes to fulfill them. Sometimes the only solution is to buy a different boat (and don't we all love *that* excuse!) but in most cases simple organizational adjustments can make all the difference.

Where there is a conflict of goals, compromises need to be worked out to ensure pleasant cruising for everyone aboard, especially if one of you wants speed and the other wants comfort. Our British friends, Brian and Dorothy on *Radnor,* are one of the most contented cruising couples we know. These two live to make each other happy. Brian is an avid racing sailor and Dorothy is a keen sailor too, but Dorothy didn't want to give up everything she loved about home life when they decided to sell their house in England and go cruising full-time. She is an excellent cook and enjoys entertaining so they made a compromise by bringing all Dorothy's specialty pots and pans as well as *a full set of china and crystal on board.* Their "deal" is that when they're going to be in port for a while, Dorothy can unpack all the china and glassware and rearrange the cupboards.

"This is our 'port boat,'" she says.

When it's time to move on, she carefully repacks everything in tissue paper and stows each item in special wooden cases that Brian, a talented carpenter, has built for her. Then she reorganizes the boat to be efficient at sea (the 'at sea boat') and off they go! They have cruised the Med and crossed the Atlantic to the Caribbean winning cruising regattas along the way.

(Note: In 1995 *Radnor* was holed by another boat when Hurricane Luis hit St. Martin/Sint Maarten. 800 out of 1000 boats sank in Simpson Bay Lagoon, until now considered one of the better hurricane holes in the Caribbean. *Radnor* sank and Brian and Dorothy lost everything when she went down. Thankfully they were insured and now have a lovely new 34 footer called *Sea Marva.* Their cruising dream continues!)

## *Efficient Organizing*

The start to reorganizing the space below for comfortable living is to store things close to their point of use. At the same time, become aware of what irritates you and take steps to develop a solution. Sometimes this requires non-linear thinking. We have a good inventory of tools which we used to stow carefully in two large heavy tool boxes under the stove. It seemed that every day we needed something from those tool boxes. It always irritated me to have to haul those heavy boxes out, unlatch them, dig through all the tools to find the ones I needed, close them, latch them again, and stuff them back under the stove so they wouldn't slide around while we were under way. After completing the job, I would have to repeat the process to put the tools away again. It was just a physically uncomfortable process when the boat was underway.

Then one day, I was cleaning out the five galley drawers beside the stove. Paul designed them to organize all our cooking utensils so they would be easy to reach when preparing a meal, even if conditions were rough. I realized that, with a bit of reorganization, I could make the bottom drawer a "tool drawer". It now holds the tools we use most often - screwdrivers, Vise grips, Allen keys, hammers and wire cutters. They are in a central location for repairs down below and close to the companionway for jobs on deck. Now, I'm more inclined to do little preventative maintenance tasks right away and don't mind pulling out the tool boxes occasionally when we need more specialized tools. Also, it is safer at sea to just grab a screwdriver from the drawer than haul out a big heavy tool box when the boat is crashing through the waves.

We wouldn't recommend reorganizing the whole boat all at once. Correct a few things here and there, then give your new arrangement a test period. Give priority to the most irritating problems and work down from there.

## *Process of Efficient Organization of Lockers:*

1.   Store items near their point of use.

2.   Analyze your storage spaces and determine their degree of accessibility. Items you use regularly should be stowed in the most accessible cupboards and lockers. To determine the best use for each locker or cupboard, think about what you're most likely to be doing when you're standing near it or where you're going when you walk by it.

3.   Consider the importance of weight distribution. Keep heavy items like canned goods low down and lighter items like pasta in higher cupboards. Similarly store heavy items centrally and keep the ends of the boat light so she can sail well and respond to the seas. Weight in the ends causes most boats to bury their bows in the waves.

## *Before You Provision*

Before loading your boat with provisions is a good time to do a thorough locker clear-out to rid yourself of unnecessary clutter and to make room for the fresh supplies coming on board. It also helps to remind you of the stores you have so you don't purchase things already on the boat. It's surprisingly easy to do this since things do settle to the bottom of lockers and erase themselves from your memory.

Checking lockers regularly means that "disasters" such as exploded soft drink cans or cracked ketchup bottles don't go undetected. It is really depressing to return to the boat exhausted from shopping and find a locker you are about to fill with groceries is in an awful mess.

But most important of all, we think, is that this is a great time to examine how well you are using your storage space and to make changes while the boat is relatively empty. Organizing the boat in a way that is convenient for you and that achieves your goals makes it a nicer place to be. The more efficiently your storage space is used, the more money you'll save, the better your boat will perform, the more comfortable you'll be and the better sense of control you will have in your cruising life. Sometimes it will seem to be the only thing in control!

# The Art of Good Stowage

*...good stowage prevents spoilage, breakage and wastage, all of which cost money and add nothing to the pleasure of cruising. It also makes it easier to run the yacht efficiently, which makes the whole business of voyaging that much more pleasant and civilized and therefore, more enjoyable.*

Annie Hill
***Voyaging On A Small Income***

Once you have cleaned and reorganized the storage space on your boat, you are ready to start loading on new supplies. This is where the art of good stowage gives you further mileage in creating a comfortable living environment.

By stowing supplies well, you protect the investment you have just made in them, you ensure that things survive the journey so they are there when you need them, and you reduce potential irritation caused by rattling cans and broken jars. (For stowage techniques of specific items, see annotations in the Provisioning Lists)

**It pays to keep a tidy ship.**
**Even protected waterways can get a little choppy.**

The art of good stowage often comes up in conversations with fellow cruisers after bouts of bad weather when poorly stowed stores have made their presence known. As a result of these discussions, we came up with eight things you are protecting your supplies from, when storing them on a boat:

1.  **Motion.** Living on a boat is often compared to being in a continuous earthquake or riding on a runaway subway and, you know, it can be like that at times! With your surroundings in a state of motion it is essential that everything is safely tucked away where it cannot be shaken loose and hurled across the cabin. Missiles are dangerous! A knock on the head is not fun. When things go flying they can break, which is a waste and broken jars or dishes can cause severe cuts. If the motion is really violent, cleaning up messes saps precious energy from the crew and adds the risk of falling as they stoop to clear the floor or bin.

2.  **Chafe.** Directly related to the motion of the boat is the damage that can be caused by chafe when goods slide around inside lockers and rub against other supplies or against the hull and bulkheads. Clothing on hangers swings in lockers and wears, plastic bottles rub through and leak, dinghy oars in cockpit lockers saw away at hoses. The best defence is immobilization. Pack clothes tightly in hanging lockers to reduce swing, or whenever possible, fold flat and store on shelves instead. Stuff plastic bags or rags around bottles and jars for chafe protection. We store wine and spirit bottles each in their own athletic tube-style sock! It stops them rattling and has prevented them from breaking (take the sock off before offering liquor to guests). Check that items with sharp edges are not going to rub against items made of softer materials.

3.  **Moisture and mildew.** Moisture can get into the boat in several ways - through condensation, deck leaks, and salt deposits. Condensation happens when warm humid air inside the boat contacts the cooler hull surface. We never have a problem with this because we have an insulative Airex™ core in the layup of our fiberglass hull. But if you do have problems, they can be solved by lining lockers with open plastic weave matting which keeps cans off the wet surface. Some people recommend varnishing cans to protect against rust damage but we store most cans in Ziploc™ bags and have never had a problem. We have enough to varnish without adding in the groceries to the to-do list.

In our first year of cruising, we had a lot of trouble with deck leaks because the builder of our hull had not sealed the hull to deck joint properly. In certain heavy weather conditions, my clothes locker became completely soggy when we sailed on a starboard tack. The source of the leak eluded us for several months and I had to store all my clothes in Ziploc™ resealable plastic bags so they wouldn't get wet and go mildewy. After some trial and error, we eventually found the water was getting in at the bow fitting and flowing through an air pocket in the sealant joining the deck to the hull. We quickly repaired it and haven't had a problem since.

Living in a salt air and saltwater environment promotes dampness. Humidity is high so we built the boat with well ventilated lockers. We also use desiccant bags in some lockers (they absorb water) to protect moisture-sensitive goods like cameras and electronic gear. We got some that can be dried out in the oven and re-used.

Salt gets tracked into the boat on shoes, clothes, bathing suits and hands and holds moisture wherever it falls. Rinsing lockers and shelves with fresh water every four to six months can reduce moisture and mildew from this source. If you do find mildew, wipe it away with a cloth dampened with vinegar to kill it and its odours. Pickling vinegar is best since it is stronger. Many people use bleach but it's so caustic I prefer to stick with vinegar.

4.   **Temperature - heat or cold.** Certain supplies are temperature sensitive such as fresh produce and medicines. This must be taken into consideration when stowing these items. Areas around the stove and engine get hot as well as those that receive direct sunlight. Heat rises so the coolest parts of the boat will be low down. Storage areas below the waterline and against the hull will be affected by the temperature of the water.

5.   **Light.** Goods such as film, fruits and vegetables are adversely affected by strong direct sunlight so be aware of the areas that receive the most light throughout the day when stowing these light-sensitive items. Special containers are available for storing film and other items that need protection from both light and humidity. We store our fresh produce in plastic open weave cartons which we store in the quarter berth. We've never had luck with hanging net hammocks. It's tough to find a spot where they can really swing free without bashing against the cabin sides or into your head as you're working in the galley. Although ventilation is good, the produce

gets too much light. In the quarter berth, it is dark and cool, the ventilation is acceptable, and our fruits and vegetables are accessible to their point of use in the galley. Look for alternatives that work for you.

6.   **Pests - insects and rodents.** We are very careful about preventing pests from getting on *Two-Step* and only once discovered cockroaches on board. This was in 1991 when we got an unexpected weather window for our passage from the Azores to Madeira. We bought fresh produce in a rush and left. Normally, we pick over our produce carefully to catch any "stowaways" before loading it on to the boat, sometimes dunking our newly purchased fruits and vegetables in a bucket of water onshore to be sure. But in this instance, we were in a hurry and threw caution to the winds. We lived to regret it. Two days out, I woke up for my night watch and saw two cockroaches on the ceiling over my head. I freaked! In two years of cruising we had never had a cockroach on board. We carried a can of Baygon™ roach killer in case the inevitable happened but the smell is so terrible I knew it would make us seasick. We still had four days to go before we got to Madeira so I didn't want to risk it. We resorted to swatting and stomping instead.

As soon as we cleared in at Funchal, I bought some boric acid powder at the local drug store. During those four final days until landfall, I had done a lot of reading about effective means of ridding a boat of cockroaches! A cruising guide recommended boric acid powder since it was odour-free and not harmful to humans. I mixed the boric acid into a thick paste with sweetened condensed milk and made little "pills" from the paste which I stuck around our produce baskets, behind the stove and in all the lockers. The roaches are attracted to the sugar in the condensed milk but the boric acid is deadly to them. It did the job. Over the next couple of days, we woke up to find little dead cockroaches on the galley counter. By the end of the week, there weren't any more and we haven't seen another one since. We were lucky that we caught them right away.

To prevent cockroaches from getting on board, check all produce thoroughly before stowing it on the boat. Paper bags and cardboard boxes harbour their eggs so never bring them on board either. If we are going to be tied to a dock where cockroaches are in evidence, we spray our dock lines with roach killer such as Baygon™.

We have never had a mouse or rat on board either but carry mouse traps, just in case. We anchor out most of the time which reduces our chances of getting rodents aboard. They usually seem to climb aboard boats tied to a dock.

7. **Children and pets.** If you are travelling with children and/or pets on board, special consideration will have to be given to their safety when stowing provisions. Pets and little people tend to get into things and their natural curiosity can result in accidents that everyone wants to avoid. Cleaning products and medications will have to be stored out of reach or in a locked cabinet. Big heavy pots need to be secured so little hands can't pull them down on little heads. We look forward to visits from our young relatives and family friends and happily reorganize our stowage system to "childproof" the boat when they come. Most of the time though, it is just the two of us on board, so we prefer to maintain a stowage system that makes life easy for our routines (cleanser under the sink, seasick pills in the unlocked galley drawer) and make temporary changes when children and pets come to visit.

8. **Black Holes.** "Black holes" are our name for those seemingly bottomless lockers that swallow up equipment and supplies. When we first started cruising, we thought they were great since they could hold so much stuff.

Our cockpit locker on the port side is so deep that, when it's empty, I (Sheryl) can stand on the bottom and close the lid without it touching my head. (I'm five foot, two inches tall.) This was a great joke when we were building the boat since I did a lot of work in that locker attaching stanchion bases and deck fittings and Paul would occasionally shut the lid and lock me in! (It was also a great hiding place when we could see chatty unwanted visitors coming down the street to see how the project was coming along. "Dive! Dive!") However, once we started living on board, that locker became a royal pain. Anything we wanted was on the bottom and it was a huge production to remove the top layers to get at what we needed. We reduced the number of things in it so now I just have to stand on my head to reach things. We have plans to build in shelves and dividers to make the space more workable.

Take a look at any potential "black holes" on your boat and avoid filling them, or come up with an improvement such as a false bottom filled with floatation material or design some kind of divider system. You'll be a lot happier and things won't get swallowed up when you stow them.

# Inventory Control

*...In a floating Utopia, the cook should keep a little book, marking each item off as it is used - a good resolution which will probably not last long. But if the basic stock is stowed in some sort of order, and transferred to a ready-use locker when needed, the cook will quickly begin to keep a mental tally of consumption and to adjust menus accordingly.*

Philip Allen
**The Atlantic Crossing Guide**

Paul and I used to waste a lot of time rummaging around in lockers looking for things until we started keeping a proper inventory list. We first tried to keep a little book and check off every item as we used it. It was a huge job to set the book up. We had everything cross-indexed by item and by locker. Then, we'd forget to make a note that we'd used another package of peppercorn sauce mix or the last can of corn and then the whole system would be thrown off. Also, it was a really tedious task.

It is important to keep track of inventory to some degree so you know what's where and if there's any left, but you've got to make it workable for your lifestyle. Now, we've simplified our methods and things are a lot better. When we provision, we divide up our shopping lists into categories such as canned fruits and vegetables, baking items, and snack foods. Those lists become our inventory list. When we stow the goods on board, we make a note on the list what locker they're in.

We label our lockers by contents which sometimes results in strange names like the "hats and finances" locker, but mostly we have sensible titles like the beverage bin, the canned meat locker, and the spice cupboard. This makes the process of maintaining inventory an easy job. Some people number their lockers but I remember names better than numbers. Do whatever works for you.

Since all our canned meat is in one locker, for example, we can tell when we open it how much we have left. We don't just throw all the cans higgeldy piggeldy into the bin; we bundle like items together in Ziploc™ bags so they are easy to find. (This is also a good way to keep them dry and a lot less work than varnishing cans. See "The Art of Good Stowage" on page 213 for more information on protecting provisions from moisture and humidity.) You can fit 9 cans of chicken chunks in a large Ziploc™ bag. Whenever we use one, we can see at a glance how many are left. If all the meat is stored haphazardly together, we'd have to do a lot more digging to find what we're looking for and it wouldn't be so easy to see how many of a particular item were still in the locker. When we use the last can of chicken chunks, the bag is empty and we know there aren't any more. Then we go to the inventory list we made when provisioning, and mark off that they are all gone instead of trying to do it every time we use a can.

We're more careful about keeping precise inventory lists before and during a passage where it could be dangerous if we're missing an essential supply. It also prevents seasickness since digging through lockers unnecessarily on a pitching boat can really do us in. I prepare a ready-use locker for passages containing most of the food items I plan to use for the trip so I don't have to go forward. When coastal cruising or at anchor we are a lot more casual about keeping track of inventory and monitor our supplies visually. We have set up our stowage system to make this possible.

I go through all our lockers about once a week to make sure there are no spills or breakage. It also helps to remind me of what we have on board. Things tend to work their way to the bottom of lockers and you can forget that you even have them. Now, if we notice we've been carrying something around for a while and are not using it, we get rid of it (unless, of course, it is some form of safety equipment.) Storage space is too valuable to clutter up with useless stuff.

Produce, I check daily when it's my turn to make a meal. (See section on Fruits and Vegetables on page 186 for more information on buying and storing produce) If things are approaching ripeness we work them into our meal plans. Paul's made it his job to turn the egg cartons over each day or two to keep the eggs fresh without refrigeration. Turning the cartons keeps the eggshells from going porous by coating the inside of the shells with the egg white. If air gets through the shell to the yolk, the eggs go bad. (See section on Dairy Products on page 182 for more information on storing eggs) We used to both turn the eggs when we thought of it, but sometimes they wouldn't get turned for days because we each thought the other had done it.

### When to Reprovision

When we're down to about a month's worth of basic supplies such as flour, canned meats and beverages, we plan a major provisioning. We do this every three to four months or if we're in a port where food is inexpensive. We feel more comfortable having the boat well stocked at all times so we have the freedom to stay longer than planned in a place we like. We shop for fresh fruits, vegetables, milk products and meats regularly when we're cruising the coast and rely on canned goods only when we're wilderness cruising or at sea. Wandering the local markets in distant lands is an enjoyable experience for us and we have discovered many new foods.

If we see a product we like at a good price we will purchase a large amount to store on board whether it's time to reprovision or not. In Spain at the central market in Seville, we discovered a delicious red table wine that came in 1 litre tetra bricks. Don Simon Tinto (red) cost 99 pesetas in 1990 or about $1 U.S. a litre! Even better, we found a little supermercado (supermarket) in Estepona on the Costa del Sol that had a sale on Campo Bello Tinto (red) and blanco (white) also in tetra bricks for 65 pesetas or about 75 cents U.S. It stowed well and we loaded enough in the bilge to get us back to Canada. Spanish olives are delicious too and you can buy them in small vacuum-sealed packages. We loaded up in the Canary islands and they made great snacks on our passages to Brazil and the Caribbean. My mother and brother met us in Grenada for Christmas and Mom really got hooked on our Spanish olives. (The ones sold in jars at home just aren't the same.) She still gets cravings for them and occasionally asks when we're going back to Spain for some more of those olives.

When it comes time for a major reprovisioning, we do a thorough check of lockers and update our inventory list in detail. That way we only buy what is necessary.

It's fun to shop in foreign ports and see your lockers full of exotic goods labelled in foreign languages. It really makes us feel like citizens of the world.

## *Inventory List*

Worksheet 5 - Inventory and Shopping List

| Category: | | | | |
|---|---|---|---|---|
| Items | Size | Number | Price | Location |
| | | | | |
| | | | | |
| | | | | |
| | | | | |
| | | | | |
| | | | | |
| | | | | |
| | | | | |
| | | | | |
| | | | | |
| | | | | |
| | | | | |
| | | | | |
| | | | | |
| | | | | |
| | | | | |
| | | | | |
| | | | | |
| | | | | |
| | | | | |
| | | | | |
| | | | | |
| | | | | |
| | | | | |
| | | | | |
| | | | | |
| | | | | |
| | | | | |
| | | | | |
| | | | | |
| | | | | |
| | | | | |
| | | | | |

Photocopy for your own use. Also available on disk. See Appendix.

# Part 6 : Cooking at Sea

# Cooking At Sea

Dusk was approaching as the Great Isaac light blinked into view off our port quarter, bringing with it the reassurance that we were a safe distance off the shoals of the Great Bahama Bank. The wind had been building nicely through the day and *Two-Step* was now dancing along under main and jib to a steady 15 to 20 knots from the south. We were at the northern-most tip of the bank and within the hour would be feeling the force of the Gulf Stream as we headed for Florida from the Bahamas. Perfect!

Paul and I had just completed a two and a half month cruise through the Exumas and Berry Islands in the Bahamas and had planned to be back in Florida over a week ago. But it was February. Winter storms, referred to as "northers" by the locals, had been rolling through in quick succession.

Although it is only a 24-hour trip from the Berry Islands to West Palm, Florida, the Gulf Stream is a powerful natural barrier in bad weather. Strong northerly winds blowing against the 3 knot current can kick up ferocious seas. Since it is our policy to never knowingly go out in bad weather (part of our "Make it Fun for Everyone" policy), we had been waiting it out in Great Harbour.

Now we were making a run for it. We had been monitoring the weather through computer fax charts and radio reports and early that morning we saw the weather window we needed. The wind was to stay in the southeast through the day and then shift to south and southwest early the next morning as a prelude to the next front that was racing across the southern states. The thirty knot north winds of the front itself weren't to arrive for another 26 hours -- the winds *before* it would make the perfect conditions for crossing the stream.

"There's the light!" I yelled down the companionway to Paul who was at the chart table double-checking our course.

"Great! Right on schedule!," he yelled back. "I'll be right up."

I looked up at the cloudless sky now fading from bright blue to sunset pinks and mauves. It had been such a perfect day. It was hard to believe that bad weather would be coming through so soon.

Paul finished plotting our new course and then came on deck to take over the watch while I went below to prepare dinner. I had baked two loaves of crusty whole wheat bread that afternoon while the winds had been light. The smell of fresh-baked bread still wafted through the cabin adding a cozy feeling to the darkening night.

Paul and I both love to cook but on passages I do most of the cooking since Paul is more susceptible to seasickness than I am. For everyone's safety and comfort, this just makes plain sense. We've seen several cruises end unhappily in the name of Equality because motion-sensitive mates were expected to work in the galley underway. Compromise is key to crew harmony.

Paul and I have been cruising now for almost a decade and have spent over 120 nights on the open sea. Our longest passage was three weeks from the Canary Islands to Brazil and we have crossed the Atlantic Ocean three times with just the two of us to run the ship. To make life easy, we have developed a few routines that make cooking at sea a pleasure, rather than a pain.

1.  **Prepare meals ahead of time**: Before we set sail, we try to pre-prepare as many meals as possible so we can relax and get into the rhythm of maintaining watches. Although this was only to be an overnight trip, we had made up several "heat-and-eat" casseroles ahead of time in case we did get caught out in bad weather and were delayed a few days. We also pre-cut vegetables such as carrots, celery, cauliflower and broccoli into bite-sized pieces for easy snacks and to throw into soups, stews and salads. The less you have to work with knives on a rolling boat, the better.

2.  **Store everything you need for meal preparation near the galley**: Of all the tasks you do at sea, more time is spent in the galley than anywhere else. Organize the galley so that everything you need is easily accessible. Running here and there to complete a simple chore is frustrating, physically tiring and dangerous at sea. We have a ready-use locker for passages. I move all the main items I need for a passage into one locker so I don't have to rummage through several bins before I prepare a meal.

3.  **Know what you've got and where it is**: Meal preparation is a cinch if you keep a good inventory book listing your supplies, handy to the galley. Before we got organized about this, we wasted a lot of time searching for things we'd already used up. Don't waste effort digging through lockers when you can just check a list. The more times you're head-down in a locker looking for something, the more susceptible you are to seasickness.

4.  **Top everything up before you leave the dock**: It's amazing how little things can be so irritating at sea. Running out of dish detergent, having to change a toilet paper roll or finding the flour canister is empty can bring me to tears if a storm is raging. The easy solution is to top everything up before you set sail.

5.  **Clean the boat like crazy**: Odors can do you in if you are on the verge of "mal de mar". Make sure there are no sour sponges, dirty dish towels, gruesome laundry or icebox gremlins on board when you sail off.

6.  **Add safety features**: The safer you are and feel in the galley, the more enjoyable your galley tasks will be. There should be lots of handholds and a galley strap available so when the going gets rough, the chef doesn't land in the soup. We have pot clamps on our gimballed propane stove, a safety bar in front (between the cook and the cooker) and lots of handholds. Protect yourself by wearing a

plasticized chef's apron if there is a danger of spills. It will prevent a nasty burn if hot liquid should spill on you and is easy to pull off quickly if, heaven forbid, it should catch afire itself.

7. **Keep it simple**: Design meals to be quick and easy. You can be gourmet at anchor. We snack a lot on passages often having several small meals rather than three major productions per day. It's easier on the digestion and easier on the cook.

8. **Come up for air**: Stick your head out the companionway occasionally if you're going to be in the galley for awhile. It clears your head and makes you feel better.

9. **Make clean-up easy**: Design your meals so clean-up isn't a major chore. One-pot dinners served on paper plates makes life easier for everyone when the going gets rough.

By the time we'd finished our meal of bread and stew, we had entered the Gulf Stream and were flying along at 6 knots. Through the night, the wind remained steady from the south southwest giving us a fast, comfortable ride. When I crawled out of the sea berth at 0300 to take over the next watch, the lights of the Florida coast were twinkling on the horizon. Then, incredibly, as we tacked at the sea buoy 1½ miles off the West Palm Inlet, the front swept in. The smoke from a huge chimney on the waterfront made an "L" in the sky as the wind shifted suddenly to north. The front was 7 hours early but we were past the Gulf Stream and had a nice beam wind up the channel to the anchorage, ablaze with the lights of West Palm Beach.

# Galley Equipment

Table 31 - Galley Equipment

| Galley Equipment | |
|---|---|
| apron | plasticized, for protection from spills |
| bread pans | for bread, meatloaf, casseroles |
| hand mixer | no battery drain |
| jar funnel | to refill jars. e.g. rice and cereal can be poured into jars. |
| plastic mixing-/measuring cups | |
| Pyrex™ bakingware casserole cake pan | most people think they will break, but they are strong and won't rust. Cooking time is faster so they save stove fuel. |
| stacking plastic bowls with lids | salads, marinades, leftovers, ½ tomato etc. also as mixing bowls. |
| stacking stainless bowls with lids | as above |
| large Dutch oven | soup, large casseroles, steaming shellfish, pot roasts, corn on cob, large quantities of sauce or stew for preserving. |
| large saucepan / lid | rice, pasta etc. Thick bottoms on saucepans retain heat so you can start rice and set aside. Then burners are free for other things. We have done a full Christmas dinner on just our 2-burner stove (plus the oven for the turkey!) |
| small sauce pan / lid | veg, rice, sauces, boiling eggs etc. |
| large frying pan / lid | meat, bacon & eggs, stir fries, stove-top biscuits |
| small frying pan / lid | single eggs, bacon, doubles as 2nd saucepan for carrots etc. |
| steamer basket | veg, fish, shellfish, doubles as a second saucepan, can steam vegetables over potatoes |
| stainless thermos | hot water for passages. Coffee, tea, soup etc. |

| Galley Equipment | |
|---|---|
| wide-mouth thermos | for stews. Also for making yogurt (see page 185) |
| pressure cooker and spare gasket | stews, meat, bread, preserving |
| pot clamps | secures pots to the stove |
| muffin tin | |
| roasting pan | |
| cookie sheet | |
| pie plates | |
| cooling rack | to cool cookies, cakes and bread |
| canning jars and lids | for preserved meats, butter, chutney etc. |
| measuring cups and spoons | |
| cooking utensils | corkscrew, can and bottle opener, wooden spoons, rubber scrapers, soup ladle, spatula, vegetable peeler, whisk, paring knives, bread knife, nut crackers, seafood picks and ice pick. |
| cutting board | protect counter when cutting vegetables |
| grater | for grating cheese, carrots, etc. |
| plates bowls and mugs | we use Corelle™. It doesn't scratch like plastic and you can heat the plates. |
| commuter mugs | these plastic mugs have a lid you can drink through. Good in a blow. |
| glasses | regular, juice, liqueur and wine glasses |
| wine carafe | |
| juice pitcher | |
| coffee pot | |
| cutlery | stainless is best in salt water. |

# Water

We could see the squall line on the horizon heading straight for us, a black wall moving across the water. Paul and I were en route to Brazil from the Canary Islands and had been at sea for 14 days. We were nearly at the equator and it was hot, over 100°F. Just to keep up with our perspiration we had each been drinking over half a gallon a day in water and other beverages.

### Water Rations

*Two-Step* was carrying 95 Imperial gallons of fresh water for the 2,000 mile voyage which we estimated would take us 20 days, all going well. There were 15 gallons in three 5-gallon jerry jugs and 80 in our four 20-gallon stainless steel tanks under the cabin sole. Two of the jerry jugs were lashed on deck at the spreaders -- one on port side, one on starboard -- where they were easy to cut loose if we had to abandon ship. **The minimum water ration for comfort at sea is ½ imperial gallon or about 2.5 to 3 litres per person per day. For survival, the ration is .5 litres or 1 pint per person per day**. The boat was also loaded with several cases of canned soda water, fruit juice and pop. We weren't worrying about going thirsty.

At the moment, we were 200 miles north of the equator motor-sailing through the Intertropical Convergence Zone (ITCZ), an area of predicted calms, unpredictable winds and electrical storms. In this zone, the trade winds from the southern hemisphere converge with those from the north, going straight up to the heavens. I had never seen clouds like the ones here -- towering black-footed monsters that grew as you watched them. At night, the sky was filled with lightning. It danced and flashed from cloud to cloud, illuminating the confused seas beneath it in silvery patches -- beautiful but frightening.

I would be glad when we got to the other side of the ITCZ. It was narrow at this time of year -- November -- and we figured we'd get from one side to the other in three days. Then, it would only be about 5 days until we made landfall in Brazil at Fernando do Noronha. But despite my anxiety, I was in awe of the magnificence of nature that surrounded me, and felt privileged to be witnessing this special place on earth.

Most of the time there was too little wind to sail and then suddenly a gust would roar out of the sky and hit us at 35 knots. We had double reefed the main and unfurled a wisp of our jib to steady us as we motored through the uncomfortable sloppy seas, but even with such little sail area, *Two-Step* leaned over, rail in the water, when the gusts hit.

## *Washing*

We prepared for the approaching squall, standing by with shampoo and soap at the ready. We weren't going to miss a free shower in this heat! To preserve our fresh water supply at sea we take saltwater bathes, dousing ourselves with buckets of seawater. Joy dish detergent and Head&Shoulders™ shampoo lather well in saltwater, but we always follow up with a fresh water rinse to prevent saltwater sores from developing on our skin and scalp. We made an economical deck shower from a 2 gallon plastic insect spray canister which we bought new for $6.00 U.S. in 1989. You can pump it to pressurize the water and it produces a fine mist so you get a good shower without using a lot of water. We also have a Sunshower™, a black plastic shower bag that absorbs the heat of the sun, that we hang up on deck when we're at anchor for a nice fresh water shower after swimming, but at sea it's not practical because it swings around too much. Using indoor showers are a great way to get seasick, and in the tropics produce a lot of mildew in the boat. We never installed one on *Two-Step* for these reasons. When we're in civilization, we shower at marinas or manage with sponge baths. We have a saltwater pump in the galley, and when offshore, use seawater for washing dishes, in bread dough and for steaming vegetables. (Note: We don't recommend *boiling* vegetables in seawater; they absorb too much salt) Our fresh water supply lasts almost twice as long when we can use saltwater in the galley.

*A 2-gallon spray canister makes an economical deck shower.*

### Collecting Water

It would be great to collect some of this rainwater, I thought as I watched the rain racing across the water towards us, but *Two-Step* is a wet boat and there is always so much salt spray when the wind and rain hits that we haven't had much luck collecting drinking water at sea. Sure enough, as the first big drops spattered the decks, we heeled to the gust. From 2 knots before, the wind rushed in at 30 knots and we shot forward, rail down under reefed sails. Under such conditions it was hard to see how to collect water.

The general rule is that it stops raining as soon as the shampoo is fully lathered but in this case we were able to have a nice shower and stand in the cooling rain for a few minutes to rinse off. We had made good use of the squall.

When we're at anchor, we collect the run-off from our sun awning or from the deck by hanging buckets under the scuppers. We let it rain for a while first and scrub the decks before collecting it, but there still seems to be fluff and other strange things floating in it. We run the water through cheesecloth and a fine steel strainer when funnelling it into our jerry jugs. This removes the "bits", but, just to be safe, we leave it in the jerry jugs, so we don't contaminate our tanks. Instead, we use it for laundry, showers and rinsing the salt off our underwater cameras.

### Purifying Water

However, if we are enjoying a tranquil anchorage and don't want to head for civilization to replenish our water supply, we purify any we've collected and use it for drinking and cooking. We add a half-teaspoon of bleach to five gallons of water (see next page) and then add it to our tanks through the deck fill. We have a charcoal filter in the line from the tanks to the galley sink which removes the chlorine taste. The end result is quite delicious.

When we got to Europe, we started going through the same procedure with the city water since often it wasn't strongly chlorinated and didn't store well for more than a couple of weeks in our tanks. It tasted beautiful, but in some ports it formed a thin layer of green algae on the walls of the tanks before we could use it up. Yuck! So for the rest of our cruise through Europe, Brazil and the Caribbean, whenever we replenished our water supply, we put the new water into our jerry jugs first where we chlorinated it before adding it to our tanks. We never pour bleach down the deck fill because we want to be sure we are mixing the correct ratio of bleach to water. This is more manageable in our jerry jugs. In nine years of cruising we have never been sick from water.

Table 32 - Treatment of Water with Chlorine

| Available Chlorine [1] | tsp. per 5 Gallon of clean water [3] | ml per 20 litres of clean water [3] |
|---|---|---|
| 1% | 2½ teaspoon | 12 ml |
| 4-6% [2] | ½ teaspoon | 2.5 ml |
| 7-10% | ¼ teaspoon | 1 ml |
| unknown | 2½ teaspoon | 12 ml |

1   Available Chlorine is listed on some bleach containers as percentage of sodium hypochlorite.

2   Javex™ and Clorox™ both have 5.25%. If the percentage is not listed on the bottle, it is likely that it only has 1%.

3   Double this amount for cloudy water. We would not use cloudy water at all unless there was no alternative.

Like most cruising sailors, we have become connoisseurs of water and before filling *Two-Step's* water tanks go through a process much like wine tasting! First, we ask around for recommendations from other cruisers. It's often known that drinking water in one port is better tasting, less expensive or more convenient than another. In the out islands of the Bahamas where R.O. water (reverse osmosis) is 40 cents U.S. per gallon (1995), there are several deserted islands where beautiful sweet water can be collected from the cisterns of abandoned resorts. We would never have known about them if we hadn't asked around.

Water makers look like an attractive idea, but they take a lot of power to operate. They are also expensive. Since we want to spend our money on other things, we stick to the jerry jugs.

Before we put any water in our tanks, we put a little into a clear glass and observe it for clarity. If it's cloudy, we go elsewhere. If it's clear and tastes good, we fill up.

The water that fell from the towering equatorial clouds was as clean and fresh as any we tasted. As the squall passed we were again left in the confused seas of the doldrums, the main boom creaking slightly as it swung back and forth. The wind dropped immediately back to 2-3 knots and we started the engine. We had planned enough fuel for 200 miles of ITCZ and it looked as if we would need it. *Two-Step* rolled so much in the seas that we couldn't really use the light wind. We motor-sailed on towards the Equator.

*Like most cruisers we have become connoisseurs of water. We check it for taste, clarity and odour before putting it in our water tanks.*

# Part 7 : Personal Comfort and Care

# Personal Items

It's easy to overlook personal items like toothpaste when your mind is on equipping the boat with new gear and major supplies for a voyage. Paul and I keep personal items stored in our shower kits which are especially handy when using marina showers. Our kits are ready to go with everything we need. They are like mini duffel bags and can be hung up so they don't get wet.

We write our boat name on our soap dishes because it is so easy to leave them in the shower by mistake. As our friend Yvonne on *Sea Spell* says, it's like leaving a five dollar bill behind. If your boat name is on your shampoo, people return it. We have met some really nice people this way!

### Table 33 - Shower Kit

| | |
|---|---|
| comb / brush | talc |
| shampoo[1] / conditioner | Skin-So-Soft™[2] |
| shower gel or soap in a soapdish | feminine sanitary supplies |
| | make-up |
| razor and shaving gel | shower cap |
| nail scissors or clippers | hair ties |
| toothbrush and toothpaste | contact lens solution |
| dental floss | tote bag for clothes & plastic bag for dirty clothes |
| cotton swabs | |
| hand and body lotion | towel and face cloth |
| deodorant | thongs (plastic sandals) [3] |

[1] Prell™ and Head&Shoulders™ work well in saltwater too

[2] Skin-So-Soft™ bath oil is effective for repelling mosquitos and no-see-ums yet smells nice.

[3] cheap beach thongs protect against athletes foot in well-used, sometimes grungy showers.

# Clothes

When long-distance cruising it is important to have clothes for all climates and occasions, yet it is a common mistake to bring *too many* clothes. When travelling and living afloat you do not need the extensive wardrobe you do when working and living ashore. Life is much more casual and, since you are not seeing the same people every day, you don't need such a variety of outfits. Then there is the question of space, which is always limited, so it is best to chose clothing that you can mix and match together easily.

We do most of our cruising in tropical climates so the majority of our clothes are for hot weather. We find the most comfortable fabric to wear is a cotton-polyester blend. It doesn't wrinkle, is cool and absorbent but moisture wicks away and it dries quickly. It's great if you have to do laundry by hand since it drip-dries nicely, especially in a trade wind. We find 100% cotton is too absorbent; it always feels clammy to us in really hot weather. It also wrinkles badly and tends to fade quickly in strong sunshine. It doesn't seem to be as hard wearing as cotton-polyester either. But what is really important is that the clothes you pack are what you are comfortable wearing and allow you to do the job at hand.

In many countries that we have visited outside North America, people dress more formally to go to town for simple chores such as grocery shopping. If you show up in shorts and a T-shirt, it is considered disrespectful. When Paul and I go ashore, we "dress to belong", especially if we are clearing into the country. You can really get off to a bad start if a customs official thinks you are not being respectful. Paul shaves and trims his beard and wears long pants and a nice shirt; I tie back my long hair and put on a skirt or sun dress, then off we go. Our friend Elizabeth on *Solstice Moon*, said wearing her "missionary dress" opened a lot of doors for her. This was an ankle-length, high-necked dress. She found when she wore it in the Caribbean, that the local women felt more comfortable with her. People invited her to their homes and she even got better prices at the local market because she was "obviously a god-fearing woman". Having known Elizabeth for a number of years, Paul and I thought this was quite hilarious.

I also discovered that wearing a dress is much more comfortable when the heat and humidity are severe. It's healthier too; wearing confining clothing in the heat (or sitting in a damp bathing suit) allows bacteria to incubate in your groin causing painful urinary tract infections (cystitis). For the same reason, you should never wear nylon underpants; cotton is safer and more comfortable.

For passage-making, we have several sets of warm clothes because at night or in bad weather you seem to need warm clothes, even in the tropics. Sweat suits are great because you can move around easily in them, they are comfortable under your foul weather gear and you can wear them as pajamas when you're off watch. If you're called on deck in an emergency, you can jump out of your sleeping bag and still be decently dressed!

Foul weather gear should be comfortable to move in so you can handle lines and sails. It should also be easy to get in and out of. If it's not, you probably won't put it on as often as you need to. If you get a douse of saltwater, your clothes will never dry and, before you know it, your teeth will be chattering. Foul weather gear doesn't need to be expensive. The sets we have only cost about $100 U.S. in 1989 and are only now ready to be replaced. They just have to keep you dry. We give them lots of ventilation by hanging them in the wet locker under the companionway. Whenever we get the chance, we give them a fresh water rinse and a little air and sunshine to keep them fresh. We also keep a set of lightweight nylon rain gear for wet rides in the dinghy or if rain is expected when we are ashore. They roll up in their own compact little pouches and are easy to store in our tote bag or backpack.

When we got work in Gibraltar, my mother shipped Paul two suits which we'd left at home (I had enough dresses with me) and we have kept them on board, as well as our briefcases, ever since. Opportunities to work in other countries are a great way to gain insights into a new culture, make some interesting friends as well as adding some dollars to the cruising kitty. We keep several sets of dress clothing since we are often invited to local events that require it. In southern Spain the expatriot community frequently host formal parties and in Bermuda, many restaurants require that men wear dinner jackets (but not ties... Paul asked, but they said "Oh no! That would be too hot"!!!).

We store all our other clothes folded on shelves in well ventilated lockers in our forward cabin. They take up less space this way and aren't as likely to chafe as when they are swinging on hangers in a hanging locker. If you fold them carefully, you won't need to iron them.

## Table 34 - Clothing

Bandannas
Belts
Shirts:
  long sleeved
  short sleeved
  T-shirts
  tank tops
Sweaters:
  fleece
  wool
  turtle neck
Sweat shirt
Sweat pants
Pants/Jeans
Shorts
Skirts
Sun dresses
Socks
Underwear
Shoes:
  Deck shoes
  Running shoes
  Dress shoes
  Sandals
  Beach shoes
  Hiking boots
Dress wear:
  Men:
    dinner jacket
    suit
    dress shirt
    neck tie
    dress socks

    briefcase
Women:
  evening gown
  dress
  lingerie
  panty hose
  blazer
  purse/briefcase
Sleep wear:
  Bathrobe
  Pajamas
  Slippers
Foul Weather Gear:
  Gloves:
    leather
    wool
    sailing
  Watch cap
  Headband
  Sou'wester
  Foul weather jacket
  Foul weather pants
  Lightweight rain jacket
  Lightweight rain pants
  Thermal underwear
  Neck gaiter or scarf
  Boots
Beachwear:
  Bathing suit
  Beach cover-up
  Sunhat
  Polarized sunglasses

# Laundry Kit and Supplies

Travelling the waterways of Canada and the U.S., we found that most marinas have laundry facilities on the premises or nearby. When this is the case, we just throw our dirty clothes and bedding into a couple of large mesh bags or pillow cases and walk down the dock. We have a "laundry kit" that we take along as well -- a small tote bag in which we keep our laundry detergent, fabric softener, spot remover, a roll of quarters, and a couple of magazines.

In the islands, laundromats are few and far between. Often the water supply is brackish so clothes don't dry very well. Many local women will do laundry but this is an expensive option and there often seem to be disputes when it is returned.

When good laundry facilities are not available, we find it's easier to do our laundry ourselves by hand. This is not as bad as we first thought it would be. In fact, now we both think of it as a relaxing activity to do on deck on a sunny day. We leave a five gallon jerry jug of fresh water on deck to warm in the sun -- enough water to do about two weeks of laundry.

We never wash clothes in saltwater. Salt holds moisture so your clothes will never dry, even in the hot sunshine in the tropics. They'll be stiff and irritating to your skin and you will probably develop uncomfortable saltwater rashes. Some people wash their clothes in saltwater and rinse in fresh, but it takes so much fresh water to get the salt out that you can end up using more fresh water than if you'd washed with it in the first place!

We have a large plastic wash basin with a five gallon capacity so there is lots of room to swish the clothes around. We fill it about two-thirds full and add a capful of liquid laundry detergent. We prefer the liquid over the powder because it mixes well and rinses out easily in all temperatures of water. It also stores better than the powdered detergent which cakes in the humid air.

We start with the least soiled, least salty items first. We let them soak for a couple of minutes to absorb the water, then swish them around. Some sailors use a toilet plunger (bought solely for doing laundry) as an agitator but we find that just squeezing the water through the clothes and rubbing at stains with a soft bristle brush does the trick. We then squeeze out as much water and soap as we can and set the first batch to one side. We continue adding clothes and repeat the process until the water starts to look grungy; then we dump the water and add clean water and detergent and continue until all the clothes have been washed. Heavily soiled clothing, such as socks, we leave soaking in a bucket of sudsy water for the day which takes out most of the dirt. We squeeze them out and then wash them like the rest of our clothes.

For rinsing, we fill our wash basin with clean water and add ½ a cup of vinegar --more if the clothes are really soapy. The vinegar helps draw the soap out of the clothes and does not leave an odour. In fact, it gives the clothes a clean fresh smell and makes them feel soft. You can use commercial fabric softener as well but vinegar is cheaper and has lots of other uses. We put a few soapy clothes in the basin, swish them around and squeeze them out. When the water gets too soapy, we dump it and start again. If we have lots of water and we're in a good mood, we'll put the clothes through a second rinse but usually once is enough. If there is a little soap left in the clothes, it is not harmful.

Squeezing clothes out by hand is usually sufficient. Our friend Glenis on *Galatea* has a wringer that she clamps on to the stern rail which speeds up the job and makes her the envy of all around. Clothes dry quickly in hot weather anyway, so even if you hang them up dripping wet, it isn't a problem.

Before pinning up our clothes to dry, we rig a clothesline from the forestay to the mast for large items such as bed sheets. For T-shirts and shorts, we wipe any salt or dirt from the lifelines and pin them there. We use lots of clothes pins, especially in the trade winds! It's really depressing to see your clean clothes go over the side and have to jump in after them. Wooden clothes pins are best. Plastic ones break down in the sun and don't seem to have as good a grip.

Socks and underwear go on what I call our "sock-topus". This is like a mini drying rack. It has one hook to hang it by, and eight short folding arms with two clothes pins per arm. This little gizmo is handy for drying clothes *inside* the boat too; useful if you are at a dock or anchored in front of a posh resort and don't want your undies flying in the breeze for all to see!

Most of our clothes are a cotton polyester blend which is comfortable and wrinkle resistant. Careful folding means we don't have to iron them very often. I used to have a 12 V travel iron but it drew so much power I got rid of it and bought an old fashioned cast iron one. I just heat it on a burner on our propane stove to press out wrinkles in 100% cotton clothes or to give us a tidy look if we're attending a formal occasion. Not all sailors go to this trouble, but my mother gets upset if we start to look "cruisey"! Besides, if you look good, you feel good (and I don't mind keeping my mother happy, even if she is thousands of miles away at the time).

Table 35 - Laundry Supplies

| laundry kit bag: | laundry bags |
| --- | --- |
| laundry detergent | clothes pins |
| fabric softener | clothes line |
| bleach | "sock-topus" |
| spot remover | |
| coins for machines | |

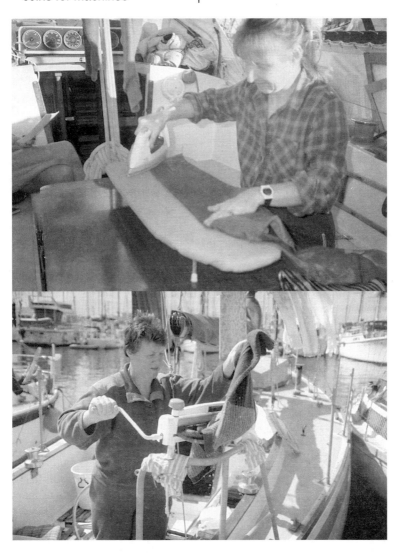

## Sewing Kit

*"A stitch in time, saves nine."*

Clothing gets a lot of wear and tear when living on a boat. Exposure to the sun, vigorous activity, and fewer clothes worn more often, seem to be the reasons. Paul and I use our sewing kit a lot when we're cruising to prolong the life of our clothes and to prevent that "scruffy" look that long-distance sailors sometimes fall victim to. In Madeira and the Canary Islands, we could tell instantly when we had fallen down on appearances -- the time-share condo sales force stopped pestering us!

I enjoy sewing and bought a brand new hand-crank sewing machine in Gibraltar. It's perfect for the boat because it doesn't draw any power! I can sew at anchor or the middle of the ocean and not worry about draining the batteries. It's heavy duty too. It can sew through 6 layers of canvas which my high-tech sewing machine at home can't do. It doesn't do zigzag or any other fancy stitch but it does the job on boat projects. It is easy to maintain and repair. Paul got really good at making courtesy flags with it and also made covers for the winches, windlass, barbecue etc. I did repairs to clothing, sails and canvas, and had fun shopping for interesting fabrics in the markets of Europe and the Caribbean when I felt like making a new outfit.

When living on board, you seem to constantly come up with canvas projects for improving the boat -- another sheet bag here, a hatch cover there -- so I recommend carrying several metres of canvas for these projects. When, I sit in the cockpit working on something for *Two-Step*, I often get requests from other sailors to sew up something they've designed for their boats. It's a nice way to earn a little pocket money!

Table 36 - Basic Sewing Kit

| Basic Sewing Kit: | |
| --- | --- |
| buttons | - spare buttons for shirts and pants. |
| elastic | - various widths. It seems to break down drying in the sun. |
| needles | - assorted sizes including a darning needle for heavy fabrics. |
| pins | |
| patch kit | |
| scissors | |
| tape measure | |
| thimble | |
| thread | cotton-wrapped polyester thread is strong and suitable for canvas projects too. Bring several basic colours that co-ordinate with your clothes. |
| Scotchgard™ | |
| shoe laces | |

Table 37 - Advanced Sewing Kit

| Advanced Sewing Kit: | |
| --- | --- |
| hooks and eyes | |
| Velcro™ | - Velcro tape and buttons are handy for repairs. |
| grommets and tools | - useful for new projects & repairs. |
| snaps and tools | - useful for new projects & repairs. |
| stitch ripper | |
| sewing shears | |
| pinking shears | |
| tailors chalk | |
| tracing paper | |
| tracing wheel | |
| iron-on interfacing | |
| ruler | |
| canvas | - keep 2-3 metres for new projects. |

Table 38 - Sewing Machine and Accessories

| Sewing machine and accessories: | |
|---|---|
| sewing machine | |
| needles | |
| screw driver | |
| sewing machine oil | |
| bobbins | |
| lint brush | |
| zipper foot | - or any other attachments your machine requires. |
| non-skid pad | - to rest sewing machine on. |

Table 39 - Courtesy Flag Kit

| Courtesy Flag Kit | |
|---|---|
| fabric scraps | - useful for making courtesy flags as well as for patching clothes. |
| liquid thread | - once I embroidered the crests on. Liquid thread is less work |
| world flag book | |

# Linens

The following is a list of the bedding and linens we keep on board. In hot climates, dish clothes and towels can go sour quickly so we keep a good supply and replace them frequently. A soak in hot sudsy water with a little bleach in it, freshens them right up and gets rid of mildew. We change the bed sheets about once a week but don't always get a chance to do laundry that often so keep several sets. We have blankets and flannelette sheets for cool weather.

We sleep in the V-berth most of the time and leave the bed made up which is convenient. If we have guests, they sleep in the berths in the main saloon, and the bedding needs to be folded up and stowed in the morning. When we're on passages and there's just the two of us, we sleep in the main saloon since there is less motion there. One of us is on watch at all times so we only make up the leeward berth and "hot bunk" it. i.e. It's still warm from the last occupant when you crawl into it. For convenience, we often just use a sleeping bag on passages, unless it's too hot.

We have two sleeping bags that zip together if we want to sleep under the stars when we're at anchor. They have also come in handy for backpacking trips when we want to travel inland. In Madeira, we left *Two-Step* in the good care of friends at the marina in Funchal and hiked through breath-taking valleys and along the spine of a jagged mountain range to reach the top of Pico Ruivo at an altitude of 1,862m or 6,109ft. Cuddled up in our double sleeping bag, we watched the sun set into the sea from the highest point in the Republic of Portugal.

Table 40 - Linens

| | |
|---|---|
| Bed sheets; regular and flannelette | Dishcloths and dishtowels |
| Pillow cases | Beach towels |
| Blankets | Bath towels |
| Duvet/Comforter | Hand towels |
| Mattress cover | Facecloths |
| Sleeping bags | Tablecloths |
| | Cloth napkins |

# Useful Baggage

Living aboard a boat you do a lot of carrying -- groceries, ice, laundry, jerry jugs, propane tanks -- the list goes on. While cruising aboard *Two-Step* we have acquired a collection of "useful baggage" that has made our life easier when doing various tasks.

We probably use our two large canvas tote bags the most. They are made of heavy duty cotton and fold flat for easy storage. The handles are comfortable to hang on to and the bags hold a terrific weight of provisions, books, ice or anything else we want to tote around. In many countries we visited, you are expected to bring your own bags to the market so our tote bags are perfect for shopping. They don't dry easily though when they get wet and tend to mildew. A good soak and scrub in hot sudsy water with a little bleach fixes them right up. We have had the same ones for six years. We got them at our local chandlers and they seem to be sold the world over in marine supply stores.

We also have a folding shopping cart. It is made with an aluminum frame and canvas and folds to the size of a handbag. The wheels aren't happy around the saltwater however, so we keep them well greased. It has been useful for transporting groceries, laundry and propane tanks but isn't too good on sand or gravel roads. We got it at a Consumers Distributing store in Canada. Many of our cruising friends have standard folding shopping carts which are stronger than ours but don't fold so compactly. We also have one of those folding luggage carriers that people use around airports. They fold flat and are good for hauling heavy cases of canned goods or jerry jugs back to the boat.

Next in line are our backpacks. They are made of water-resistant nylon and are hard wearing. I have had mine for 16 years and it's still going strong, although the colour has faded somewhat. On the boat, I have to lubricate the nylon zippers with candle wax since they seize up in a saltwater environment. They seized up twice before I learned the waxing trick, but I got them sliding again by soaking them in fresh water and working at them. Paul and I each have a backpack with padded shoulder straps and an adjustable hip strap which make them more comfortable for carrying heavy loads. We use them mostly for trips to the market. We also wear them for day hikes to carry our lunch, a water bottle, our lightweight rain gear or an extra sweater. Paul's pack is large enough to carry an 11 lb. propane tank which has been helpful when we need a refill.

Something else we both have and find invaluable is a fanny pack. It clips around your waist so your hands are free to grab shrouds or life lines when you're climbing into the dinghy. They are small enough not to be a nuisance and yet large enough to hold a lot of useful little things you always seem to need, but don't usually feel like carrying around. Ours contain our wallets with I.D., a pen, our boat cards (like a business card with our names, our boat name, Paul's radio call sign and our address on them), sun block or lip balm, a pen light, a safety pin, a paper clip, an elastic band, an emery board, a Band-Aid, a pen knife, a map of the port we're in, a small orienteering compass, and a foreign language dictionary or phrase book if necessary. I also carry a small point-and-shoot camera in mine. I've got some of our most interesting photos with that little camera just because we were in the right place at the right time and had a camera.

We also have several nylon duffel bags which we use to store seasonal clothing and as overnight bags when we get an invitation for a weekend visit somewhere. They are also useful for toting laundry. We have a couple of very small duffels that we use as toiletries bags for carrying to the shower. (See Personal Items on page 239)

Something else we have found useful is mesh bags. We have several sizes of them and use them for storing small items like socks in our clothes locker. They keep things organized and you can see what's in them. The large ones are good for stowing dirty laundry which can go mildewy if not well ventilated in a hot humid climate. We have also used mesh bags for chilling wine -- we pop a bottle or two in a bag and hang it over the side. We have kept conch fresh in the same way until we were ready to clean them for a meal. We have even seen sailors use them for doing dishes. They put the dishes in a mesh bag and tow them along under sail until they're clean! They tend to lose dishes though.

We have also sewn up some custom bags using synthetic canvas. Paul made one for our Danforth anchor so it wouldn't catch on everything in the cockpit locker. It's much easier to pull it out now and carry it around on deck when we want a second anchor. We also made one for our dinghy anchor that holds the rode too and several for stowing dock lines. You can never have enough bags, it seems.

Table  41  -  Useful  Baggage

| | |
|---|---|
| canvas tote bags | fanny packs |
| folding shopping cart | duffel bags |
| folding luggage carrier | toiletries bags (shower kits) |
| backpacks | mesh bags |

## Important Documents

It is a good idea to make two photocopies of all your important documents. Leave one set of copies with someone at home and keep the other set on the boat *in a separate place from the originals.* Include a page with useful phone numbers, such as "lost card" phone numbers for your credit cards, with each set. In the event that your boat is broken into or your wallet is stolen, there will be a complete record of all your documents and the necessary phone numbers to arrange their replacement. We store all our documents in Ziploc™ bags since the salt air can make them go moldy.

We find it is useful to have separate credit card accounts so if Paul's wallet was stolen, we can freeze his card and still have the use of mine. It is also good to have <u>different</u> cards, e.g. Paul with Mastercard and me with Visa, since some places take Visa but not Mastercard and vice versa. We once got into a cash flow problem in Brazil because the bank and local shopkeepers on the island of Fernando de Noronha only took Mastercard and we both had Visa. At that point we had cruised North America, the Caribbean and Europe and had always been able to use our Visa cards to access our accounts or make interest-free cash advances. (see the Cost of Cruising for more information on transferring funds, page 35) Subsequently we were not able to stay as long as we would like to in this idyllic place.

*Paul registers our camera equipment with Canada Customs before sailing across Lake Ontario to the US on our trip south.*

Table 42 - Important Documents

| Important Documents | |
|---|---|
| Crew list | the name, address, nationality and passport number of every crew member. Some countries require you to make up this list yourself. Most have a special form for this information which you fill out when you check into the country. |
| Papers required for pets | |
| Ship's registration papers | |
| Passports | |
| Credit Cards | |
| Customs Registry | These forms prove that high priced items such as cameras are duty paid before you left home. Contact customs before leaving on your cruise. |
| Receipts | e.g. of items purchased on route, or still under warranty. |
| Birth Certificates | |
| Marriage License | Sometimes required for work permits. |
| Cruising permits | Where required. Purchase when entering the country. |
| Fishing permits | |
| Vaccination Certificates | |

# Medical

One of the things we worried about before sailing away on our first cruise was how to maintain good health while travelling. Would we be susceptible to strange tropical diseases? How would we handle a medical emergency at sea? What would we do if we needed a doctor or ambulance in a foreign country?

On the advice of our family doctor, we made an appointment at the Travel and Inoculation Clinic at the Toronto Hospital. What a valuable service! At the clinic, we talked to a knowledgeable counsellor about our concerns, the countries we were planning to sail to, our mode of transportation, the duration of our cruise, and what inoculations we required.

She reassured us that voyaging in our own boat was probably one of the healthiest ways to travel since we would control the sanitation of our living quarters and the purity of our water and food supply. She showed us several methods for purifying water, instructed us on how to store it safely (see Water, page 231) and explained how to prevent and treat travellers' ailments. We also discussed what to do in an emergency when sailing offshore and she made up a list of medical supplies to have on board (see below). She would have given us vaccinations but none were required for the countries we were planning to sail to.

The Toronto General Hospital also has a Travel Information Line. Using a touch-tone phone you can get recorded information on water purification, treatment of common travellers' illness, inoculations and specific information on continents or countries you are planning to visit. Call (416) 340-4030.

We left the clinic carrying a package of informative literature which included the valuable list of prescription and non-prescription drugs for "high risk isolation travel". Since we were planning to cruise in remote areas and make ocean passages, we would need to be able to treat ourselves in an emergency. We have included that list but recommend that you go to a travel clinic near you and talk to your doctor to get specific information for your cruise.

After showing the list to our family doctor, she wrote out the prescriptions we needed and we arranged with Sheryl's mother, a pharmacist, to have the prescriptions filled. She made sure that the drugs were ordered new, so we could carry them for the maximum time before their expiry dates were up. If you explain your plans to your pharmacist, he or she will gladly do the same and educate you on the best way to store and administer them. Our bill for medical supplies was over $1,000 CAN. (1989).

We took first aid training and a CPR course before we left. We keep our first aid manual in our medical kit on board, as well as a sailors' first aid book called *Advanced First Aid Afloat.* We purchased a first aid book for divers too, on treating injuries caused by marine plants and animals since we love to snorkel and scuba dive.

After nine years of living aboard, we have never been healthier! We hardly even get a cold when we're cruising. Fresh air, exercise, reduced stress and a controlled environment make for healthy living. It is only when we are home, riding crowded subways in the wintertime that we seem to get sick.

As with all things about cruising, if you prepare well you can look forward to a healthy and happy voyage!

### The Golden Rule of Preventing Dehydration

Sheryl's cousin, Dr. Euan Carlisle, a nephrologist (kidney specialist) at St. Joseph's Hospital in Hamilton, Ontario, warned us to drink lots of fresh water and stay well hydrated while living on the boat. Apparently sailors are susceptible to kidney stones because they get dehydrated so often. This is because they don't keep up with the fluids they lose through perspiration (caused by the increased physical activity of running a boat and being in the outdoors) which is compounded by the fact that they are trying to conserve their fresh water supply.

We heeded his advice and feel it is fundamental to the good health we enjoy. Two-thirds of the human body is made of water. By keeping "topped up", we have lots of energy and a better resistance to illness. Even if we're not feeling thirsty, we can tell if we are dehydrated when, for no apparent reason, we feel tired, "headachy" or irritable. A big glass of water is an instant cure. Fruit and vegetable juices are the next best alternative. Tea, coffee and alcohol are diuretics and stimulate the kidneys to *pass* water rather than to *restore* it so make the problem worse. Try to avoid these beverages until you are properly hydrated. (See Beverages on page 180)

Another way to judge if you are keeping up with your fluid loss is to follow the Golden Rule: If your urine is dark yellow in colour and scant, it is concentrated with metabolic wastes due to dehydration. Time for a big glass of water. (Note: Some vitamin supplements make your urine appear bright yellow too. If you are taking vitamins, the best way to judge if you are dehydrated is by the *quantity* of your urine.) If you are voiding regularly and your urine is clear and pale yellow in colour, you're fine.

## Common Ailments When Cruising

A survey amongst long-term cruisers resulted in the following list of common ailments:

- dry eyes from wind and sun
- splinters
- saltwater rashes
- athletes foot and jock itch
- minor burns including sunburn
- coral burns and jellyfish stings
- insect bites
- cuts, scrapes and bruises
- stiff or strained muscles
- yeast infections and urinary tract infections (cystitis)
- constipation or haemorrhoids
- seasickness
- headaches from dehydration, salt deficiency, eye strain or over-indulgence of alcohol
- swimmer's ear

A first aid manual will tell you how to treat most of these problems. Talk to your family doctor for his or her recommendations as well.

## Medical Supplies

The following is a list of medical supplies we keep on Two-Step. The asterisks (*) indicate medications that require a prescription. We recommend going over this list with your doctor so he or she can adapt our list to your individual needs. Also, investigate the limits of your provincial health insurance plan. You will probably require additional health insurance when travelling outside your province especially when cruising in the United States where medical fees are astronomical.

| Medical Supplies | Use |
| --- | --- |
| **Eyes and Ears and Mouth** | |
| saline solution | Sterilized. For rinsing irritated eyes and ears. e.g. Tears Naturelle™ or Isopto Tears™ |
| eye ointments | For infections of the eye or eyelids. e.g. Polysporin™ ophthalmic ointment |
| eye drops | For infections of the eye. e.g. Polysporin ophthalmic drops. |
| ear drops | Dilute hydrogen peroxide makes a good antiseptic ear drop for swimmer's and other ear infections. |
| ear wax remover drops | Cerumenol™ dissolves wax. Light mineral oil is a gentle alternative. |
| canker ointment | e.g. Orajel™ relieves pain of cankers. |
| toothache medication | e.g. Oil of clove or Orajel. |
| cold sore ointment | e.g. Zovirax™ or rubbing alcohol. |
| lip balm | e.g. Blistex™ or zinc oxide (for sun protection) |
| dental pick and mirror | For on board dental check-ups. |
| dental repair kit | For temporary repairs to lost fillings, knocked-out teeth, etc. |
| **Respiratory Ailments** | |
| cough medicine: suppressant expectorant | DM for suppressing dry coughs and expectorant for breaking up congestion. |
| cough lozenges | To soothe coughs. |
| cold medication | For reducing congestion and easing aches and pains. e.g. Neo Citron™ |
| throat lozenges | To soothe sore throats. e.g. Cepacol™ antiseptic throat lozenges. |
| throat gargle | To reduce pain of sore throat. e.g. |

| Medical Supplies | Use |
|---|---|
|  | Tantum* |
| oral antibiotics | To fight infection - strep throat, upper respiratory tract and earache. e.g. Amoxicillen* or Penicillin*. If have Penicillin allergy, use Erythromycin*. For children, ask your pharmacist to sell the antibiotic unreconstituted and to show you how to make it up with water. Bactrim™* and Novotrimel™* are good for urinary tract infections (cystitis) and diarrhoea. |
| antihistamines | For minor allergic reactions - hay fever and other allergies. e.g. Allegra™ and Clariten™ are non-drowsy formulas and are safe for people on heart medication. Benydryl™ is good for skin allergies but causes drowziness. |
| bee-sting kit | For severe allergic reactions or acute asthma where life is threatened. e.g. Ana kit™ or Epi-pen™* |
| **Skin Irritations** |  |
| sun block |  |
| aloe vera gel | Soothes minor burns and skin irritations. |
| insect repellent | Avon's Skin-So-Soft™ effectively repels insects but has a pleasant smell. |
| head lice kit | E.g. Nix™. |
| petroleum jelly | Protects skin. |
| barrier cream | As above but not so greasy. e.g. Barriere Cream™, Prevex™. |
| first aid ointment | Soothes minor burns and speeds healing of cuts, scrapes and skin irritations. e.g. Ozonol™. |
| antibiotic ointment | Prevents infection of cuts, scrapes and skin irritations. e.g. Polysporin ointment. In the heat of the tropics Polysporin is not strong enough so use Bactroban* or Fucidin* ointment instead. |
| oral antibiotics | For more serious skin infections, like a boil or wounds with pus use Cloxacillin* until you can get to a doctor. |
| burn ointment | For severe burns. e.g. Flamazine™* |

| Medical Supplies | Use |
|---|---|
| calamine lotion | Relieves the itch of skin irritations e.g. Caledryl™ |
| cortisone cream | For rashes. e.g. Cortate™* |
| anti-fungal powder | For athlete's foot and jock itch. e.g. Desenex™ |
| **Digestive** | |
| nausea control:<br>   pills<br>   suppositories | e.g. Gravol™ or Stugeron™ (available in E.C. countries) to prevent seasickness. If crew member is violently ill, suppositories may be necessary. Alka Seltzer™ is good for upset stomach caused from over-eating. |
| diarrhoea control | e.g. Imodium™ |
| antiprotozoal | For treatment of internal parasites. e.g. Flagyl™*, Novonidazol™* |
| **Infection Control** | |
| rubbing alcohol | For sterilizing instruments like thermometers |
| alcohol swabs | For sterilizing skin. |
| hydrogen peroxide | For sterilizing skin and cleansing wounds. Not so harsh as rubbing alcohol. |
| antibacterial skin cleanser. | Phisohex™, Betadine™ or Savlon™ |
| **Muscle Strain** | |
| liniment | To warm and relax muscles. e.g. |
| hot/cold packs | To control stiffness and swelling. |
| muscle relaxants | e. g. Parafon Forte™ |
| **Pain Control** | |
| Coated Aspirin™ | Controls pain without upsetting stomach. |
| Panadol™ | Controls pain and inflammation. |
| 222's | Contains codeine. Stronger than aspirin or acetaminophen. |
| Tylenol #3™ | Contains 30mg of codeine for serious pain. |
| **Urinary and Reproductive** | |
| Monistat™ | For treatment of vaginal yeast infections. |
| antibacterial tablets | For treatment of urinary tract infections (cystitis) e.g. Bactrim™*, Septra™* |

| Medical Supplies | Use |
|---|---|
| contraceptives | For birth control. Condoms prevent the spread of Aids and other venereal diseases. |
| **Bandages** | |
| Elastoplast™ bandages | Stays on the best in a wet environment. Hard to find outside Canada. |
| liquid skin | |
| gauze pads | |
| adhesive tape | |
| elastic bandages and clips | |
| triangular bandage | |
| **Tools** | |
| fine needles | To remove splinters |
| tweezers | For splinters |
| small mirror | For self-examination |
| cotton swabs | |
| tongue depressors | |
| thermometer | |
| syringes | In some countries you are expected to provide your own. It also insures that it is sterilized properly. Our doctor wrote a note to this effect on her letterhead which we keep with the syringes in case of interrogation during a customs inspection. |
| suturing kit | |
| ring cutter | It's important to be able to get rings off swollen fingers. |
| finger splints | |
| wrist splints | |
| neck brace | |
| inflatable cast | |
| hot water bottle | |
| cold packs | |
| sling | |

# Recreational Gear

While cruising, you have more time to enjoy hobbies and activities that complement sailing. We are avid divers and photographers so we make space on *Two-Step* for this type of gear. After our first winter cruising in the Bahamas, we got interested in fishing and have added a fishing kit and hand spear to our list of recreational equipment. Many of our cruising friends carry surf boards or windsurfers on their boats. All sailors seem to be avid readers and trading books is part of Happy Hour activities. We have discovered many new authors this way. Video swaps are becoming common as well.

If at all possible, continue the hobbies you enjoy at home. You'll miss them if you are cruising long-term. Whatever your pleasure, look forward to enjoying the leisure time that the cruising life provides!

The following is a list of some of the recreational gear Paul and I keep on our boat:

### Recreational Gear

Diving and snorkelling equipment (including wetsuits)
Fishing gear
Cameras and film
Hiking and camping equipment
Beach chairs, beach mat and sun umbrella
Folding bicycles (no longer have; too heavy and took up space)
HAM radio equipment (also consider this a safety feature)
Sewing machine and accessories
Cards and board games
Books and videos

# Part 8 : Appendix

# Call of the Ocean - Excerpt Chapter 7

The following is an excerpt from our new book, *Call of the Ocean*, the story of our three-year cruise to 23 countries around the Atlantic Ocean, Mediterranean and Caribbean Seas. The book is planned for publication in the spring of 1999.

At the beginning of this chapter we are in Bermuda. *Two-Step* is tied to the town dock in St. George's Harbour and we are nervously waiting for good weather to begin our first transatlantic passage to Europe. Rafted up to us are a young couple in their 20's, our new Australian friends, Matthew and Lisa Buckle, aboard their Nicolson 32, *Caribee*, and rafted to them is British friend, Keith Braint, aboard his Nicolson 32, *Happy Girl*. Keith, a retired engineer, is a very experienced sailor. He has made numerous bluewater passages over the 25 years he has owned *Happy Girl*, and at this point in the story, is completing the last leg of an Atlantic Circle back to England. Matthew and Lisa have only recently purchased *Caribee* when they flew to Florida a few months previously. Like us, they are facing their first trans-oceanic voyage.

## *Onward Across the Ocean*

I watched Matthew cycle down the dock and out onto the narrow road which buzzed with passing scooters headed for town. Riding out to the Air Force base to get the latest weather information had become a ritual for Matthew this week. It helped him burn the adrenalin he felt - we all felt - as we prepared our boats to go to sea.

We had been in Bermuda for three weeks now, rafted four deep at the town wall in St. George's Harbour and, for the last few days, had been "watching the weather" for a good day to start our first trans-Atlantic passage. It would take us nearly three weeks, all going well, to sail the 1,800 nautical miles from Bermuda to the Portuguese islands of the Azores. Our feelings about the passage were a mixture of excitement and trepidation; excitement at the adventure that lay ahead and fear of the vast loneliness and danger of the sea.

"I hope he brings good news today," said Paul as he stowed the sun awning in the cockpit locker. "The waiting is killing me."

"Me too," I replied.

But looking at the colour of the sky, it seemed unlikely that we would be leaving today. The sun was blocked by a thin cloud cover and there was a misty feel to the air. Still, there was lots of work to be done so I continued stowing gear, just in case. We wanted clear decks for this voyage after our experience with the run-away propane tank on the passage from Fort Lauderdale. We also wanted to place our cargo weight as low in the boat as possible. A top-heavy boat rolls from side to side. Not only is this uncomfortable; it's dangerous too.

Together, we worked steadily for the next forty minutes sorting lines and re-organizing the cockpit lockers so the gear we needed most at sea would be easily accessible. Things tend to work themselves to the bottom of lockers if you aren't using them regularly and, since arriving at the island three weeks ago, diving equipment and beach bags occupied the top layer, taking priority over such important items as flare kits and abandon ship supplies. As I put things back in order for a safe passage, I saw Matthew come gliding back down the road and onto the pier.

"I've got the weather charts, Mates. Skippers' meeting on *Caribee*," he called as he locked his bike and scaled down the wall.

Keith popped his head out of *Happy Girl's* companionway.

"I'll be right over," he called. "It's good news, I hope."

Keith, Paul and I crammed into *Caribee's* saloon and began looking over the weather package with Matthew and Lisa. Keith's daughter Ann and her husband Robert, had just flown in from England to join Keith as crew for the passage home, and with the lack of space, opted to continue loading provisions onto *Happy Girl* rather than join our meeting.

Matthew spread the weather chart on the table. The U.S. Air Force base in Bermuda supplied this information free to visiting yachtsmen, in hopes, I was sure, of preventing the need for rescue.

"Here's the situation," said Matthew, serious for once. "There's a front coming off the north eastern states but it's not due here until tomorrow. If we leave now, I think we can nip out from under it."

"What speed is it travelling at?" asked Keith.

"Three knots," answered Matthew. It's a close thing but I can't see that it would catch us."

"You're right," Paul agreed, sharing Matthew's enthusiasm. "If we wait for it to pass, it might be another few days before we can go."

Lisa and I looked at each other. We were still feeling anxious about the passage and could have been persuaded to delay departure for another day or two. Being stuck in Bermuda was not too hard to take. But the prospect of more days of stomach-churning anticipation was more than we could bear.

After a lot of discussion, it was decided that, for better or worse, we were going to set sail that day and begin our passage across the Atlantic. Our departure time would be 1400. Although it wasn't as good a weather window as we'd been hoping for, a great weight was lifted from our shoulders. With the decision finally made, we had a new spirit of purpose and set off enthusiastically to complete our tasks.

Paul, Matthew and Keith headed over to the customs dock to clear us out of the country and retrieve our flare guns. The flare guns had been held by customs since our arrival as a national security precaution. In Bermuda, flare pistols are classified as weapons so are confiscated and held in bond during your stay. None of us were carrying fire arms onboard as some sailors do, put if we had, they would have been confiscated and held in bond as well. This is the law in many countries.

The rest of us headed for the nearest grocery store to stock up on perishables. We always purchase fresh fruits and vegetables, bread and eggs just before leaving so they are in good shape for as long as possible on the voyage.

"Matthew!" Lisa yelled from the dock when we returned with our loaded grocery bags. "We can't leave today. They were out of apples. No Granny Smiths."

Matthew rolled his eyes but continued to lash down jerry jugs of extra fuel. "I'll live. Get a move on."

She winked at me. "Aw, well, it was worth a try."

Robert and Ann struggled along the pier behind us with paper grocery bags full of packaged bread.

"Great stuff," said Robert catching one of the spongy loaves as it nearly fell from the bag. "So full of preservatives it'll last the whole way across."

Despite the joking around, Robert had a very worried look on his face. He stood on the pier and scanned the sky. It was getting noticeably cooler and the grey clouds had thickened up, casting a dismal gloom over the bay.

"You know it really doesn't look like that great a day," he said. "I was talking to some locals at the market and they said we were crazy to leave today. Maybe we should listen to them."

"Oh, they're just upset because there's no sun for the beach," I said, full of bravado now that I was psyched up for leaving. "We'll have a great sail once we get out there."

"That's right," Matthew joined in. "Dry decks all the way!"

With one last glance at the sky, Robert climbed down the wall and clambered over the rafted boats back to *Happy Girl*.

At 1400 we were ready to go. *Happy Girl* cast off first and headed for the fuel dock. There was a good wind whipping across the water now and as we circled, waiting for *Happy Girl*, we heard a horn blast from the visiting Canadian submarine at the pier.

"Hey Paul!" I shouted above the wind. "We're going to have an Canadian Armed Forces escort. The sub's leaving too."

The wind was really picking up so Paul decided to put a reef in the mainsail before we left the harbour. This should have been a clue about the kind of night we were about to have but there was no turning back. The adrenaline was flowing and *Happy Girl* joined in the flotilla.

Then a familiar voice came over the radio.

"Have a good sail, chaps. Thanks for visiting Bermuda!" came the voice of Bermuda Radio as we sailed out the inlet and into the vast ocean.

The wind was blowing a stiff 20 knots from the south as we set our course at 095T and pointed our bows for Faial in the Azores. The submarine was just behind us and to the north we could see other war ships preparing for the day's exercise. Ahead, *Happy Girl* and *Caribee* tried to out sail each other and we all chatted and joked over the radio.

Our spirits were high and we were excited about being under way in such fine company. Sailing with others would be fun for this long lonely passage but little did we know that the night ahead would be our last together for some time to come.

Bermuda quickly faded from sight. After being so deeply involved with the community there these past weeks, we'd forgotten what a little dot in the ocean Bermuda is. Seeing it again from the water, so isolated and vulnerable in the vast ocean, put the country's trials and tribulations into a whole different perspective.

While Paul adjusted the sails, I put on the kettle to make tea and we settled into our "at sea" routine. Paul was wearing his new scopolamine patches - whole patches this time - to combat potential seasickness for this long passage. We both had butterflies in our stomachs but felt it was nervous excitement more than anything else. We were at the start of the voyage we had dreamed of for a long time.

The wind remained at a steady 20 knots with overcast skies for the afternoon and we sat in the cockpit reminiscing about Bermuda and wondering about the adventures that lay ahead. Our little fleet travelled happily together and every couple of hours we would give each other a call over VHF radio.

By dinnertime, Paul wasn't feeling like eating since the seas had been growing rougher through the afternoon. We had reefed the headsail and were travelling along with *Happy Girl* and *Caribee* at a good 5 knots. I gave Paul lots to drink to keep him hydrated, confident that in time he would adjust to the motion.

At 1000 GMT, we checked on the sideband radio with our friend Herb Hilgenberg back in Bermuda for a weather update. It was great to hear his friendly voice over the airwaves. What a different passage this was going to be with friends within view and on the radio! Herb's news, however, was not good. The front we thought we could sail away from had picked up speed and was almost right on top of us. We had gambled on the weather hoping to prevent further delay in Bermuda and were going to pay for it now. It was going to be a long night.

"Let's go back!" I said when Paul signed off with Herb. "We're only 6 hours out from Bermuda. We can let the storm pass and start fresh."

"We can't go back," he stated plainly. "We'd be going right into the wind. We're better to ride it out and make miles towards the Azores. The front will most likely pass us tonight. I'd better call the others and tell them." I could just imagine what Robert was going to say.

Through the evening the wind and sea continued to build.

*Two-Step* rolled and pitched as the restless landscape heaved up ever-growing mountains of water. Occasionally we would see Matthew through the spray struggling to the foredeck in the pitching seas to make a sail change on *Caribee*.

Paul hailed Matthew on the VHF radio when we saw that he was safely back in the cockpit.

"Hey, Matthew! Whatever happened to, 'Dry decks all the way!?'

We heard Robert on *Happy Girl* pipe in, "Yes, Matthew. What was that you said about 'dry decks' this afternoon?"

I cringed, remembering my own cavalier remarks when Robert had expressed his doubts about the weather.

"Well, you know. Committee decision," Matthew replied cheerfully. "But what are you blokes complaining about? Now we have wind! Right up the bum! We'll be in Horta in no time!

By nightfall, the winds were blowing 30 knots and the waves were sporting crests of foam as they rolled by. *Two-Step* tracked stalwartly through them and the Autohelm creaked and groaned in response. Leaning against the galley strap to prevent myself from falling, I fought the motion to prepare an evening meal of stew and mashed potatoes but Paul felt too nauseated to eat and my appetite was not good either.

Suddenly I felt the vulnerability of our situation and a chill ran up my spine. We were so close to land and security yet it was safer to sail for 1800 miles in the opposite direction. Despite the scopolamine patches, Paul was feeling very ill and at 2200 he went below to get some rest before his 0200 to 0600 watch. The wind was howling through the rigging and, as I pulled myself up the companionway ladder into the cockpit, I was greeted with a douse of spray. I planted my feet firmly on the cockpit floor and with my gloved hands gripping the handle of our spray dodger, I peered anxiously through the darkness.

Ahead, I could see *Happy Girl*'s mast light bouncing through the blackness as the boat rode the waves. To port and slightly aft I could see *Caribee*'s light. Assured they were a safe distance away, I wedged myself in under the dodger to get out of the spray. We were bowling along at 6 knots with a reefed main and reefed jib. I looked at the windometer reading and my stomach tightened. It registered 30 knots. *Two-Step* rolled with the gusts. I could handle this on a daysail but we had never sailed in building winds like this on the open ocean at night. What kind of punishment would *Two-Step* stand up to and for how long?

I looked around again for *Caribee*'s and *Happy Girl*'s lights. At least we wouldn't be alone if something happened. If only we hadn't been so anxious to get going. I thought of the others who had remained behind, now asleep in a secure anchorage or swapping tales over a brew at the White Horse Tavern.

I stood through the first half of my watch with a death grip on the dodger, peering constantly into the churning darkness. The blowing spray reduced the visibility even further and I strained my ears to make up for my sense of blindness, a tiring and futile gesture in the high winds. The shrouds were singing with every shrieking gust.

Throughout my watch I furled the jib smaller and smaller as the winds rose. The reduced sail area at the bow increased the boat's tendency to turn into the wind which put an additional strain on the autopilot. I really needed to put a second reef in the main to balance the helm but Paul was finally getting some sleep and I didn't want to wake him. "When in doubt, let it out," goes the saying, so I kept easing the mainsheet to let the wind spill out of the mainsail to compensate.

Although I was grateful for the companionship of the other two boats, I now felt nervous having them so nearby with the visibility reduced. It is difficult to determine distance when all you can see is a dot of light in the darkness and at one point *Caribee*'s bow loomed out of the spray close to our stern. In a flash their power lights went on and they charged away to port to stay out of our path. Then Matthew's voice came over the radio.

"Sorry about that, Sheryl. Didn't realize we were gaining on you so quick. We're going to take a more southerly course so the three of us are a little more spread out. The visibility is too bad for us to be this friendly."

"Roger," I replied both anxious and relieved. "We'll keep our regular radio scheds with you and, if you get out of range, you can listen in to our scheds with Herb."

"We'll do the same," came Keith's calming voice over the radio. "It's getting rather nasty out here, wouldn't you say? Hope you're all keeping warm and dry."

"Affirmative," I replied. "Just feeling a little green around the gills."

Keith laughed. "Admiral Nelson had the same affliction. This is certainly a rough start to a passage. I think we all got too charged up about leaving. It will soon pass though. Maybe we'll have blue skies tomorrow."

"Can I get that in writing, Keith?" This time it was Lisa's voice.

Again, Keith laughed. "Well, no one seems to have lost their sense of humour."

"No Keith, just our appetites," she shot back.

"Right then," said Keith. "Everyone have a good night. We'll all leave our radios on and stay out of each other's way. Over and out."

Lisa and I said our goodbyes and I watched as their lights faded into the spray.

Then heard Paul's sleepy voice calling out from below. "What's going on? Is everything okay?"

"Everything's fine," I shouted back.

"It doesn't sound fine. What's the windspeed?"

I looked at the windometer.

"Thirty knots with higher gusts," I said bleakly.

"My god! Reef!"

He was up on deck like a shot.

"Are you crazy?!" he yelled above the wind as he clipped on his safety harness. "You can't leave this much sail up in these conditions. You'll tear the sail to shreds! Man the winch and I'll go forward."

"I didn't want to wake you," I yelled back defensively but realized how stupid I sounded. I took my position at the winch near the companionway and watched anxiously as Paul crawled along the wet heaving deck towards the mast.

When he was ready, I turned the boat into the wind a little to take the strain off the sail and released the mainsail halyard. With great difficulty, Paul hauled down the angry flapping sail to the second reef point and gave me the hand signal to adjust the halyard. I winched cautiously until the luff looked set and then Paul worked his way back to the safety of the cockpit. He was soaked and shaking with the effort.

"You've got to wake me up if you need help," he gasped. "I'll sleep better knowing you're not taking chances on my behalf. We can't compromise in these conditions."

He was looking very pale. I nodded agreement and he went below and was very sick.

The wind speed continued to climb and by midnight it was blowing 35-40 knots. We altered course and reefed again. *Two-Step* battled on through the roaring seas and when I went off watch at 0200 it was blowing a sustained 45 knots with gusts to 51. Paul dropped the main sail completely and reefed the jib to the size of a handkerchief. The result was more comfortable motion but the effort, so soon after he woke up, started his seasickness cycle again.

"Are you alright?" I yelled from below where I had started to remove my foul weather gear. I hauled myself back up the companionway ladder to find Paul lying in the cockpit, retching and miserable.

"Yes. Yes. I'll be fine," he said wearily. He sat up and checked that his safety harness was clipped on securely. "Get some sleep in case I need you later."

I passed him a mug of water to rinse his mouth and some paper towels. Just at that moment, a wave crashed over the deck and, despite my handhold on the companionway ladder, I was sent sprawling backwards onto the floor below. Luckily, I didn't hit the table and pulled myself up again fearing Paul's fate on deck.

"Paul!" I screamed. "Paul!"

Relief flooded me when I heard a string of curses from the cockpit and saw his drenched silhouette in the companionway.

"I'm alright," he sputtered. "Are you okay?"

"Fine," I said gulping back tears and seasickness.

"Good. Now get some sleep. I'll keep watch for as long as I can, then I'll call you. You've been great, Sher'."

I didn't feel so great. I realized how much I depended on Paul and what a strain it was on him to be running the boat when he was so seasick. I resolved to take on more responsibility with sail changes and navigation to relieve his burden.

I lowered myself back down the ladder and sat on the floor. It was useless trying to stand with the pitching motion of the boat in the angry seas. I wriggled out of my foul weather gear and crawled fully clothed into the lee berth.

"Teach Your Wife, It Could Save Your Life," was a sailing motto we had lived by. We had done all our sailing and navigation training together; sailed our first boat, *Engaged*, together; crewed as a team for club races, and spent two happy summers giving *Two-Step* her shakedown on Lake Ontario. We both loved the boat and being under sail, but it was Paul who best loved to trim the sails and plan course tactics for our trip. He had become an expert at judging when to reef, what sail plan to use and when. In this respect, my skill was inferior to his and as I collapsed into the bunk I vowed to get my act in gear.

The warmth and cosiness of the sleeping bag was such a contrast to the maelstrom outside. I could hear the Autohelm grinding along, seemingly unaffected by the huge wave that had momentarily sent us reeling. The wind howled in the rigging and the churning seas pounded against the hull beneath my pillow. I had a momentary flash of vertigo, thinking of our little ship suspended on the surface of the waves nearly two miles above the earth's crust. I shuddered and soon dropped off into a fitful sleep.

Meanwhile, Paul kept watch in the cockpit fighting back the seasickness that engulfed him with each rising wave. As the seas increased, he was frequently hit with blankets of water that were flung from the breaking wavetops. Great hissing rollers prowled through the darkness around him, pouncing on deck and knocking him from his feet in a rushing sweep of the deck. The autopilot fought on and *Two-Step* maintained her course despite the sea's attacks.

As the night wore on, the waves grew fiercer and Paul began to fear that the breaking seas would be too much for the Autohelm. To have to steer the boat ourselves for hours on end would be an exhausting task in these conditions. The boat was tracking well now, the keel slicing cleaning through the waves but, every once in awhile, waves would join together and their combined size and power would create an avalanche of water and spray. So far, none of these rogue waves had hit us but Paul knew it was just a matter of time before *Two-Step* would be put to the real test. So he watched, and waited.

The minutes passed like hours. The size of the seas were difficult to see in the dark. Our 10 watt masthead light cast a faint glow that dimly lit the nearest of the foaming crests. We could see nothing further and the wave tops appeared like white wraiths groping towards us.

Then, over the roar of the wind, Paul heard the low rumble of an approaching wave, far bigger than the rest. He braced himself and prepared for a knock-down.

The wave struck. A mountain of water roared over the boat completely submerging the deck. The Autohelm screamed as it strained against the force of the wave and there was a horrifying sound of ripping canvas. Paul held on for dear life. The water foamed and boiled around him, filling his boots and grabbing at his legs, and he felt the boat going over, over, over ...

# Inventory Lists on Floppy Disk

### Overview

If you have access to a computer, the checklists, worksheets and hints from this book are available on a 3.5 inch disk for use on IBM-PCs. Using the disk, its easy to customize our lists to fit your own needs.

The lists print out on standard 8 ½ X 11 inch paper so you can insert them in a binder and create a personal inventory manual designed for your boat.

### System Requirements

IBM-PC or compatible with one of the following word processors: Microsoft Word-for-Windows Version 2.0 or higher, WordPerfect Version 5.1 or higher, or Microsoft Write Version 3.1 or higher.

### To Order

To order the disk, see the form at the back of the book to mail order from *Pelagic Press.*

# Recommended Reading

## Provisioning

**The Care and Feeding of the Offshore Crew** by Lin Pardey with Larry Pardey: 1980. (New edition available in May 1995)
This book follows the Pardeys' 60 day passage from Japan to Canada and is a reference book on how to buy, provision, store and prepare food for extended voyages. Although the recipes don't suit our tastes, it is the best book we have found on what it is like to cook in various conditions and what routines have to be kept at sea with regard to provisioning.

**Cooking On the Go** by Janet Groene: 1987, 1st rev. edition.
An excellent guide to preparing foods without an oven or icebox written by a veteran sailor. Includes a "Failsafe Guide to Provisioning".

**The Cruising Cook** by Shirley Herd Deal: 1993. (Continually revised)
This book is full of tips, checklists, guidelines and 300 galley-tested recipes. It's in binder form so you can add your own recipes and provisions lists. Many long-term cruisers have this book onboard.

**Good Food Afloat, Every Sailor's Guide to Eating Right** by Joan Betterley: 1986.
"Tasty and healthful alternatives to the usual shipboard fare." Recipes are also easy to prepare onboard. Useful tips for storing fruits and vegetables and designing meal plans. The author is a registered dietician as well as a sailor. (No longer in print but available in some libraries.)

**The Joy of Cooking** by Irma S. Rombauer and Marion Rombauer Becker :1981.
For world cruising, we find this book to be an excellent reference guide to have on the boat. We rarely use the recipes since they are just too complicated for our style of cruising but, if we come across new foods in foreign markets, this book usually helps us identify them and gives us an idea of how to prepare them.

We also carry a selection of regional cookbooks which we purchase along the way as well as specialty cookbooks on pressure cooking, canning, grilling, and entertaining. Any cookbooks you use regularly at home should come aboard for extended cruising.

## *Outfitting*

**Offshore Cruising Encyclopedia** - By Stephen and Linda Dashew, 1996. A great reference for anyone outfitting for serious cruising. The Dashews have a wide variety of experience both building and sailing different boats. Although much of their sailing is in larger yachts (50-85 feet) they have a lot of good advice, on seamanship as well as equipment, for people on any size vessel. The second edition is over 1200 pages!

**The Self-Sufficient Sailor** - by Lin and Larry Pardey, 1982. Although somewhat traditional in their methods this cruising couple give concise information on all aspects of cruising.

**Spurr's Boatbook: Upgrading the Cruising Sailboat** - Dan Spurr, 1990. Full of great ideas for projects to upgrade the cruising sailboat. Fantastic illustrations.

**Marine Diesel Engines**, Nigel Calder, 1987.
This is a comprehensive text covering both diesel theory and useful troubleshooting information. A great place to start if you are not a diesel mechanic. Nigel also wrote the **Boatowner's Mechanical and Electrical Manual** - another very worthy addition to the bookshelf.

**Seven Seas Cruising Association: Equipment Survey,** S.S.C.A, 1996 (every few years) The Seven Seas Cruising Association (described below) conducts a survey every few years, asking their members how they rate different brands of gear. What works, what doesn't, from windlasses to propellors, dinghies to fuel filters this guide rates a wide range of cruising gear. The **best** source of opinions from people who really know!

## *General Cruising*

**All About Cruising -** Walter Gleckler, 1998
An good all-round guide about cruising by this experienced west coast yachtsman.

**All in the Same Boat** - Fiona McCall & Paul Howard, 1988
A fun read, especially good for children. The Howard/McCall family circumnavigate in their 30 foot steel junk rigged boat. Lots of information for people planning a cruise. Also the sequel, *Still in the Same Boat.*

**Heavy Weather Sailing** - K. Adlard Coles, 1981
In-depth descriptions of some of the worst gales yachts have encountered this century. It is the standard work on seamanship in gale conditions.

**Just Cruising** - Liza Copeland, 1993
An entertaining and informative story about the first half of the Copeland family's 6-year voyage around the world. The second half of their trip is covered in *Still Cruising*.

**Once is Enough** - Miles Smeeton, 1959
The exciting story of Miles and Beryl Smeeton and their boat *Tzu-Huang*, attempting to round Cape Horn. Their boat is pitchpoled and the conditions they describe will give all sailors pause to think before heading off around the Horn.

**Reed's Nautical Almanac** - Reed's, issued annually.
A great resource. It has tide and current tables as well as some harbour charts, radio station listings, light list, etc.

**Saga of a Wayward Sailor** - Tristan Jones
*ICE* and *The Incredible Voyage* are also well worth reading. Actually, all of the late Tristan Jones' books are very entertaining! Not good for provisioning though -- in ICE, he lived for a year in the Arctic, eating burgoo (a mix of porridge, bacon-fat, and rum)!!

**Sailing Alone Around the World** - Joshua Slocum, 1905
The first sailor to circumnavigate alone, Slocum was also a great story-teller and this book is still easy to read almost a century after he wrote it.

# Magazines

Canadian Yachting
Cruising World
DIY Boat Owner
GAM on Yachting
Ocean Navigator
Pacific Yachting
Practical Sailor
Sail
Sailing Magazine

# Associations

**Bluewater Cruising Association** 1905 Ogden Avenue, Vancouver, BC., V6J 1A3   Phone: 604-266-3361
An association of world cruising sailors. Monthly newsletters and meetings. Informative publications and seminars.

**Canadian Power and Sail Squadron** 26 Golden Gate Court, Scarborough ON M1P 3A5 call 1-800-268-3579 FAX 416-293-2445
Formerly known as the "Power Squadron", sailors are now well represented in this organization. It offers excellent classroom courses in all aspects of yachting, all across North America.

**Ontario Boat Builders Co-operative** 2265 Royal Windsor Drive, Unit 6, Mississauga, ON. L5J 1K5 Phone/Fax 905-403-0549
A group of amateur boat builders who meet monthly to discuss boat building and arrange bulk purchases of products. Guest speakers. Monthly newsletter.

**Seven Seas Cruising Association** 1525 South Andrews Ave, Suite 217, Fort Lauderdale, FL. 33316   Phone 954-463-2431   Fax 954-463-7183
Email: ssca@bcfreenet.seflin.lib.fl.us
This group of cruising sailors keeps each other up-to-date through monthly bulletins on developments in the world cruising scene. They have the least biased, most current information on destinations and also publish guides such as the Equipment Survey described above.

**Travel Advisory** 1-800-267-6788
A 24-hour phone service for Canadians travelling abroad on travel preparation, information and awareness.

**World Cruising Club** 199 Sutherland Drive, Toronto, ON., M4G 1J1 416-421-7352
Based in Toronto, this group offers a seminar series each winter for sailors planning to go off cruising. Monthly meetings and guest speakers.

**United States Power Squadrons** USPS Headquarters, 1504 Blue Ridge Road, P.O. Box 30423, Raleigh, NC 27622 Phone 1-800-336-BOAT.
Local Power Squadrons all over the USA offer very good classroom training in navigation, seamanship, engines etc.

# Index

## U

## V

## W

## Y

## Z

# About the Authors

Paul and Sheryl Shard have been cruising internationally aboard their self-built Classic 37 sailboat, *Two-Step*, for nearly a decade. In that time, they have sailed over 30,000 miles including three transatlantic passages and have visited 23 countries around the Atlantic Ocean, Mediterranean and Caribbean Seas.

The Shards combine their love of sailing with their work and are award-winning marine filmmakers and writers. Their documentary on their first Atlantic cruise, *Call of the Ocean*, was broadcast across Canada on the Discovery Channel and was part of *Discovery's Search for Adventure* series. Their current television series, *Exploring Under Sail*, which they co-produce with Peter Rowe Productions, documents the Shards' new cruising adventures and those of other intrepid sailors. The pilot episode of *Exploring Under Sail*, won the Gold Award for Best Sailing and Watersport Documentary at the Charleston International Film Festival. The Shards also produce informative specialty videos for sailors, the most popular being *Cruising the Bahamas.*

Avid scuba divers and underwater photographers, the Shards have filmed and photographed a myriad of colorful marine life during their voyages. Their most exciting footage includes underwater encounters in the open sea with dolphins, sharks and pods of pilot whales and sperm whales.

The Shards also write for numerous sailing magazines including *Cruising World, Sailing, Canadian Yachting* and *DIY Boatowner.* Their bestselling book, *Sail Away! A Guide to Outfitting and Provisioning for Cruising* is now in its Second Edition and their new book, *Call of the Ocean*, which is the story of their 3-year Atlantic cruise, will be published in 1999.

When the Shards are not filming or living aboard they reside in Mississauga, Canada, where they are active in the Port Credit Power and Sail Squadron and are members of the Port Credit Yacht Club. Popular speakers, they travel extensively each year inspiring sailors everywhere with their dynamic multimedia presentations and seminars.

**www.interlog.com/~shard**

Cruising the

# Bahamas

60 Minutes

With
Paul and Sheryl Shard

Sail and dive the spectacular waters of the Bahamas with international cruisers Paul and Sheryl Shard. Expert advice on piloting, anchoring, navigating and planning a cruise.

**60 Minute Video**

## $29.95

*A real taste of Bahamas cruising. Beautiful footage and useful hints make this a great souvenir for sailors who've been to the Bahamas, and a good introduction for those planning to go.*

Pam Juryn - Commodore, World Cruising Club

# Cruising the Bahamas
## with Paul and Sheryl Shard
### Video

International cruisers and award-winning filmmakers, Paul and Sheryl Shard, bring you the first in a new series of cruising videos. Using unique underwater footage, the Shards demonstrate techniques for anchoring and piloting the shallow waters of the Bahamas.

They take you to their favorite destinations, introduce you to local characters, show how to read the color of the water, interpret the weather and find protected anchorages. Watch for spectacular footage of a dismasting in Nassau harbour and the Shards' encounter with Hurricane Bertha!

The Shards are avid divers as well as keen sailors and take you below the crystal waves to explore vibrant tropical reefs. They show basic snorkeling techniques and how these skills can help you clear a line from your prop as well as introduce you to the fascinating marine life beneath the sea.

If you are dreaming of a cruise to the beautiful islands of the Bahamas this delightful video will whet your appetite for adventure while providing valuable tips for a safe and enjoyable voyage.

# Exploring Under Sail

## The Sailing Adventure Series

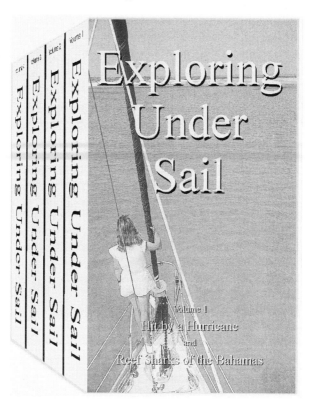

Volume 1
Hit by a Hurricane
and
Reef Sharks of the Bahamas

Charleston International Film Festival Gold Award

50 minute videos

Each volume contains 2 half-hour episodes.

**1 video $29.95**
**Set of 4 videos $89.95**

# Exploring Under Sail

*Travel with a group of global adventurers exploring remote corners of the world under sail. Winner of the Gold Award for Best Sailing/Watersport Documentary at the Charleston International Film Festival. Each volume contains 2 half-hour episodes from this exciting television series.*

## Volume 1 - Hit by a Hurricane/Reef Sharks of the Bahamas.
"Hit by A Hurricane" follows Paul and Sheryl Shard on voyage down the Inland Waterway from Lake Ontario to Florida. En route, they run for shelter from an approaching hurricane. In "Reef Sharks of the Bahamas" the Shards sail to an island populated by giant iquanas and dive in the midst of a dozen grey reef sharks.

## Volume 2 - Cape Horn Challenge/Antigua Sailing Week
"Cape Horn Challenge" is the story of Georgs Kolesnikovs, a middle-aged cruising sailor from Niagara Falls who breaks the 135 year-old record for the fastest time from New York to San Francisco. In "Antigua Sailing Week", sail with keen racing crews aboard maxi yachts in a tropical island paradise.

## Volume 3 - Islands of the Whales/Mysteries of the Atlantic
In "Islands of the Whales", Paul and Sheryl arrive in the Azores after a transatlantic passage and discover a land of lush green hills exciting underwater creatures. They meet a retired whaler and sail an original whaling canoe. In "Mysteries of the Atlantic" the Shards cook a meal in hot volcanic mud and Paul runs with the bulls in the streets of the village. They attempt to dive on an active underwater volcano in the open Atlantic.

## Volume 4 - Voyages to Newfoundland/Frostbite Sailing
In celebration of the 500th Anniversary of John Cabot's voyage of discovery to Canada, a flotilla of 100 boats from Toronto and New York battle cold, fog and icebergs to sail to Newfoundland. In "Frostbite Sailing" we sail at top speeds over the frozen water of northern Canadian lakes aboard ice boats, windsurf in the snow, break through ice to sail radio control boats and race aboard 8' dinghies in a blizzard.

# Call of the Ocean
## Video

An inspiring one-hour documentary on the Shards' three-year, 20,000 mile voyage aboard their self-built sailboat to countries around the Atlantic Ocean, Mediterranean and Caribbean Seas. Interviews with family and friends combined with the Shards' beautiful footage, result in a vivid account of what it's like to build a boat and go cruising. Highlights include underwater footage of the Shards' encounters with dolphins, sharks and whales in the open sea. Part of the Discovery Channel's "Search for Adventure" series.

*I feel like I've had a vacation everytime I watch this video!*
Eileen Clarke
Mississauga, ON

*Fantastic underwater footage!*
Fernando De Oliveira
Commercial Photographer
Toronto, ON

*Better than antibiotics for curing a winter cold!*
Steve Johnson
Oakville, ON

**60 minute video**
**$29.95**

# Order Form

Name: _____ Phone: ( ___ ) _____ - _____

Address: _____

_____

_____

City: _____ State/Prov: _____ Postal Code/ZIP: _____

**Videos**
  **Cruising The Bahamas** ___ copies X $29.95 CDN = _____
  **Exploring Under Sail Volume 1** ___ _____ copies X $29.95 CDN =

  **Exploring Under Sail Volume 2** ___ _____ copies X $29.95 CDN =

  **Exploring Under Sail Volume 3** ___ _____ copies X $29.95 CDN =

  **Exploring Under Sail Volume 4** ___ _____ copies X $29.95 CDN =

  **Call of the Ocean** ___ copies X $29.95 CDN = _____

**Video Special - Any four videos for the price of 3** ___          **$89.95**

**Sail Away!** Book only:          ___ copies X $24.95 CDN = _____
**Sail Away!** Computer disk only:          ___ copies X $19.95 CDN = _____

**G.S.T.** (Canadian orders only - GST#895 325 942 RT)add 7 % _____
**Shipping and Handling**          (add $4.00) _____
                                        Total          _____

Please make your cheque or money order payable to Pelagic Press and
mail with your order form to:  Pelagic Press, 3376 Enniskillen Circle,
Mississauga, Ontario, Canada  L5C 2N1.

**Orders will be shipped within 48 hours.**

# For Credit Card Orders Call Toll-free 888-319-2365
## (8am to 4pm EST)